DEATH BY THE POWERFUL

Studies in Social Harm

Series editors: **Christina Pantazis**, University of Bristol and **Simon Pemberton**, University of Birmingham

---

The Studies in Social Harm series seeks to understand the production of harm within contemporary society. The series offers comparative and international perspectives to understand the distribution of harm and combines new theory and empirical research.

Also available in the series:

Crime, Harm and the State
by **Lynne Copson**, **Eleni Dimou** and **Steve Tombs**

Social Harm and Neoliberalism
by **John Gregson**

How Technologies Harm
by **Mark Wood**

The Harms of Beauty
by **Sam Barnes**

Border Harms and Everyday Violence
by **Evgenia Iliadou**

Against Youth Violence
by **Luke Billingham** and **Keir Irwin-Rogers**

The Harms of Work
by **Anthony Lloyd**

Labour Exploitation and Work-Based Harm
by **Sam Scott**

Harmful Societies
by **Simon A. Pemberton**

Environmental Harm
by **Rob White**

Find out more at:

bristoluniversitypress.co.uk/
studies-in-social-harm

DEATH BY THE POWERFUL

Invisibility and Social Harm

Katy Snell

BRISTOL
UNIVERSITY
PRESS

First published in Great Britain in 2026 by

Bristol University Press
University of Bristol
1–9 Old Park Hill
Bristol
BS2 8BB
UK
t: +44 (0)117 374 6645
e: bup-info@bristol.ac.uk

Details of international sales and distribution partners are available at bristoluniversitypress.co.uk

DOI: 10.51952/9781529233971

British Library Cataloguing in Publication Data
A catalogue record for this book is available from the British Library

ISBN 978-1-5292-3394-0 hardcover
ISBN 978-1-5292-3396-4 ePub
ISBN 978-1-5292-3397-1 ePDF

Cover design: Bristol University Press
Front cover image: Stocksy_A I E
Bristol University Press uses environmentally responsible print partners.
Printed and bound in Great Britain by CPI Group (UK) Ltd, Croydon, CR0 4YY

FSC www.fsc.org MIX Paper | Supporting responsible forestry FSC® C013604

Bristol University Press' authorised representative in the European Union is:
Easy Access System Europe, Mustamäe tee 50, 10621 Tallinn, Estonia,
Email: gpsr.requests@easproject.com

To all the families I met whose lives
were split into before and after – you did
everything you could.

Contents

Series Editors' Preface

Christina Pantazis and Simon Pemberton

The Studies in Social Harm series provides space for scholars to develop novel theoretical and methodological approaches to advance understanding of the production of harm in contemporary societies. The series is co-edited by Christina Pantazis and Simon Pemberton, along with an international advisory board that includes some of the leading thinkers in the field.

While the debates surrounding social harm are familiar to many criminologists and, in particular, critical criminologists, the central aim of the series has been to extend the notion beyond these disciplinary boundaries. By drawing together a range of scholars from multiple disciplines, it is hoped that we might develop unique interdisciplinary conversations, which are more effective in accurately detailing the harms that impact our societies, as well as offering solutions to these issues. Thus, the emphasis within the series has fallen on providing cutting-edge research that illuminates the existence of complex aetiologies, of injuries in relation to the contemporary workplace, migration and environmental policy. The point being many of the harms that are explored in the series are often 'hidden'. They are 'hidden' because they are viewed with societal indifference or as a 'given', an unavoidable consequence of the 'natural order' of societies. Thus, the work in this series seeks to challenge the 'common sense', academic, policy and public orthodoxies that surrounds these harms.

Much of the initial work in this area focused on the definition of social harm and argumentation surrounding the boundaries of the term. It is notable that as the field of study matures, that focus has moved beyond these now staid debates of definition. Instead, fine-grain empirical analysis in this series has given rise to theoretical refinement and advancement, specifically in relation to the aetiologies of harm production. Work in the series will then continue to contribute to our understanding of the production of and societal responses to social harm. While disparate empirical focus might exist, contributions to the series converge around key issues:

- an appreciation of harm which is socially mediated, produced and sustained through unequal social structures (such as gender, sexuality, race and class);
- the methodological approaches required to better understand the extent, nature, experiences and causes of harm within contemporary society;
- an understanding of responsibility for harms at different levels of society (such as at the individual, organizational, institutional and structural levels);
- an understanding of the different ways in which harms are represented and reproduced in academic, legal and media debates;
- a critical understanding of existing policy responses to harms and alternative policy approaches.

The issues the series grapples with have gained greater importance as our societies continue to transform at pace. Whether we are wrestling with the pernicious effects of neoliberalism on the Global North and South, the enduring legacy of the global COVID-19 pandemic or the impacts of the culture wars on women and gender-diverse individuals – the social harm framework has much to offer. We are encouraged by the contributions of social harm scholars to these debates, and we hope the series can continue to contribute meaningfully to remedying these harms.

About the Author

Katy Snell is Lecturer of Criminology at the University of Hull. She began studying criminology in 2000 and went on to develop an interest in corporate and safety crime. Following her graduation, she worked for eight years in a prison as a Treatment Manager and then in FE while studying part time for a PhD. After being awarded her PhD, she moved to UCNL (University Campus North Lincolnshire) and joined the Open University, before also joining the University of Hull in 2022. She has a long-standing interest in crimes of the powerful, corporations and prison abolition.

Acknowledgements

The most important part of this book is the testimonies from the families – thank you to each of you. I'll always remember the kindness you showed me while describing the indescribable. Remembering your words and the love that was evident for your son/brother/father/partner was the main reason I wanted to do this. While this can never repay the debt, I hope it does something useful with your words.

Thank you to Bristol University Press and specifically Grace and Zoë for getting this started and seeing it through to the finish. Also 'thank you' to the anonymous reviewer; your comments made me cry, in a good way!

Steve, thank you for what is now more than a decade of replying 'no worries if not' to my emails when there was never any worry. For every journal article, pointer and consideration – thank you.

Thanks to Joe, Janet and Helen for your support and encouragement, which I probably brushed off but kept for later, who along with Steve have seen me go from a single woman with a bug bear about corporate crime to a mother with a PhD (and a bug bear about corporate crime). To colleagues and friends at the University of Hull and OUT; Jo, Darren, Alice, Jon, Daniel, Nicola and Simon, thank you for your understanding and advice. Thank you, Catherine and Linda, for your genuine enthusiasm and encouragement.

Thanks to Suzy for finding the time to read a chapter and offering encouragement when I was flailing and unsure and for responding to the voice notes when you barely have time to crack a chocolate orange.

Mum, thank you for reading the first draft with no notice, carefully marking typos and returning it to me in a folder. It's the small things as much as the huge things.

To Chris, Juliet and Briony, I hope you think this was worth my time away in the office, despairing over the order of my words interspersed with singing along to George Michael and Self Esteem. I'm so grateful and happy to be here with you, doing this, with Timber at my feet. Love you always.

Introduction: Aims, Methodology, Chapter Outline

This book can be traced back to 2000, when I was sitting in a lecture theatre and heard about the death of Sidney Rouse, who was killed at work through no fault of his own. I was confused that someone could be killed so casually and that no one was held responsible. I had never questioned whether my father and partner, who work in similar industries, would come home from work at the end of the day. As conscientious workers in what I believed to be an overcautious environment, I had never worried about them. Yet I left the lecture theatre thinking maybe I should – if Sidney Rouse had not been safe, neither were they.

My interest in the topic did not wane, so I chose to do my dissertation on corporate crime and the railways. This did not lead to any further comfort as I realized members of the public were also more at risk, whether they were using medication, attending football matches or travelling in general – the reach of the powerful was wide and unavoidable. The disasters I had read about in the newspapers were not random tragic events, and the professionals I thought would help should I need them were not always the knowledgeable and astute people I had assumed them to be. My interest continued because of curiosity and a need to find answers to questions I had previously not realized needed asking, and as with any good study, the more I researched, the more questions I had.

This book starts and ends with the experiences of families like the sister of Sidney Rouse. People whose experiences are still shocking to me, even though I have read and heard them a hundred times. Before the death of their loved ones, many were like me and did not imagine that those with more power would be able to act with impunity. It is one thing to experience the pain of bereavement and quite another for it to have been avoidable and for no one to admit the truth or be held responsible. These deaths occur frequently enough to be routine, and this book will argue that the responses are routine too.

Deaths such as Louise Adamson's brother, Michael, an electrician who was killed in 2005 following an electric shock. He had been connecting cables above a false ceiling and cut through a wire that was marked 'not in use' but was still connected. Louise found out the corporation did not provide 'lock-off' devices for live cables, nor did they provide testing equipment or maintain up-to-date risk assessments. In the first year after Michael's death, Louise had to continually ring up to find out what was happening; when the first preliminary hearing happened, the family was told to 'strain to hear' because they could not hear what was going on. The family travelled over 60 miles to hear the pleas being entered but were told they were a week late because the hearing had been moved and the trial postponed at the request of the defence. This was the woeful level of care extended to the family during the trial.

At the trial, three years after Michael had died, the case against two directors and a senior manager was not heard in front of the jury due to insufficient evidence. The corporation was fined £300,000. Prior to this, the defence had argued they had agreed to plead guilty on the condition no charges would be raised against individuals. Michael's death was not a one off: seven workers died in similar circumstances between 2004 and 2006, before and after his death. This was an avoidable death that the family were left to cope with, in addition to the way they were treated by the corporation. Described by Louise as '26-years old, engaged to be married … his whole life ahead of him to live. Michael was a son, a brother, a fiancé, and he didn't live to become an uncle, a husband, or a dad', having been denied the chance by those with the power who did not keep him safe.

Pauline Campbell's daughter Sarah died in HMP Styal in 2003 after swallowing 120 sleeping tablets on the first night of her sentence. HMP Styal was aware that while on remand at the same institution, Sarah had committed 28 acts of self-harm, yet no risk assessment was carried out, and she was placed in harsh conditions in the segregation unit. Staff wrongly identified her as being on the unit for disciplinary reasons. At the inquest, Pauline heard two strip searches had failed to find any drugs, and staff had not been trained in suicide prevention – many believed that if women wanted to commit suicide, they should be able to (Hattenstone, 2006). There was little emergency response as the ambulance was delayed by 20 to 40 minutes. Pauline shared in an article in the *Guardian*: 'In the end [Sarah] was vomiting and fitting … when she actually died, she was bleeding from the nose and mouth … And I'm supposed to come to terms with that?' (Hattenstone, 2006).

The inquest recorded that a failure in the duty of care and lack of communication contributed to her death in an institution that put auditing assessments above looking after prisoners. Sarah was one of six women who died at HMP Styal within the same 12-month period. Pauline's worst fears came true when her daughter died, and afterwards she herself began to suffer from post-traumatic stress disorder, describing how she would wake her neighbours up in the night with her screams, unable to 'believe Sarah's dead' (Hattenstone, 2006). In 2008, Pauline died by suicide at her daughter's graveside.

In very different circumstances, both Michael and Sarah were killed under the care of more powerful institutions they had to rely upon to keep them safe. The people who loved them experienced grief because of their sudden and violent deaths. In addition to the traumatic bereavement that comes with this, both learnt that these deaths – which irrevocably changed their lives – were avoidable. Yet, despite this, they witnessed a process that failed to send anyone to prison and ultimately harmed them. Further to this, they realized their loved one was not the last person to die in that way, which both Louise and Sarah fought to resist on behalf of others in the years that followed. The principal concern of this book is secondary victims, people like Louise and Pauline – family members whose lives were changed when someone they love and who loved them was killed.

Accidental

In 1988, as part of his employment, Sidney Rouse was instructed to dig a trench under a pavement to clear a path for a gas main (Bergman, 1991). A potential hazard of this work was the presence of pre-installed electric cables, negated by the 'ways' and 'mains' maps, which detailed where to avoid. However, the ganger supervising the work that day had only been given the 'ways' map (Bergman, 1991). Oblivious to the risk and dependent upon those who employed him, Sidney's spade struck an underground electric cable, and he suffered 80 per cent burns due to the subsequent electric shock. Sidney was taken to hospital, where he later died. His sister reflected: 'The worst thing about it was to see him in hospital for over a week. He was in a terrible condition' (Bergman, 1991: 7). An inquest returned a verdict of 'accidental death'. Both the Crown Prosecution Service and Health and Safety Executive (HSE) decided not to prosecute, so the company was neither put on trial for corporate manslaughter nor fined (Bergman, 1991). Sidney's sister did not see any justice in the months and years that followed her brother's death.

One cannot say that what happened to Sidney was criminal. Any person who may have been held responsible was deemed innocent by the lack of official response – they were never even under suspicion of wrongdoing or subject to any process that might have entertained this notion. Although Sidney was denied the information he needed to prevent his death and was acting on instructions as part of his job, his sister can only officially claim that what happened to her brother – that his premature and horrific death – was an accident, chalked off as 'one of those things'. No one was responsible; no corporation would have to change its procedure to keep future workers safe, and no public outrage would be expressed because a man had been electrocuted at work after simply following orders.

Academics have worked to collect quantitative data to demonstrate how many people are like Sidney, whose deaths are not recorded or are recorded in a number of different places (Slapper and Tombs, 1999). They have examined whether such deaths should have led to a charge or at least a day in court (Slapper, 1999) and examined the experiences of victims of larger-scale instances of fraud and gathered information about how they felt in response to what had been taken from them (Spalek, 1999). Researchers have borrowed concepts from academics who have sought to explain fraud and business deviance (Punch, 1999) and applied these to the deaths of workers (Slapper and Tombs, 1999). They have collected evidence, using different types of white-collar crime from across the world to show that corporations and workers are committing crime (Croall, 1992).

What has not been established as clearly are the experiences of the families of those who have been killed at work in the UK. Family members like Sidney Rouse's sister, who saw him suffer and witnessed the official responses to his death, which ensured anyone responsible would avoid justice and punishment. What this research documents are their experiences as secondary victims: how the family members have to suffer to ensure the innocence of the corporation – as a powerful perpetrator, rather than a powerless perpetrator, the blame is shifted to the dead. This leads the families to question what they could have done differently to secure justice for their loved one, causing irreparable harm that makes any type of return to normal life even more difficult.

This research was informed by talking with secondary victims who had lost loved ones who had either died at work or as a member of the public, and with those involved in social movements campaigning for change. My aim was to gather missing qualitative data to provide detail behind the limited number of prosecutions that follow the high numbers of those killed almost routinely in the UK. Such detail sheds light on when and why each case avoids justice and the effects of this on the families. Families of those who have been killed have been largely invisible in mainstream criminology and silenced in debates about crime and justice. Their experiences both deserve and need to be heard as part of a larger group of people who have the misfortune to be harmed by the powerful rather than the powerless. The secondary victims remain isolated, and their experiences are minimized and/or pushed to be invisible from mainstream concern. Their existence as victims is disregarded by those with the power to support them, chalked up as the result of unrelated and spontaneous 'accidents'. The way they are treated and their resistance urgently require inclusion in the criminological literature to strengthen and illuminate the need for a social harm approach that is not preoccupied with categories defined, in part, by those causing the gravest of harms.

Initially, my research had not been on social movements but solely on families as they navigated through the various agencies, such as the police, HSE and the court system. However, it became clear that the social movements were a significant response to the lack of justice and required further investigation. This was a part of the families' response and therefore required inclusion in this research to examine the success of a number of groups and the value in such resistance. The groups studied made up the movement for corporate accountability that began at the end of the 1980s. This research examines the origins, nature and aims of this movement. Each group that formed part of this movement has been described by their members in a plethora of ways. For example, the members of one group covered in this research, Disaster Action, described it as an 'organisation' (Eyre and Dix, 2014: 11), a charity and a 'special kind of family' (Eyre and Dix, 2014: 14). It was created out of a combination of 'family and support groups' (Eyre and Dix, 2014: 12), 'self-help support and action groups' (Eyre and Dix, 2014: 19), 'trusts' (Eyre and Dix, 2014: 27), 'associations' (Eyre and Dix, 2014: 28) and 'action groups' (Eyre and Dix, 2014: 20). For consistency, I have chosen to focus on groups that share the goal of supporting and working to alter the representation and treatment of the victims of corporate and safety crimes. Each group chosen was highly visible in the movement for corporate accountability.

Their experiences demonstrate the limitations of a criminal justice process that 'when threatened sacrifices the principles of justice' (Scraton, 2009: 267). I argue that reform of the system and policy change may be possible, but immediate and meaningful change is better sought elsewhere, where harm is recognized and remedied outside of the official processes that offer false promise of retribution and deterrence. A new approach is needed to prevent secondary victims from blaming themselves and from going through the process in isolation, enduring more harm and pain at an unimaginable time in their lives. When 'an ordinary life is hard enough' (Tombs, 2019), bereaved families should not be sacrificed for the innocence of corporations; those with less power should not suffer for the benefit of the powerful and be further harmed.

This book highlights the suffering of individuals affected by a powerful offender (Gouldner, 1973). Researching the experience of the families of the victims of safety crime is a way to negotiate the problems of observing corporate criminality while acknowledging but navigating debates over whether they should be subject to criminological study. As an interviewer, a researcher, I am borrowing and taking the time of family members and requesting they recall painful memories for academic research, the results of which most people will never see. Since the desire for this research comes directly from the experiences of those interviewed and in response to their suspected poor treatment, which I am gravely concerned about, it is unrealistic and misplaced for me to claim neutrality was highly important or something I attempted to maintain. This was replaced with the need to listen, understand, draw out and voice their experiences. Being impartial and detached was never an aim nor a requirement I placed on my behaviour. I did not attempt to be 'professional' or assume the role of a friend. It was my intention to listen and assume enough confidence so that the family members would not try to censor difficult memories. The fact I was not impartial and therefore genuinely interested was conveyed. Nothing, beyond the sterile nature of the interview, was false.

My own position originates from a genuine curiosity to understand why people can be killed and yet their loved ones are denied the right to find out what happened to them and have no assurances that it will not happen again when this is entirely possible. I am in agreement with Carson (1982: 301) that the criminal justice system should be open to debate, and if 'saying this consigns me to the company of those whose criminology was once castigated for being based on a "mindless and atheoretical moral indignation", I can only say that I hope there will always be room for some moral outrage in criminology and sociology alike'. Accepted definitions of crime should be challenged (Hillyard, 2003), along with what we have within criminology: a summary of the process of victimization and less about how being a victim is experienced (Spalek, 2006). Feminists have taken up similar challenges in the past and revealed inequality that may otherwise have lain dormant (Walklate, 2007). Such researchers recognized that what is held as common knowledge exists within, and maintains, power structures. It is crucial that this common knowledge is interrogated (Harding, 1991). It is important to challenge those who perpetuate safety crime and question the structures that facilitate it to scrutinize the powerful and present alternatives to the dominant discourse. This research hopes to add to this tradition.

A note on definitions

The definition of safety crime has emerged from the work of Sutherland's focus on 'crime in relation to business' (1940: 1). He was one of the first to look at crimes committed by those in the 'upper or white-collar class' made up of the respectable and the 'least respected business and professional men' (Sutherland, 1940: 1).[1] Sutherland refined the concept as 'a violation of the criminal law by a person of the upper socioeconomic class in the course of his occupational studies' (1941: 112). Corporate crime itself 'developed out of Sutherland's original claim and its allied conceptual ambiguities' (Snider, 2003a: 51) when he referred to an 'offender active in the corporate world' (Melossi, 2008: 139). A more 'counter-hegemonic concept' (Snider, 2003a: 52) linked to profit, it makes the role of the corporation explicit, moving away from a focus on the individual.

Corporate crime includes crimes as well as omissions made by legitimate, formal organizations (Pearce and Tombs, 1998). The most suitable definition for the purposes of this research defines corporate crimes as: 'Illegal acts or omissions, punishable by the State under administrative, civil or criminal law, which are the result of deliberate decision making or culpable negligence within a legitimate formal organisation' (Pearce and Tombs, 1998: 107–10). This definition includes all the corporations registered in the UK under the Companies Act 2006 and discounts those corporations created with the intention of breaking the law. It also includes those who could and are punished by regulatory means, which Sutherland recognized (Tombs, 2005). This is relevant to the cases in this research.

In *Corporate Crime*, Slapper and Tombs (1999) note four subcategories of corporate crime. This research focuses on the second category, safety crime, which arises out of 'the employment relationship … crimes against employees … by employers' (Slapper and Tombs, 1999: 45). In outlining this subcategory, Slapper and Tombs cite the work of Carson (1980, 1982), Bergman (1991, 1993, 1994), Pearce (1990), Pearce and Tombs (1993, 1997), Slapper (1993), Wells (1995) and Box (1983), all of whom use characteristics of what they term 'health and safety crime' (Slapper and Tombs, 1999: 46). Tombs and Whyte (2007) refined this to safety crime, focusing on victims who are 'immediately apparent', for example when a worker is killed in a factory as a result of their employer violating the law. This is in contrast to many victims of health crimes who are created over a long period of time – for example, the latency period of mesothelioma caused by exposure to asbestos is 20 to 50 years (Mesothelioma Center, 2017).

Additionally, Tombs and Whyte (2007) use the Health and Safety at Work Act 1974 to extend the remit of safety crime to include members of the public who are affected by the 'decisions and omissions' of corporations as well as direct employees. In this, they exchange the 'corporate' in Pearce and Tombs' (1998) definition with 'safety'. This includes many more victims, such as those associated with 'disasters', for example members of the public killed in the *Herald of Free Enterprise* disaster. This is both helpful and crucial to this research, covering those involved with both private and public institutions. As per this research, Michael Adamson was a victim of safety crime involving a private institution and Sarah Campbell was a victim of safety crime involving a public institution. Every person who was involved in this research was involved because of their proximity to victims of safety crime, either as a family member (secondary victim) or because they were involved in a social movement as part of the movement for corporate accountability.

Chapter outline

This book tells a story of an episode in the UK's history prior to the enactment of the Corporate Manslaughter Act in 2008. By gathering and documenting the experiences of secondary victims, it details what happens to people when they are subject to a system that is designed and operated by those with power. The experiences of secondary victims of safety crime demonstrate terms of engagement for future victims, illuminating that they are subject to processes that will, first, harm them further to establish their own innocence, which is not dependent on their personal skill, tenacity or individual efforts. Second, the book draws together victims of safety crime as part of a larger group of victims who have also been harmed by a perpetrator with power. Finally, it suggests that the criminal justice system does not offer suitable solutions for such secondary victims, and other social arrangements are necessary.

Chapter 1 – Safety Crime: Criminology and Social Harm

Criminology has incorporated various theoretical approaches to explain crime and the behaviour of criminals. This has moved from classicism to positivism to victimized actor approaches with a preoccupation on the crimes of young men (Burke, 2019). Sutherland's introduction to white-collar crime in 1939 was a watershed moment: choosing instead to focus on the powerful, as a concept it was challenged as being too subjective and not able to withstand the rigorous standards of law makers, who were better placed to decide the concerns of criminologists (Croall, 2003). Following decades of silence on the matter as criminological explanations preferred to explain crime by focusing on positivism and pathological reasons that located fault in the individual, critical criminology attempted to look in another, less popular direction, drawing back on Sutherland: redefining and expanding the definition of white-collar crime. Literature from Pearce (1976), Box (1983), Slapper and Tombs (1999) and Croall (1992) revealed further crime and harm carried out by those neglected by mainstream criminology, culminating in the study of safety crimes (Tombs and Whyte, 2007) and, latterly, zemiology. This chapter will discuss whether the move to zemiology is the answer to the challenges Sutherland responded to almost 100 years ago. Zemiology, a social harm-based approach (Soliman, 2021), permits the exploration of such collective harms as corporate killing, focusing on how the harms can be resisted away from the criminal justice system and further legislation (Canning and Tombs, 2021).

Chapter 2 – A Biography of Harm, Victims and Secondary Victims of the Powerful: Deaths by Private Institutions

Thousands of workers and members of the public are killed every year around the UK and globally. The 'continued neglect or indifference' shown by social scientists towards victims 'may play a part in denying legitimacy to them and their suffering' (Shover et al, 1994: 96). The first half of this chapter will focus on such people and the effects of their deaths, adding to a biography of harm located within a zemiology that permits and encourages their examination (Copson, 2011). Drawing on known victims of safety crimes between 2005 and 2015, it will detail the circumstances of their deaths, the nature of their employment, the nature of their contact with the various institutions and the official responses. This research emphasizes the experiences of individuals who face grief and harm as individuals. Initially isolated, their grief and struggle may feel unique even though they are one of thousands across the UK.

Chapter 3 – A Common Response: Deaths by Public Institutions

This chapter draws on relevant areas from critical criminology, which include the Hillsborough Disaster, the Grenfell Disaster and deaths in custody. The inclusion of examples drawn from these areas will demonstrate how the powerful harm and the consistent official responses to such harms, echoing the findings of Chapter 2.

Chapter 4 – How Victims and Secondary Victims Are Pushed to Invisibility

This chapter will move on from the context covered in Chapter 3 to focus on how the harms of the powerful are pushed to become invisible. The debate about whether criminologists should study behaviours that are 'illegal but not outlawed by criminal statute' belies a real problem the families are forced to experience in the Coroner's Courts, Magistrate's Courts and parliament (Croall, 2003: 52). Those who are harmed must be invisible and officially diverted away from the criminal justice system and the status it provides. Through a collective examination of 'the processes, structure and policies which produce' and enable these responses, it becomes apparent they are not random but an operation of power (Canning and Tombs, 2021: 109). There are notable similarities in the operation of power as it seeks to avoid accountability and remain invisible. This is a process that shuffles and diverts individuals out of the system, legitimately and illegitimately, as each case passes a series of obstacles that ensure only a small number of cases reach the criminal justice system at all and those that do are likely to fail. There are a multitude of options available to the powerful to avoid blame or responsibility – for example, delay is a powerful tool that is visible in almost all cases. This chapter combines these instances to demonstrate the tools that are used by power that causes further harm when threatened, despite justice rather than in the pursuit of it (Scraton, 1999).

Chapter 5 – Harmful Effects on Secondary Victims

The tools and processes that block justice and potential punishment, outlined in Chapter 5 (such as delay), are part of an autopoietic process that not only ignores but causes further harm to the bereaved (Canning and Tombs, 2021). Such tools serve the corporation's pursuit of official blamelessness at the expense of those who loved and feel responsible for the person who has been killed. When this process fails to reach culmination, the loved ones feel they have failed, that 'this is the last thing [they] can do for them' and yet they have let them down (Dannemiller, 2002; Snell and Tombs, 2011: 217). This is a further harm that is experienced as those in power attempt to avoid responsibility. Examining the different cases together will demonstrate how, irrespective of scale, power has caused further harm when threatened. Various examples will be explored and built upon to demonstrate that the processes that embolden the powerful to claim their innocence further harm the families of those who were killed.

Conclusion – Alternative Social Arrangements as the Counter to Invisibility and Harm

Just as criminology is not designed to meet the needs of widows and bereaved mothers but of law makers and the criminal justice system, zemiology provides an alternative space to create solutions rather than prioritizing and accommodating the needs of faceless and often nameless employers and corporations (Todd, 2015). Zemiology is in a better position to explore alternative social rearrangements that would reduce and eliminate the experiences of secondary victims because it is not singularly focused on traditional perspectives of justice (Garside, 2013). The final chapter looks at alternative social arrangements which have worked in the past and what is needed in the future to reduce the harm experienced by secondary victims.

Note

1 A note should be made on Sutherland's reference to 'businessmen' with no consideration for gender. While I do not assume gender, to continue to refer to men is appropriate since in 2019 an analysis of the CEOs in the UK's top 100 corporations found a CEO is more likely to be called Stephen than be a woman (Bergman, 2019). However, when not quoting Sutherland, the gender-neutral 'corporation' or 'business' will be used.

1

Safety Crime: Criminology and Social Harm

The reorientation within criminology that can be traced back to Sutherland's address to the American Sociological Society in 1939 led to the discovery of the victim of safety crime, the principal interest of this research. This chapter argues that critical criminology has worked hard to take what Sutherland first named and legitimate it as an interest. However, the study of social harm is better placed to continue the study and to move away from comparison with common crime.

Social harm and zemiology can legitimately expand upon what victims of white-collar and corporate crime express about perpetrators who are unpunished. For many 'hidden' victims (Spalek, 1999: 213), it is clear who is criminal and who has harmed them, irrespective of official judgments made by the criminal justice system and those unaffected, as this victim of the Robert Maxwell pension fraud states: '[B]ut I never swore like I swore about Maxwell, because I thought he was a criminal, a real criminal … a far bigger criminal' (Spalek, 1999: 226). This chapter will first examine what critical criminology has established out of Sutherland's original assertions. The chapter then goes on to highlight what criminology cannot solve which social harm can and, finally, will justify how this is the next stage of reforming criminology in the name of the victim of corporate and safety crime.

White-collar crime is real crime

Sutherland asserted that '[w]hite collar crime is real crime … because it is in violation of the criminal law' (Sutherland, 1940: 5). The term 'crime' should be applied to unlawful acts, focusing on acts which are socially injurious and *could* be followed by a penalty, which is just as important as acts that *are* followed by a penalty. He asserted this is acceptable because there may be unlawful behaviour that meets the requirements of being socially injurious and potentially followed by a penalty which is not pursued/approached in court, failing to end with a successful prosecution. Sutherland noted that while prosecution is important for those administering punishment, it was also the duty of scholars within criminology to study criminality that met the first two conditions (Sutherland, 1983). He pushed against the 'inherent biases of the "scientific" criminology of his time' (Friedrichs, 2017: 58) with a desire to expand how crime was defined and the types of crime that was studied within the 'ambit of "crime" and thus criminology' (Tombs, 2019). He urged criminologists to study unpunished criminals, asserting they were criminals nonetheless (Geis and Goff, 1983). This received pushback in sociology and criminology.

Within criminological texts, Sutherland's name is often followed by two of his critics, Tappan (1977) and Shapiro (1983). For Tappan, Sutherland was inviting claims he was making a 'value judgement', which should be avoided by relying on the authorities to define what is criminal with appropriate 'rigour and precision' (1977: 281, 279). A criminology that focused on those who had been punished by the authorities drew a firm boundary within which to observe, document and explain the behaviour of officially defined criminals and criminality. This was a legitimate pursuit, upholding crime as an expected blip in an 'otherwise efficient, fair and just social system' (Sim et al, 1987: 3). Sutherland's inclusion of the white-collar 'criminaloid' and his focus on harmful crimes that were unpunished deviated from this established routine (Geis and Goff, 1983: xvii). In unmasking the white-collar criminal, his 'pursuit of studying scientific, objective … criminological phenomena' was called into question (Friedrichs, 2017: 58). For academics such as Tappan, Sutherland's assertion of the existence of the white-collar criminal was not a legitimate area of study but 'currently fashionable dogma' (Tappan, 1977: 98).

As with Tappan, Shapiro called for academics to favour objective, neutral investigation, led by the law. This was not only preferred but the responsibility of academics in order to avoid 'fuel[ing] an unfair stereotype … of the sociologist as superficial and incapable of acquiring legal knowledge, and as a purveyor of the obvious' (Shapiro, 1983: 306). It also prevented those carrying out research on corporate crime from expressing 'moral outrage', which clouded their sociological good sense (Shapiro, 1983: 306). Instead, Shapiro called for academics to work on conceptualizing white-collar crime given that 'scholars … have been embroiled in terminological disputes' (Shapiro, 1983: 306) that had not been resolved. Referring to both criminologists and sociologists, Tappan similarly took issue with the lack of definition on what is injurious, which 'invites the subjective value-judgements of the investigator' (Tappan, 1947: 97). Pre-dating debates on crime having no ontological reality (Hillyard and Tombs, 2005), Tappan refuted the idea that the law is an 'artificial category' in support of the creation of laws that are not created out of 'fortuity or artifice' (Tappan, 1947: 98). Criminologists should work with the resources available to 'develop intelligent theories of phenomena covered by current definitions' (Shapiro, 1983: 307) and not expand the definition based on their own belief. To do so would be to become the moral entrepreneurs of old, moving from harm to crime based on personal judgements of what is offensive.

Tappan's rebuttal demonstrated his contempt: 'Off with the old criminologies, on with the new orientations, the new horizons!' (Tappan, 1947: 96). He reasserted that conviction was essential to define who is criminal, emphasizing the legal nature of this distinction: 'Criminals … are a sociologically distinct group of violators of specific legal norms, subjected to state treatment' (Tappan, 1947: 102). Those who differentiate between people who breach the law and those who are convicted enjoy 'damning as criminal most anyone he [sic] pleases' (Tappan, 1947: 99). This was an ideological jump from Sutherland's inclusion of unconvicted law breakers to anyone in the population an academic wished to brand as criminal. For Tappan and Shapiro, using the law as a site of analysis is essential to remain morally neutral and suitably restrained within rational, defined parameters. The legal definition of criminal behaviour was '[p]recise … and [the] least ambiguous' (Michael and Adler, 1933, cited in Bottomley, 1979: 5), a standard that was both amoral and neutral.

Yet calls for academics to look at unrecorded crime were made a hundred years prior to Sutherland by Quetelet (1984) and Guerry (1829); the former was astonished that unknown crime was neglected (Bottomley, 1979). In their search for a theory of crime, they recognized official statistics were incomplete and assumed a real figure that was yet to be uncovered (Sellin and Wolfgang, 1964, cited in Bottomley, 1979). Quetelet's, Guerry's and Sutherland's (1939) focus on the punishable foregrounded work of Realists, who drew from 19th-century statisticians with the creation of the National Crime Survey in the 1960s in what was a 'hold my beer' moment within criminology. Designed to collect the 'dark figure of crime' (Coleman and Moynihan, 1996), victimization surveys asked members of the public whether they had been victims of crime that they did not report. These have since been embraced by criminologists and legitimized by the Home Office, gathered annually and incorporated into official statistics in Britain since 1984. Realists answered Quetelet's and Sutherland's criticisms while avoiding accusations of expressing personal moral outrage. Indeed, Tappan's calls for definitions of crime to stick to the punished is 'little more than a historical footnote today' with few supporters (Geis, 2016: 33, 45).

This accepted turn in criminology – the collection of data via national victim surveys – does not resolve Sutherland's call because this larger sample still fails to examine 'persons of respectability' and those of high social status (Sutherland, 1940: 4). Criminology has accepted that it is legitimate to draw data from those who are unconvicted, supporting what Sutherland and his proponents spent decades defending. Yet the victim surveys do not seek to measure victims who are the focus of this research: hidden data now found in the Crime Survey for England and Wales neither establish white-collar crime as crime nor seek to uncover it, a crucial aim Sutherland did not deviate from.

Providing proof rather than illustrations

While the white-collar criminal was strong as a concept, the evidence presented by Sutherland was based on the results of lie detector tests on employees, remarks from mayors and included assertions such as '[w]hite-collar criminality in politics … is generally recognized as fairly prevalent' (Sutherland, 1940: 4). Sutherland (1940: 3) provided 'illustrations … rather than … proof' of the scope of white-collar criminality. Hindered by the novelty of his own concept, he conceded that '[a]n accurate statistical comparison of the crimes of the two classes is not available' (Sutherland, 1940: 3). This was inadequate for the study of criminology during the latter part of the 20th century, when 'the conservative tinge of the political climate [and] the priorities of sociology went through a period in which highly quantitative, supposedly value-free empirical investigation was prized' (Geis and Goff, 1983: xxx).

Criminologists studying common crime are comparatively resplendent with potential quantitative data to explore the motivations of mostly poor people committing a number of different state-sanctioned crimes with access to government-collected statistics, the dealings of the courts and the content of prisons. This is 'convenient' for criminologists who agree with the values of law makers (Sutherland, 1940: 9). However, for those studying corporate crime, it is something they must resolve because, first, the data are not readily available, and, second, even though focusing on the unconvicted is standard within criminology, the data collected by those studying white-collar crime remain contested. By looking at criminality outside of agreed parameters for crime committed by those who were not lower class, Sutherland's original aims were part of 'a fierce, long running, and contemporary, dispute' (Slapper and Tombs, 1999: 5). Nevertheless, several criminologists endeavoured to establish and evidence the existence of the respectable criminal and provide proof that corporations and the respectable persons who ran them were committing crime at a higher rate than those in the lower class. This required a robust definition to scope the prevalence of white-collar crime.

Sutherland's first definition reflected his wish to look at criminals who were in a class as defined by their occupation and 'of low socioeconomic status' (1940: 1). In a footnote, he qualified the term 'white collar' as referring to those who were 'respected, socially accepted', and not necessarily those who are well dressed, well paid and well educated (Sutherland, 1940: 4). A year later, Sutherland clarified white-collar crimes as 'a violation of the criminal law by a person of the upper socioeconomic class in the course of his occupational studies' (Sutherland, 1941: 112). He immediately criticized his own definition as being 'arbitrary and not very precise' (Sutherland, 1941: 112) but asserted that the creation of the term had a greater purpose – to draw attention to a section of barely mentioned criminality that poured cold water over popular explanations of criminality. Sutherland's work did indeed draw attention to crimes that had been hitherto ignored, yet his definition also drew just as much attention, receiving criticism and revision in the intervening years. Sutherland's focus on the perpetrator was seen as problematic, as explored further in the next section.

Criminality, not the criminal

Sutherland's focus on the perpetrator and the inclusion of class was seen as empirically weak, but both were essential to the definition as they are integral to the unmasking of the white-collar criminal (Geis, 2016). For example, Sutherland argued it was the status of business people which meant they were less likely to be subject to enforcement and punishment (Sutherland, 1945, cited in Slapper and Tombs, 1999). The removal of class and respectability would abandon a critical point and focus of analysis. Shapiro (1990: 350) argued that 'conceptions of white-collar crime or corporate crime are preoccupied with actors rather than with acts', which means they focus on 'malevolence'. She called for criminologists to avoid this by not focusing on the class of the criminal, or even on the criminal at all, and instead focus on the criminal act. This would avoid missing the crimes of people who are not upper class and from making generalizations about white-collar criminality based on those 'whose wrongs are so egregious' (Shaprio, 1990: 362).

Croall (1992) agreed, arguing any definition should not be linked to the high status and respectability of offenders, because people who commit crime can be found throughout the occupational hierarchy. It may still be true that offenders in the higher classes have greater opportunities (Shapiro, 1990, cited in Croall, 1992) and enjoy 'structural advantages' in the criminal justice system (Croall, 1992: 165), but focusing on class ignores different levels of power found throughout the hierarchy, as explored in 1982 by a series of publications that formed the Yale White-Collar Crime Project. Neither Croall (1992) nor Slapper and Tombs (1999) abandoned Sutherland's aims: the former continued to use the term 'white-collar crime' because it is recognizable to both academics and the public, while the latter focused on corporate crime, moving away from individual offenders who share social characteristics to legitimate (and respected) organizations.

This move to corporate crime was logical since Sutherland's definition of white-collar crime referred to individuals committing crime, yet his subsequent case studies were based on corporations and businesses (Cressey, 1989; Geis, 2016). The distinction between white-collar and corporate crime furthered the endeavour of critical criminology in its critique of the existing law and by highlighting its inadequacies (Slapper and Tombs, 1999). In doing so, it moved Sutherland's study from a focus on theory to observations on law and policy, challenging 'powerful political and economic interests' (Michalowski and Kramer, 1987, cited in Tombs and Whyte, 2003a: 37; Tombs and Whyte, 2015). The study of corporate crime maintains an interest in those who use their power drawn from their status to refute the law because it focuses on the law as 'capitalism's law' (Slapper and Tombs, 1999: 18) and as 'bourgeois legal categories' that 'capitalist corporations by and large do not and cannot … routinely adhere to' (Slapper and Tombs, 1999: 19). Corporations are afforded status, both in their position as legal organizations and in the (lack of) response of the law. In this, critical criminologists focused on criminality and established parameters for the study of crimes committed by those who were likely to be drawn from the higher socioeconomic classes, continuing in Sutherland's tradition.

This definition was built upon and broken down into smaller categories that permitted further analysis which both Sutherland (1939) and Clinard and Yaegar (1980) made use of in their research (cited in Slapper and Tombs, 1999). The creation of subcategories of crimes that do not equate to criminal offences (for example grievous bodily harm) are used by criminologists to provide a smaller group of offences to focus upon and compare (Croall, 2001). Similarly, in critical criminology, researchers sought to define and map the scope of subcategories of corporate crime, observing the search for 'observable causes of crime' as per the foundations of criminology (Garland, 1985: 129). In the 1990s, there was a proliferation of typologies, including consumer crime (Croall, 1989), food crime (Croall, 1993) and safety crime (Tombs and Whyte, 2007). In one example, Slapper and Tombs (1999) defined different types of corporate crime, identifying the four most frequently used subcategories of corporate crimes: financial, offences against consumers, crimes against employees and environmental offences. Of concern here is the penultimate category, 'crimes against employees', which includes the failure to provide a safe working environment, leading to the deaths of workers. These established crimes committed by corporations as objects of study and enabled a clearer distinction of parameters which criminologists could use to qualify Sutherland's assertion that 'the illegal behaviour [of businessmen] is much more extensive than the prosecutions and complaints indicate' (Sutherland, 1983: 228). The victim of corporate crime was now clearly defined and about to be counted.

Legitimizing the existence of corporate crime

Out of Sutherland's white-collar, and then corporate crime, researchers had a clearer distinction of parameters of study but still could not draw wholly on official statistics. Instead, they had to use them in 'critical and creative' ways (Croall, 2016: 50). Collecting data that was not collected by the state, nor of interest to them, was complicated and time consuming. For example, researchers who study fraud, a type of corporate offending that has 'the highest political and legal profile' (Slapper and Tombs, 1999: 56), require a combination of data from at least 11 different bodies (Levi and Pithouse, 1992, cited in Slapper and Tombs, 1999). Slapper and Tombs (1999) devoted a chapter in *Corporate Crime* to mapping the extent of 'crimes against employees', drawing on data made available by regulatory bodies but acknowledging they are likely to be underestimates. Indeed, Sutherland (1983: 44) concluded that 'official decisions against a corporation is not a good index of the extent to which it obeys the law'. By getting creative with official statistics, critical criminologists pre-empted claims that in doing so they were moving away from science. Rather than going no further, they began with a caveat that a level of uncertainty is certain, similar to qualifications made in the face of 'enormous problems with official recording of conventional crime' (Slapper and Tombs, 1999: 56).

In order to count deaths at work, data was gathered using official data taken from the Reporting of Injuries, Diseases and Dangerous Occurrences legislation, which compels the Health and Safety Executive (HSE) to record the number of annual fatal injuries. This examination demonstrated the partial recording of deaths in favour of what they called a 'headline figure' since it neglected to include the deaths of many, such as those who had been killed as a result of gas, in the sea and those on the road (Slapper and Tombs, 1999: 68). To represent the numbers of people who had been killed because of their contact with a corporation, figures would have to be collected from other bodies such as the Department of Transport and the coronial system. This figure then had to be interrogated further to determine what proportion was likely to be corporate crime – for example, not every death at work is a corporate crime, and not every death in a prison is a state crime.

To accurately map crimes against employees, Slapper and Tombs (1999) again turned to official sources and combined what they had collected with investigations carried out by the HSE and reports such as Commissions of Inquiry and Accident Investigation Reports. Aware of potential claims of moralizing (Shapiro, 1983), Slapper and Tombs (1999) used data collected by legislators, potentially minimizing accusations of moralizing and of being biased and unscientific. This process led to a 'conservative estimate' that the number of deaths at work were 'four times greater than homicide' and that 'two out of three fatal injuries appear to occur as a result of criminal acts of omissions on the part of employers' (Slapper and Tombs, 1999: 78). By using data not usually examined, the activities of corporations were being qualified as a necessary topic within criminology, and researchers demonstrated at the end of the 20th century what Sutherland had pressed for in the early part of the century: corporations and the respectable persons who ran them were committing crime at a rate higher than those in the lower class. The perpetrators of safety crime were many, and, further, their acts went unconvicted and unpunished. Critical criminologists looked for reasons to explain why this was the case.

Cultural immunity

Sutherland acknowledged the inequality of the application of law because 'the upper class has greater influence in moulding the criminal law and its administration to its own interests than does the lower class' (Sutherland, 1940: 9). Corporations make the rules of the game, and 'the greatest opportunity lies in their ability to prevent their actions from becoming subject to criminal sanctions in the first place' (Box, 1983: 59). It is not that they play the game well, with excellent legal representation, but that they make the rules of the game in the first place. Sutherland included the now oft-quoted words of Daniel Drew, 'a pious old fraud': 'Law is like a cobweb: it's made for flies and the smaller kind of insects, so to speak, but lets the bumblebee break through. When technicalities of the law stood in my way, I have always been able to brush them aside as easy as anything' (Daniel Drew cited in Sutherland, 1983: 57). Sutherland (1983) argued that due to a shared class status and the distance between corporate criminality and popularly perceived criminality, the corporate criminal does not perceive themselves as criminal, and while the smaller, common criminals are caught, the larger, corporate criminals are not.

From within academia, scholars working in socio-legal studies created a body of work after the 1970s that focused on business regulation (Tombs, 2018). Proponents of 'regulatory orthodoxy' supported the tone of the Factory Acts that suggested the selective use of the threat of prosecution as a 'last resort' in favour of regular inspections and punitive measures (Almond and Colover, 2012, cited in Tombs, 2017: 77). This is in part based on the acceptance of limited resources being dedicated to reducing and controlling corporate crime in the future and the failure of enforcement and punishment in the past (Tombs, 2017). Those endorsing 'regulatory orthodoxy' called for the weight of regulation to be concentrated on those corporations who 'play fast and loose' (Ayres and Braithwaite, 1992, cited in Tombs, 2017: 81), drawing direct similarities to what factory owners agreed to 170 years earlier. The notion that there was a time in the past when corporations were heavily controlled belied Sutherland's (1940: 8) insistence that crimes of the 'upper class' were handled by 'inspectors' and often there was 'no official action at all'. It 'serves the function of a myth … or a sacred narrative which explains … the way it is and why it has to be so' (Tombs, 2017: 83). One assumption of regulatory orthodoxy – that business would comply and cooperate following persuasion (Braithwaite, 2002, cited in Tombs, 2017) – which Sutherland (1940) referred to as cultural immunity, fitted well with business.

Corporate crimes have continued to avoid being associated with clear criminal liability and are instead categorized as offences that are based on the breaking of regulations, irrespective of the nature of the deaths or the circumstances that led up to the deaths (Gunningham and Johnstone, 1999; Wells, 2001, cited in Almond, 2009b). Health and safety offences are judged as doing something lawful with a degree of carelessness, reinforcing a dominant assumption about those capable of committing violence (Wells, 2001). The term 'business regulation' stands outside of criminal law and 'crime control' (Croall, 1992: 143), which belies the existence of legal categories that could, on paper, respond to corporate criminality in the Crown Court. Much criminological research outside of the proponents of 'regulatory orthodoxy' has worked to highlight the daily response (and non-response) to corporate criminality (Bergman, 1994), as seen in the administration of the laws that affect corporations. Criminologists highlighted the consequences of corporate criminals not being arrested by the same agencies, nor counted by the Home Office or treated the same way as conventional criminals (Slapper and Tombs, 1999).

Researchers have reiterated Sutherland's point: in court, the judges bestow 'light' punishment as they benefit from a measure of 'social capital' and admire and respect owners of corporations, reluctant to see them as criminals (Punch, 2009: 51). In this, the law does not reflect the want of the public; indeed, there is no evidence that the legal system reflects the importance the public attach to crimes (Almond, 2009a), refuting Sutherland's point that law against corporations is inept because of the lack of calls from the public. The law is distinct from crime – it is an interpretation of experts, judges and solicitors (Snider, 2003a) who are less likely to see corporate criminality as a matter for the law. Criminologists continued to highlight how labelling certain crimes as less important and therefore unworthy of examination on the premise of how they are responded to is 'historically and culturally contingent' (Wells, 2001: 7); adherence to law is a moot point since dictators in history have committed acts of mass harm yet have acted within legal limits. Despite the existence of laws aimed at controlling corporations, Sutherland (1940) noted the reluctance of courts to impose punitive measures and that no 'effective method of dealing with corporations under the criminal law has yet been devised' (1940: 114). Almost 100 years later, this remains unresolved, and the failure to prosecute corporations can be explained by the lack of scrutiny of the state, something he did not acknowledge directly.

Sutherland focused on finding a 'hypothesis that will explain both white-collar criminality and lower-class criminality' (Sutherland, 1940: 10) without an examination of the state. This preoccupation of criminology ignored the state and its 'structures of power, domination and control … [which are left] unresearched and untouched' (Sim et al, 1979: 8). Critical criminology instead attempted to examine the structural context from which crime arose, moving away from the interpersonal to the economy, state and ideology (Scraton and Chadwick, 2009). It defined the state as a collection of institutions that maintain order through coercion and consent (Coleman and Sim, 2019). Critical and radical criminology scrutinized institutions, including universities, the police, courts and prisons, to demonstrate the power of the state (Sim et al, 1987), moving their efforts out of the margins and from 'abnormal' individuals to focus on violence condoned and committed by the state (Sim, 2010: 6). The absence of the state in widely used criminological texts has implications for many undergraduates who consequently believe 'state crime does not exist' (Hillyard, 2003: 206). When the state is not considered, it can operate as something intangible that appears as naturally neutral and objective, betraying the role it plays in criminalization and non-criminalization, a denial of the existence of a status quo (Solnit, 2004). Studies in safety crime drew from this interest in the state to explain the lack of prosecutions and to explore the ongoing and symbiotic relationship between state/public actors and corporations (Kramer et al, 2002, cited in Bernati and Whyte, 2017). Critical criminologists had established that safety crime existed, there was more of it than expected and that it was going unpunished. Only a connection to the state explained its invisibility in the long arm of the law.

Congressmen and businessmen

For Sutherland, the criminal law was underpinned by the relationship between congressmen and businessmen, with a direct link to the president rather than the state per se. He referred to 'those who are responsible for the system' and are 'afraid to antagonise businessmen' because of the potential consequences, including 'a reduction in contributions to the campaign funds needed to win the next election' (Sutherland, 1983: 55). Therefore, change the individual, change the enforcement of the law. Sutherland illustrated the importance of this link with the example of the Sherman Antitrust Act 1890, which he claimed was influenced by who was president at the time, arguing that it was not enforced when those who were 'friendly toward business' were in charge (Sutherland, 1983: 58). He gave the example of the Pure Food and Drug Law passed through Congress in 1906 which did not create a new law but tried to re-implement a state law that was already in place; however, it was not enforced because of the pressures raised by the 'offenders ... the head of the Dept of Agriculture ... congressmen ... and by others' (Sutherland, 1940: 8). He appeared optimistic about the possibility of change, noting that following the Great Depression, which began in 1929, there was an increased desire to enforce the laws that existed and implement new ones (Sutherland, 1983).

Writing with the memory of the depression, Sutherland did not foresee the global domination of corporations or the aggressive pursuit of a neoliberal agenda. He considered that in 'the conflict between the government and the corporations, the government has lost' (Sutherland, 1983: 78), viewing the two as competing, not in collusion. For him, the corporation was linked to the state via cultural homogeneity due to 'intimate personal friends ... families which have other members in business' (Sutherland, 1983: 251). Yet he sowed the seeds for the research completed since that has filled in gaps on endemic issues, expanding upon his brief mention of 'capitalistic enterprises' (Sutherland, 1983: 251). Critical criminologists have highlighted the complicity of the state in morally elevating corporations to a position where they can define their own status (Tombs and Whyte, 2010). This has gone beyond what Sutherland (1983: 233) noted as the 'rationalizations' that those in charge make to conceal crime.

Corporations have been promoted to a position where they are included in governmental reviews which seek their advice on health and safety, thus granting them prestige rather than stigma. The report that preceded Health and Safety at Work Act 1974 was headed by Alfred Robens, who was the chairman of the coal board at the time of the Aberfan disaster that killed 116 children and 28 adults, a board that was held responsible by the official tribunal (Institution of Occupational Safety and Health, 2022). Indeed, it was this public disaster in 1967 that led to calls for a strengthening of the legislation. Similarly, a review in 2005 was headed by Philip Hampton, the financial director of British Gas during the time their subsidiary, Transco, caused a gas explosion that killed a family of four (Tombs, 2017). He was the Director of Lloyds TSB when the bank was involved in falsifying its records (Tombs, 2017). The Chairman of Bowles Transport company was awarded the Most Excellent Order of the British Empire award for services to the Road Haulage Association, despite the fact his company had been found to have been involved in systematic rule breaking which had led to an employee falling asleep at the wheel, killing two people on the M25 (Gobert and Punch, 2003). Foot summarizes: 'Again and again in different industries and enterprises the regulators and others responsible for supervising industries and services were chosen from the boardrooms of the most successful and powerful companies' (2012: 417). This public celebration and delegation of power demonstrate the lack of stigma attached to corporations and those at the top. Critical criminologists pointed to longer sentences and a widening of the net of the criminal justice system for powerless perpetrators, while, at the same time, the 'persistent' efforts of powerful corporations secured 'differential advantages' in pursuit 'of their interests' (Sutherland, 1983: 197), supported by the public, who perceived it as 'bothersome', related to 'red tape' and in direct opposition to entrepreneurialism, which supported the continual reduction of regulation (James et al, 2012). It is with no irony that people who have been publicly linked to the deaths of workers are rewarded with the top seat at the table tasked with reducing further deaths.

Neoliberalism

Sutherland did not predict the power of the corporation, which, facilitated by the state, has expanded under neoliberalism. Under the ideology of neoliberalism, it does not matter who is in charge because their interests are built into the structure of the state. Whatever is good for business is good for society, and the state is surplus to requirements (Michalowski and Kramer, 1987, cited in Tombs and Whyte, 2010; see also Tombs and Whyte, 2010). The union movement, a key protection offered to workers from safety crime, was promoted as an unnecessary hindrance to business and a thorn in the side of the state.

Under neoliberalism, the power of trade unions diminished from a prominent position post-WWII (Chomsky, 2003). Under Thatcher's control, employers gained more power to attract workers with the promise of lower wages in exchange for flexibility and fragmentation. As a result, union membership in the UK reduced from its peak of 13 million when she became prime minister in 1979 to 6.4 million in 2014 (Hodder et al, 2017). With the explosion of sub-contractors working zero-hour contracts and the slashing of union power, workers became more vulnerable and were placed in a 'relatively subordinate economic position' (Whyte, 2007: 455), while capitalism, revered by Hayek (the pioneer of neoliberalism), was barely threatened (Foot, 2012). As neoliberalism accelerated, critical criminologists emphasized that workers killed are 'more likely to work in smaller rather than larger workplaces, or to be self-employed or on short- or fixed-term contracts, to be non-unionised, and receiving low levels of pay' (Tombs, 1999: 91).

The price of flexible labour was the safety of the workers; the social contract was attacked, exchanging short-term profit for the public good and diminishing the safety net the state had provided since WWII (Giroux, 2005). The isolation of workers in itself increases risk, which can be seen between sectors as exemplified in the multibillion-dollar company Amazon, which outsources labour to agencies who can take disciplinary action when workers are late or ill (Shears, 2018). In 2018, GMB used ambulance statistics to demonstrate that workers at Amazon were making a disproportionate number of emergency calls. One site in Staffordshire had 115 callouts in three years compared to just eight callouts in the same period at a similarly sized site owned by Tesco (Shears, 2018). While neoliberalism has increased the wealth of the richest in society, it has also increased levels of inequality and left those at the bottom more vulnerable to harm, both physically and mentally.

Innovative entrepreneurs

Neoliberalism strengthened the link between the state and business, which had loosened in the post-war period, enabling the plundering, building and extraction of profit. The blending of public with private expanded, reaching a zenith in 1992 with the opening of Europe's first private prison. At a time when in the US, 'Wall street and Washington have become sutured together as never before' (Peck, 2010: 109), the state purposefully blurred the line between corporations and the use of public money, subsiding the rich. This continued in the UK. Whyte (2015) highlights how 142 peers who had connections to private healthcare corporations were eligible to vote on an Act that sought to increase the use of private services in the NHS (Whyte, 2015), writing that it is 'nothing short of incredible that in liberal democracies … so much public funding could be so simply transferred from government to the "private" sector … negotiated with a hand-picked group of elite bankers over a Balti takeaway' (Whyte, 2015: 11, 12).

While the corporations benefit handsomely from their links with the state, the public are encouraged to view this as a cheaper and more efficient way to spend public money. Corporations and the people who run them have increased in stature, elevated to a position as a public good and a panacea for social problems. Television programmes promote private corporations and chief executive officers, such as the BBC programme *Can Gerry Robinson Save The NHS?* Public services are viewed as wasteful and businessmen as enigmatic saviours. Critical criminologists have highlighted this sleight of hand: put simply, business is good, private ownership is more efficient and regulation unnecessarily restrains the conditions for profit. This is promoted while the state transfers money from the taxation of the public to private corporations, which wilfully avoid paying taxes in return (Giroux, 2005).

The contempt 'businessmen … feel and express … for law' (Sutherland, 1983: 299) is less necessary due to the pro-business stance political parties have expressed since the 1970s. The effects of neoliberalism have meant that the HSE, like many other sectors, has reduced workers to be 'thankful they've still got a job' (Tombs, 2017: 169), streamlining the service to remove the most expensive employees (those with years of experience) and leaving those who have general rather than specialist expertise. With fewer employees, who are paid less and with more to do, the HSE is ineffective, with no time to complete even basic training (Tombs, 2017). Regulation has been reduced and made ineffective, yet publicly the HSE is perceived as having been expanded and over-zealous. Critical criminology emphasizes that the state is an 'ally of corporate power' (McCullagh, 2016: 103) which acts like 'the executive committee of the ruling class' (Bukharin, 1929, cited in Foot, 2012: 432) to further the interests of those in power at the expense of those who do not have power.

Critical criminologists draw from other disciplines to explain the historical link between the corporation and reveal its collusion and dependence on the state, which from Sutherland's point of view in the US appeared intimate and dependent upon social networks. Tombs (2017: 15) drew on the earliest example of a corporation, the East India Company, which was 'created for the mobilisation, utilisation and protection of capital within socio-historical state formations'. Bound up in colonization and the theft of capital, the East India Company depended upon the state and in turn was tasked with military action, much like the British Navy expanded to protect the empire in the 1690s (Andreas and Nadelmann, 2006). In 1857, an Act was passed that explicitly linked the two and facilitated the theft of £1.65 million from India to England and contributed to a famine that killed 30 million people in Bengal (Elkins, 2022). The first corporation and its role in the murder of civilians, enabled by the state, emboldened the worst crimes committed under imperialism as 'a political and economic system of violence' (James, 2015, cited in Elkins, 2022: 299). James Fitzjames Stephen described India as 'a belligerent civilisation' (Mazower, 2008, cited in Elkins, 2022: 304) that was in need of control via the legislation he was writing. His view of the law sums up how it can be used against people judged as inferior – in his words, 'law is nothing but regulated force' (Elkins, 2022: 303). Critical criminologists began to highlight and then explain the reluctance to apply the law, as regulated force, against the powerful.

Embryonic law

Sutherland (1940) described those with the power legislate as reluctant to believe businessmen needed more than slight encouragement to conform and as undeserving of the stigma generally attached to those who break the law. Academics began scrutinizing regulation and law as indicative of this social order to examine what the state permits and what it prohibits (Pearce and Tombs, 1989) The political, legal and ideological processes that empower corporations to cause large-scale social harm require a great deal of state work (Tombs and Whyte, 2015: 93). Wells (2001) concluded that members of corporations are enabled to exploit the gap between the corporation and its members to avoid conviction, using the law to avoid any stigma and punishment. Corporations and those who work within them can present incidents as 'one offs' (Croall, 1992) and be given the benefit of doubt. The law works in favour of corporations: for example, after the sinking of the *Herald of Free Enterprise*, jury members were invited to judge whether P&O (called Townsend and Thoresen at the time of the incident) was prudent based on the interviews of employees (past and present). Wells (2001) likened it to a jury being asked to judge the morality of a person charged with robbery by interviewing their family and friends. To extend this to a corporation following the deaths of 193 people was incomparable to usual proceedings in common manslaughter charges. Lord Justice Taylor went on to conclude that the risk was not obvious because the *Herald of Free Enterprise* had sailed without similar tragedies for seven years, which is akin to a person accused of burglary claiming they entered many houses without ever burgling them. These instances show how the state uses its power to create legal systems that protect the power of corporations, as they did during colonization to murder citizens, both inside and outside of its borders (Elkins, 2022). The law is not impartial in its approach to corporate criminals: it is not merely that corporations play the game well, or that they know individuals whose help they can call on. Instead, the law is structured not only to find them innocent but to increase the likelihood of harm.

If there is ever a time that laws and regulation might change, it is following public disasters, such as those involving members of the public. However, researchers including Snider have concluded that 'cultural permission to proactively scrutinise the practices of dominant economic actors is short lived following corporate disasters' (2009: 27). This was seen following the Ladbroke Grove train crash in 1999. John Prescott visited the Paddington site and promised an inquiry to 'get to the bottom of everything that happened' (Tran and Pulham, 1999) and that money was of no object in ensuring the safety of the railway (Wolmar, 2001: 152). He met with victims' groups, such as the Marchioness Campaign Group, yet it took two elections for a Corporate Manslaughter Act to materialize, an Act which failed to fulfil its promises and protect the public, along with the law relating to corporations which are 'treated as an important historic species, to be preserved in their embryonic form, never allowed to develop a bite' (Wells, 2001: 113). The courts have prevented the law from evolving to reflect modern corporations and are therefore unable to hold corporations criminally responsible. Along with children under the age of ten, the insane and animals, corporations are not held morally to account (Wells, 2001). Deaths and disasters offer a period when change seems possible, but business soon resumes until the next brief break in the corporate veil. The state is reluctant to refuse the needs of corporations and profit and tries instead to attract their influence, investment and confidence (Snider, 2003b). By analysing the state and the law that it creates (Harvey, 2007), critical criminology encouraged the study of the structure of both the state and the corporation to explain the continued immunity of respectable persons.

A victim of the powerful

In the latter half of the 20th century, academics began to unravel why there was a gap between 'what actually occurs' and the way things should happen (Pearce, 1976, cited in Tombs and Whyte, 2015: 29). Similar to the lack of convictions for rape or deaths in police custody compared to their prevalence, academics and activists asked why people were dying but no one was being prosecuted. For example, Slapper (1999) and Bergman (1991) asked how it was possible that no director had been convicted of corporate manslaughter in England and Wales prior to 1994. Cross-referencing official data with the revealed scope of corporate crime, Tombs (1991, 2003) pointed to the five prosecutions and two convictions brought between 1965 and 2003 compared to the more than 20,000 deaths at work in the same period. Each study pushed the reader to be compelled by the seriousness of corporate criminality, to concur with the statement that 'corporate crime kills!' (Box, 1983: 23). By highlighting both the dearth of prosecutions and the experiences of victims, researchers and campaigners shifted the burden away from criminologists who had been tasked with providing proof of the existence of the corporate criminal. It questioned the failure of criminology to interrogate the likelihood that corporations never commit crime. Feminists had explored the same discrepancies in relation to the low rate of convictions for rape in the same period.

In this work, feminists centred the victim in the decriminalization of rape in the 1970s. By highlighting the experiences of the female victim in the criminal justice system, they documented how woefully inadequate the process was at recognizing certain crimes and in the delivery of justice (Davies et al, 2005). Their research demonstrated that the success of cases in court was dependent not upon the act itself but how the event was framed within the criminal justice system. The criminal justice system relies upon various rape myths in its interpretation of the truth, used by defence barristers in court to undermine the credibility of the complainant, deny victimhood and crucially 'make her appear unworthy of the protection of the law' (Lees, 1996: 2). These myths include the failure to resist, that sex offenders are different from ordinary people, 'kissing as consent' and that rape is an easy allegation to make (Temkin et al, 2016). Victims of rape were disadvantaged due to the nature of the offence committed against them, and the defence counsel has 'at his fingertips a history of misogynist thinking to draw on about women's mendacity, untrustworthiness, spitefulness, impurity, provocation, wildness, unpredictability, irrationality and general unreliability … the idea that all women are "whores" who cannot really be raped as they want it anyway' (Temkin et al, 2016: 261–2). Lees comments: 'The image of the law is one of impartiality, objectivity, rationality and neutrality. Traditionally, the law is supposed to treat all who come before the courts equally, regardless of class, race, sex or creed. This is far from the case' (1996: 130). Until the work of feminism in the 1960s and 1970s in naming 'that which had gone without a name' (Mawby and Walklate, 1994: 11), the court was empowered to claim to be a bastion of the truth as presented and dissected by the neutral agents of the court, determined to home in on the facts. Feminist research demonstrated its inept response to cases of rape, how it blocked justice and damaged victims.

It is a body of work which demonstrated the way the law operated via the court to victimize the victim and worked to change perceptions of the legal system as being a force in which it works to 'subjugate other discourses (namely law's version of rape versus women's version)' (Smart, 1995: 8). This is significant for victims of corporate and safety crime, whose experiences in the legal system share commonalities with victims of rape (Shover et al, 1994) in that the inaction and processes of the court reveal their inherent biases. The inclusion of the victim was something Sutherland did not cover in his work, which is in keeping with the context of criminology at the time of his writing, being concerned with the perpetrator and finding the causes of crime to enable reforms of the criminal justice system (Sim et al, 1987). However, critical criminologists drew attention to the victims of crimes, intent on both proving their existence and that their experiences are worthy of study.

Carson (1982) was one of the first to consider safety victims in his collection of qualitative data from workers extracting oil in the North Sea. He compelled scholars to connect the personal troubles of workers 'whose deaths are now anonymously enshrined in the statistical records of North Sea casualties' to public issues (Carson, 1982: 296). Similarly, Spalek's work on victims of financial crimes (1999, 2001, 2006) made it difficult to deny the experiences of people who had their money stolen, whether that was retirement savings by Maxwell or money for children's Christmas presents in the Farepak scandal. This type of research established that victims were worthy of academic study and public concern and provided proof of what Sutherland noted was an effect of white-collar crime – 'the violation of trust that creates distrust' (Sutherland, 1940: 5). This shift of focus to the forgotten victim examined the criminality of respected criminals, voicing the experiences of their 'invisible' victims.

Resistance

Sutherland had briefly mentioned the white-collar victim in relation to their 'weakness' against the 'power' of the white-collar criminal (1940: 9). He noted that the corporate criminal, Daniel Drew, had resolved to take money not from his peers but from those less powerful who 'wouldn't be able to organize and fight back' (1940: 9). He claimed that '[w]hite-collar criminality flourishes at points where powerful business and professional men come in contact with persons who are weak' (Sutherland, 1940: 9). Sutherland rightly highlighted the difference in power between the corporation and the safety crime victim. What he had not foreseen was the centrality of the victim and the impact of strong victims and campaign groups who mobilized in response to various injustices and what 'can't be silenced when the victims exist' (Whyte, 2007: 200).

In the 1980s, Phil Scraton was approached by a 'weaker' victim (the family of Jimmy Kelly) for advice on the inquest system, assuming he and other experts could apply their knowledge to help them answer their questions. Instead, they realized they knew little about it and applied for internal funding to attend to this gap (Ryan, 1996). The victims were not waiting to be uncovered and were not weak but took a highly active role. This led to the creation of INQUEST in 1981 to provide people with the 'emotional support and legal expertise they need to help piece together the circumstances that surround the death that has transformed their grief into anger' and make it a 'public concern' (Ryan, 1996: 1). INQUEST blurred the line between activism and other recognizable full-time roles as academics, solicitors, journalists and charity workers worked with bereaved family members. This was continued following several disasters in the late 1980s and 1990s, when several groups were created. Where Sutherland (1983) considered a lack of conflict between government and business was because of a lack of organization by the public, groups instigated by bereaved families demanded the attention of the press and the government. Their testimonies 'were transformed into public issues' and became a 'spur to ... political action' (Rolston, 2000: 319) in a manner that Carson (1982) pushed for. Families of victims of safety crime were making themselves visible and became part of a movement that included other interested parties.

Families and survivors demonstrated strength at the most difficult of times, creating and steering social movements while dealing with their sudden bereavement. Groups responding to corporate crime included Disaster Action (DA) and the Herald Family Association. They shared experiences, outrage and distress at 'a total lack of information from official sources ... a lack of legal guidelines' (DA newsletter, 1992, cited in Eyre and Dix, 2014: 11, 18). They stayed 'outside the ideological terrain of the state and at the same time' engaged 'on the terrain of the policy world or within the current political system' (Eyre and Dix, 2014: 179). They coalesced around one goal – forcing corporate killing on to the political agenda in the 1990s (Whyte, 2007), pushing for the term corporate manslaughter to enter public consciousness. They demanded change at a time when there 'was a genuine possibility to pierce ... the de facto veil' (Tombs and Whyte, 2015: 175), which followed years of campaigning, high-profile public cases and a change of government. This culminated in new legislation and the Corporate Manslaughter and Corporate Homicide Act 2007.

Victim groups campaigned for 20 years for this change in legislation, but its original aims had been significantly watered down by the time the Act was passed. In the years since, there have been a lower number of prosecutions than predicted, and directors and managers have been able to use the law to argue that individual charges should be dropped (Roper, 2018). The Act excludes the possibility of directors being prosecuted (Tombs, 2018) and continues to prosecute smaller corporations while failing to deal with large corporations (Parsons, 2018), which is the same issue that led to calls for the Act in the late 1980s, as identified and fought for by the aforementioned groups. For example, in the first nine years there had been 21 prosecutions using the new legislation, all of small corporations employing fewer than 150 employees, with one exception that employed 550 people across four different locations (Tombs, 2018). Why these have not been resolved in the creation of the Act despite years of struggle points to the influence and connection between the state and corporations, as those with power still possess immunity from scrutiny (Sutherland, 1983). Tombs (2018: 500) describes this as a 'double injustice', where 'complex organisations and their directors retain relative immunity'. Victim groups powerfully 'force the state's agenda, threaten legitimacy, and arouse and channel dissent' (Wells, 2001: 3) at times when the status quo is demanded by those with power, signified by a lack of accountability and change. Critical criminologists who worked with them demonstrated the inequity and mobilized to enact change, including as part of the Centre for Corporate Accountability, covered in the final chapter. However, this hard work did not lead to a law which saw more perpetrators punished, nor did it lead to an increased interest within criminology.

Working with campaigning groups is at odds with the requirements of university research, which is increasingly sponsored by private businesses and consultancy. Neither sits comfortably with research into the crimes of the powerful and, notably, safety crime (Slapper and Tombs, 1999). Researchers are vulnerable when they collaborate with trade unions and campaign groups to work towards 'a more just and humane social order' (Tombs and Whyte, 2002: 232) and examine a state that has internationally 'repositioned labour markets and labour processes in favour of capital' (Tombs and Whyte, 2007: 49). Severing a link with and criticizing the state opens the study of corporate crime up to further disapproval and exclusion. Within criminology, this breaks with the 'social institutional and intellectual conditions' that separated 'the rich or the poor or the law-abiding or the masterful' that originally made criminology 'desirable' (Garland, 1985: 117).

Sociological theory

It is of note that in the 1920s Sutherland was not writing strictly from within criminology. In his 1940 paper, he drew together economics and sociology and attempted 'to integrate these two bodies of knowledge' (1940: 1). This reflects his experiences within academia: he started working under a political economist (Gaylord and Galliher, 2020), becoming a sociologist principally focused on solving social problems. He sought to develop theories of crime that explained white-collar criminality, which came under the remit of criminologists because it was a violation of the law (Sutherland, 1940). In his practice, Sutherland drew from other disciplines to develop behavioural theories of criminal behaviour, moving away from economic and biological explanations (Gaylord and Galliher, 2020). He remained firmly rooted in sociology and what was an expanding discipline. Unlike criminologists, Sutherland did not seek to predict and control crime but to make propositions about society.

The rise and establishment of criminology, in part, depends upon its reliability in examining and controlling criminals drawn from the lower socioeconomic classes. Theories that explain corporate crime tend to focus on explanation and resolution and treat it as an aberration. This research concurs with Bernat and Whyte (2017: 77), who argue that corporate crimes are 'interruptions or unplanned phenomena that arise from the normal conditions of doing business'. This recognizes corporate crime as part of a process, based on social relationships that are inherently flawed rather than focused on unique moments in time (Laslett, 2010, cited in Bernat and Whyte, 2017; Tombs, 2013). Sutherland's (1940) focus on solving social problems (Gaylord and Galilher, 2020) is incompatible with criminology's tendency to look to state interventions and criminal justice.

Sutherland was a firm defender of sociological boundaries, and within that chose to focus on criminological issues, examining labour unions, farmers' organizations, employment agencies and socialism (Gaylord and Galilher, 2020: 158). Sutherland (1940) compared the high-status criminal to the low-status criminal. However, mainstream criminology was not persuaded, and, as previously discussed, the definition he introduced was highly criticized. It became a sticking point for many working within criminology, despite the fact he recognized its fallibility, put aside for a larger project: 'The purpose of the concept of white-collar crime is to call attention to a vast area of criminal behaviour which is … overlooked … seldom brought within the scope of the theories of criminal behaviour, and which, when included, calls for modifications in the usual theories' (Sutherland, 1941: 112). White-collar crime has continued to be overlooked and has not been brought into the scope of theories of crime. It is often an addition to theories that dominate criminology, offered as a criticism, useful for undergraduates and A-Level students. As Hirschi and Gottfredson claim, 'no topic in criminology can be discussed without the spectre of white-collar crime hanging over it' (1987: 949). Indeed, the study of the powerful exists on the periphery. Justifying its existence and integration has taken up much time of those who picked up where Sutherland left off. Despite critical criminologists establishing it as a legitimate focus of study, its absence in the criminal justice system remains a problem in a criminology that is focused on the criminal justice system and policy recommendations.

Criminal justice studies

Criminology is now an established discipline that is distinct from sociology, with thousands of undergraduates and postgraduates studying it at university with a plethora of professors of criminology. While Sutherland's criminology was 'generously accommodative to the concepts and perspectives of sociology' (Gaylord and Galilher, 2020: 159), criminology has since moved further towards the criminal justice system. The top ten universities offering criminology, according to the *Guardian* guide in 2021, focus on sentencing, desistance, the prevention of crime, criminal justice policy and police, courts and prison. Only one of these ten universities diverged from centring criminology around the criminal justice system. There are few questions posed about the centrality and necessity of such a system: we may study miscarriages of justice but do not theorize justice; study institutional racism in the police without questioning power. Academics' acceptance of the criminal justice system provides a 'spurious legitimacy' (Muncie, 1999: 128, cited in Scraton, 2013: 19) to an institution that has been crafted and created, 'an ideologically wrought destination that does not necessarily capture activities that cause harm' (Kramer, 1985; Michalowski, 1985; Schwendinger and Schwendinger, 1970, cited in Presser and Sandberg, 2019: 135).

There is little doubting the popularity of criminology, as seen in the comparatively large student numbers and popular interest in crime. An acceptance of what crime and criminals are has created a scholarship that is diverse and widespread. It remains crucial to protect individual interest in a particular topic as the need for securing funding and publication preoccupies the time of every research-active academic. The law continues to be an obvious frame of reference; there is much that can be studied and supported within the law that avoids the criticism of Tappan, Shapiro and others. Criminologists strive to be able to lay claim to objectivity by operating within the realm of faceless law and 'avoid a moral position or just avoid the word "moral"' (Coleman, 2017). To be able to excel in criminology, it makes sense to do so, and to avoid what Christie called for in the final paragraph of *Crime Control as Industry*: for academics to keep the debate in the cultural arena, because the 'delivery of pain, to whom, and for what, contains an endless line of deep moral questions' (2000: 202). As Sutherland found, moving outside of the law and, further, being critical of the status quo, opens any subsequent scholarship to increased criticism, which makes being an academic more difficult and with added layers of labour and questions of legitimacy.

Sutherland's introduction of the white-collar criminal occurred towards the end of his career, during his presidential address to the American Sociological Society, two years after his contract at Chicago University had ended (Gaylord and Galilher, 2020). It is comparatively difficult for academics to focus on the corporate criminal for their entire career. As a discipline, sociology has seen a reduction in student numbers compared to criminology. Tombs (2018: 12) states from personal experience, 'and through what felt like a series of intellectual gymnastics, I was constantly seeking to legitimate the area of harm-producing social life with which I was concerned as the proper stuff for criminology and, indeed, for the criminal justice system'.

It is now almost 90 years since the white-collar criminal was named, and scholars are still required to justify its inclusion into the discipline despite the exponential growth of white-collar crime. Crime as defined by the criminal justice system continues to be a boundary for criminology and criminologists that is experienced by those who agree with Sutherland's address. There has been a 'vast amount of energy devoted to attempting to include white-collar, corporate or state crimes' (Hillyard and Tombs, 2005: 20). Critical criminology offered some protection to theorists who were 'simply *ignored*, at times crudely parodied, or simply, and contemptuously, dismissed' (Pearce, 2003: xi, emphasis in original).

Muting the chat: social harm and zemiology

The problem of adhering to legalistic definitions and, more recently, the link between the criminal justice system and criminology, poses a problem for safety crime. Criminologists can argue that corporate criminals do not feature enough in the criminal justice system while also being critical of the system's potential to resolve corporate criminality or, indeed, any criminality. Yet from within criminology, the criminal justice system and the definition of crime remain central. Moving critical criminology to a different discipline would leave criminology to explicitly reflect the status quo and to fulfil its 'whole raison d'etre' of addressing crime (Smart, 1990: 159) as defined by the state. Those who want to 'deconstruct crime' (Smart, 1990: 160) can examine topics that harm but are unlikely to be viewed popularly as a problem for society. They can focus on being idealistic, campaigning and opposing dominant political ideals that side line harm (Scraton and Chadwick, 2009) without spending time justifying their inclusion into a discipline that has moved closer to psychologists, psychiatrists and other 'outsiders' (Gaylord and Galilher, 2020). The neoliberal era has made it almost impossible for 'the basic assumptions of corporate ideology … as well as its social consequences' to be challenged (Giroux, 2005: 15–16).

With its focus on the criminal justice system, criminology in its various iterations supports dominant structures (Copson, 2018) and as a discipline has been in service of the powerful (Hillyard et al, 2004). Criminality identified by Sutherland has not led to justice in the criminal justice system, and activists who worked hard for a change to the corporate manslaughter law have been disappointed. This lack of redress creates social problems and contributes to doubts about the equality of the agencies that form part of the criminal justice system, including the coronial system. Feminist researchers have focused on the inadequacy of the laws relating to rape within academia, publishing research that has demonstrated this inequality, yet this has not altered the law or criminal justice system to an extent that it has been resolved. The notion that there will be a tipping point, where, in the face of unequivocal research, the criminal justice system will start to provide satisfactory outcomes for victims and hold the courts accountable, is arguably more utopian than the desire to abolish capitalism. In continuing to include these subjects in criminology, researchers risk becoming 'scientific alibis' (Garland, 1992, cited in Copson, 2018).

This is not without problems. The neoliberal context that has made work precarious for potential victims of safety crime has also affected academia, which depends upon student numbers and funders, making it difficult to recommend abandoning a subject that is popular with students. The fear and obsession with crime has led to healthy student numbers and a discipline that has expanded. Criminologists compromise between two opposing forces, appeasing populist notions of crime with elements of criticality that oppose 'common sense' notions; occupying a space between perpetuating the official discourse on crime and punishment and subverting it entirely. Research works twice as hard: for example, a research paper at a conference presents a highly critical version, while feedback to public bodies and the university emphasizes achievable, practical reforms.

This is preferable to abandoning criticality altogether and instead legitimating the criminal justice system as it is, producing what Sim (2023: 527) refers to as 'snake oil' research. It is an 'official criminology that fits our deeply divided and increasingly anxious society' (Garland, 1997: 198) that recognizes the value of 'progressive social change' but ultimately maintains the 'political arrangements which lie at its centre' (Garland, 1997: 198). This is perhaps understandable given the subject can be purged, as radical analysis was across the US in the name of McCarthyism (Sim et al, 1987), which would have affected Sutherland had he lived to see it, and in the UK in favour of postmodernism under Thatcher. But it is questionable whether it is acceptable to sustain study for the powerful at the expense of the powerless (Becker and Horowitz, 1972, in Carrington and Hogg, 2013). Perhaps a move to a different discipline would be an imperfect but useful response to these problems (Copson, 2011).

Sutherland (1983) attempted to use the same techniques and considerations of criminologists of conventional crime, including arguing it was organized crime. He searched for a theory to explain all crime, as he stated:

> The definition should not be the spirit of the law for white-collar crimes and the letter of the law for other crimes, or in other respects be more liberal for one class than for the other … the criterion of white-collar crime must be justified in terms of the procedures of those criminologists in dealing with other crimes. (Sutherland, 1983: 5)

However, this was not accepted within the discipline – as discussed, he was criticized for a weak definition, moralistic assertions and relying upon questionable data. Critical criminologists almost 100 years later will still recognize these criticisms despite the progress they have made in establishing white-collar crime as a typology that is included in the criminological canon.

Beyond the experiences of critical criminologists, the victims of white-collar and corporate crime are pushed further to invisibility under neoliberalism and the expansion of the criminal justice system. Their needs and experiences – what they endure – is unlikely to be legitimated by a discipline that is bound up in the needs of the state, a crucial link that cannot be undone. Without the defence of the state, critical criminologists have continually responded to problems endemic to criminology and still exist as a complement or haunting opposition to the main work of the discipline. Time spent justifying the inclusion of corporate crime into criminology could be better used under the remit of social harm and zemiology working with other disciplines to explore means to reduce harm and alter the experiences of those who are harmed by the powerful, even at an individual level.

A form of criminology that focuses on the reform of the criminal justice system and individualistic theories of crime is likely to remain popular with the state. In this, what criminology has to offer those studying safety crime is stability. The costs of participating in this include claims of being subjective and disdain for examining what Shapiro (1990: 350) 'sarcastically labelled … All the Bad, Offensive, Hurtful Things Corporations Do' (Shaprio, 1990: 350). Indeed, as part of critical criminology, it included the 'unfounded allegation that radical theory was abstract and could not be subjected to empirical investigation [which] was, in later years, repeated so often that it became accepted' (Schwendinger and Schwendinger, 2014: 61). The claim that a criminology which studied white-collar criminals could be dismissed as non-scientific is presumably not what Sutherland would have wanted since he pushed for sociology to be 'an effective spokesman for sociology as a scientific enterprise' (Gaylord and Galilher, 2020: 159). Returning to feminism for inspiration, Smart (1990) asked whether criminology had anything to offer feminism, and a similar question could also be asked: what else does criminology have to offer the study of safety crime? Would it be better placed to return to sociology or move to zemiology rather than legitimize what is ultimately the study of the criminal as defined by the state; a natural reflection of the father of criminology, Lombroso, when he 'discovered' the criminal in southern Italy (Garland, 1985)?

There is less hope of an internal revolution and transformative change as expressed by critical criminologists during the 1970s and 1980s (Carrington and Hogg, 2013) and instead a creeping acceptance that criminology is unable (and in part, unwilling) to push for equality and less division (Garland, 1997). In the case of safety crime, the state has not stepped in or curtailed what Sutherland referred to as the 'persistent … effort to secure differential advantages and ruthless … pursuit of their interests' (Sutherland, 1983: 197). Instead, the state has preserved 'political arrangements' (Garland, 1997: 198) and further empowered corporations. Critical criminology has examined the equity between corporate and common crime, pushing for its inclusion as a legitimate crime and worthy of public scrutiny. It has sought reform of the criminal justice and regulatory system to reflect the harm it causes. Yet, the criminal justice system functions in response to what zemiologists believe are 'ultimately social problems' (Copson, 2018), which leads me to an unlikely agreement with Tappan (1977) that the criminal justice system cannot handle powerful criminals. Working within criminology and calling for the inclusion of corporate crime into a flawed system that demonstrates its reluctance to accept it is both frustrating and laborious.

The impact of neoliberalism, the enduring and enmeshing of the state with power via corporations, the lack of developed law directed at those with power, the impact of victim movements and criminology's relationship to the criminal justice system was not foreseen by Sutherland when he unveiled the white-collar criminal almost 100 years ago. These issues have been explored by critical criminologists, working within criminology against the continued pull of positivism. Social harm and the potential of zemiology offer a chance to move beyond criminology and explore further the experiences of those harmed, to focus on social problems and social solutions and break from the state, redirecting efforts into activism. It is a commitment to working with those who are affected, not as a viewer but as an active partner, and not negotiating the results if they contradict what is desired (Tauri, 2018).

Social harm is defined as 'actions, omissions, policies, conditions, states of affairs, assumptions, ways of doing things and dominant structures which contribute to the absence of or distortions in self-actualisation' (Tombs and Canning 2021, cited in Davis and White, 2023: 89). It should include 'significant examples of human suffering' (Pemberton, 2007: 29) and develop elements of critical criminology (Copson, 2018), moving away from the criminal justice system to refocus on strategies outside of policy change, as they are reliant upon the state (Sim et al, 1987). It breaks with the legal definition of crime (Tombs, 2018), removing the natural progression from the act (whether it is criminal or not) to prison/punishment. Social harm research moves away from calling for reform and instead offers the chance for alternatives to counter harm outside of the criminal justice system (Pantazis, 2008). It unpicks the assumption that common crime is the main source of harm to society (Pemberton, 2008a), ripe for the study of crimes of the powerful, including safety crime.

Breaking from the criminal justice system

Moving outside of criminology would enable a move away from the state and policy as a legitimate and pivotal focus of study. In the same way that those studying rape chose feminism and gender as areas of study, the study of the powerful and corporations should look to criminology only in relation to the operation of the criminal justice system. It should not be limited by a discipline that forces it into a cul-de-sac forced to justify its existence and to look for reformist solutions.

If the study of safety crime has been neglected because ignoring it 'contribute[s] to the reproduction of the power structure in society' (Ruggiero, 2015: 132), working with an alternative discipline would open up solutions that have hitherto been sidelined (Alvesalo and Tombs, 2002). Radical criminologists have demystified and exposed the workings of state power (Sim et al, 1987) and contributed to the conclusion that solutions need to be found outside of the limits of law and punishment. Zemiology offers the theoretical paradigm to develop this potential. Safety crime and the harm it causes can be studied without the limitations of criminology and the assumed positivist lens this demands (Billingham and Irwin-Rogers, 2022).

Issues around the definition of social harm continue to be refined and debated, as a relatively new and contested concept. This is ongoing to establish 'clear and well-established ontological, epistemological, or ethical underpinnings' (Raymen, 2022: xvi). It has been argued that theorizing should relate both to rejecting 'the capitalist order as the only possible mode of social organisation' (Garside, 2013: 252) and to revise its origins 'towards decolonial ends' (Wright, 2023: 140). For Garside (2013), neoliberalism is an inadequate base for understanding social harm, but for Wright (2023) taking neoliberalism as a point of analysis ignores the debt owed to colonialism and the harms experienced by those in former colonies. Indeed, there is a tension between the need for clear boundaries while also encouraging the widening of topics to look for further explanations of the harms people experience and endure. As a perspective, social harm has yet to provide an 'exhaustive or definitive account' (Pantazis and Pemberton, 2009, cited in Garside, 2013: 254), instead offering one that is 'subject to review, augmentation, refinement, and challenge' (Garside, 2013: 254).

This research examines social harm as an effect of power focused on 'practices where crime and social harm happen to coalesce' (Lasslett, 2010: 14) aligned with studies where this is not the case which go beyond criminology as a much-needed perspective to examine why justice is seemingly unachievable. It is recognizing 'harm when we see it' (Raymen, 2022: 134) in accordance with the parameters established in Chapter 4. It is part of the need to 'understand qualitatively what constitutes harm and the mechanisms by which harm can be produced and experienced in individuals' everyday lives' (Mason, 2020: 386).

Biography of harm

As a perspective, social harm allows for the effects of all victims to be documented as 'biographies of harm' and to explore the violation of trust that creates distrust (Sutherland, 1940: 5). In its aim for legitimacy and to resolve the aforementioned methodological problems, criminologists working on corporate and state crime have focused on large cases where there is agreement on wrongdoing and scandalous behaviour, if not crime. Two examples include Spalek (1999) on Maxwell and Scraton on the Hillsborough Disaster (2009). The reflections of otherwise 'hidden' victims (Spalek, 1999: 213) demonstrate a recognition of criminal offenders by the victims. When invited and permitted to share their thoughts, such victims are clear that what has happened to them is criminal and extremely harmful. Moving towards social harm and straying outside of criminology would necessitate the gathering of these hidden experiences, without the need to justify their inclusion or derisory accusations of partiality. Time would be better spent 'making an injury visible' as the 'first step in remedying it' (Solnit, 2004: xiv) and seeking solutions that do not begin with explaining why the harm is not in the criminal justice system and then arguing that it should be, especially when it is a further site of harm. Consideration of moving outside of criminology to another discipline entirely such as zemiology would not act as a counter or oppositional force to it as a discipline but create a separate focus of study altogether. While there may be overlapping elements, one does not have to be compared or be reduced in the face of the other.

For victims of safety crime, studying their experiences within social harm would acknowledge that the harm they suffered was preventable (Billingham and Irwin-Rogers, 2022) and foreseeable within both a capitalist society (Mason, 2020) and racist institutions. Social factors should be interrogated to gain insight into how 'invisible social harms' are 'normalised' against 'marginalised and minoritised individuals' (Addison, 2023: 297). The deaths are not an 'act of god' or random bad luck but the result of decisions taken or not taken by individuals. The study of social harm has the potential to oppose the status quo that compels secondary victims to accept a fate that has been written for them because the harm they experience does not fit that which is deemed as a legitimate focus of the criminal justice system. It creates distance between knowledge and its misuse by the state, which has historically created policies that criminalize relatively powerless groups, including indigenous groups (Tauri, 2018).

Crucially, victims can demonstrate their experiences in ways that the law has refused to acknowledge and analyse the effects of this in terms of needs that are unfulfilled (Billingham and Irwin-Rogers, 2022) that not only prevent flourishing but de-humanize them in their time of need. The harms secondary victims of safety crime experience are dispersed, hidden and viewed as an acceptable consequence of industry. Social harm offers a perspective that could unify these experiences and reduce this isolation and normalization (Atiles, 2024) that benefits those with power.

Activism

The work of critical criminologists who join movements such as INQUEST would be encouraged since the study of social harm and zemiology demands that critical criminologists commit to an activist position. This would avoid perpetuating social inequalities as reflected and upheld by the state (Presser and Sandberg, 2019), continuing what Sutherland (1940: 1) called for when he referred to 'reforming criminology'. Working with those who are harmed and interrogating their questions is both democratic and necessary, using knowledge of the movements that have gone before to consider solutions that can be useful to those who have been harmed and are likely to be harmed in the future.

This book contributes to uncovering the victims of corporate crime and ultimately the harms caused by corporations that have remained on the periphery of criminology and the criminal justice process. It recognizes that those who are held in prison have far from a monopoly on causing serious harm inflicted upon society. It explores the additional impact of excluding victims of the powerful from the various institutions the state employs to respond to serious harm. As part of social harm, it recognizes implicitly 'the symbiotic relationship between the state and corporations' that facilitates harmful practices (Aldini, 2024: 6). This is not an aberration but an extension of a state that has been systematically violent in 'ancient and modern history' (Davis and White 2023: 97) and used the law to reproduce inequalities (Aldini, 2024) that have been experienced by citizens and workers that require examination and 'resistance by [forming] coalitions and alliances' (Agozino, 2018: 12).

As a body of work, it offers an opportunity for students to read alternative accounts and for these to be developed in future studies, outside of, and complementary to, criminology. As part of the study of social harm and as an opportunity for zemiology, it is a commitment to 'achieve the ends to which we are committed' (Copson, 2018: 52) and highlight that which is denied and unseen. Taking inspiration from feminists, it stands outside of the discipline that reproduces the exclusion faced by victims of safety crime in public life. In the absence of meaningful or effective progression in law or policy, time should be spent documenting the current situation, the operation of power and searching for alternative solutions that acknowledge the history and limitations of the criminal justice system, ultimately refusing to accept the dehumanization of people whose loved ones should still be alive. Neither their profound loss nor their inhumane treatment was inevitable.

Conclusion

In this chapter, I took Sutherland's assertions and examined the extent to which criminology successfully answered his main propositions. Critical criminologists took up where Sutherland left off, and in almost a century, they have developed and provided evidence which supports his work. White-collar crime has been defined and redefined to include many other crimes committed by the powerful. The scope of such crimes has been mapped, demonstrating the large numbers of victims who are affected by otherwise hidden crimes coupled with the inadequate response of the law.

In an era of neoliberalism, the corporation, and its link to the state, has expanded beyond Sutherland's expectations. Criminology has focused on predicting and controlling crime, a difficult fit for a topic that is not a feature of the criminal justice system. Moving to social harm and zemiology permits an examination of the harms caused by corporations and those with power, as Sutherland (1940) intended. Including harms caused by the powerful under social harm as an organizing concept for zemiology (Pemberton, 2016) could mean that more time is spent working with those focused on changing the outcomes for future victims.

This chapter argued that the study of social harm and consideration of a move to zemiology is best placed to further the debate and to break from the state and its response to crime, the legal process. Just as Sutherland's move from sociology to criminology was motivated by 'disillusionment' (Gaylord and Galilher, 2020: 5), employing social harm as a perspective and considering zemiology is a progression of what Sutherland intended when he referred to 'reforming criminology' (Sutherland, 1940: 1). As a discipline, it offers a theoretical paradigm to document the harms of white-collar crime and the ways in which it remains invisible, almost 90 years after Sutherland unveiled it.

Chapter 2 aims to add to a biography of harm that is excluded from official statistics on crime and criminality. As in the manner of Punch (1996), the research in Chapters 2 and 3 has been designed for use in teaching, and the information can be tailored to the audience. The experiences documented in Chapters 2 and 3 demonstrate how society responds to those who are harmed by corporations and the subsequent harms caused by the operation of the criminal justice system. These biographies break with the legal definition of crime as they profile what the families of victims of unconvicted safety crime experience as they are led deliberately and inevitably away from justice.

2

A Biography of Harm, Victims and Secondary Victims of the Powerful: Deaths by Private Institutions

As outlined in the introductory chapter, the research in this chapter is focused on safety crime, defined as '[i]llegal acts or omissions, punishable by the State under administrative, civil or criminal law, which are the result of deliberate decision making or culpable negligence within a legitimate formal organisation' (Pearce and Tombs, 1998: 107–10, cited in Tombs and Whyte, 2007: 3). This expands the definition of crime beyond the criminal law and criminal justice system to a focus on 'acts and omissions ... which have not been interrogated as, let alone proven to be, violations of the criminal, or indeed any other form of law' (Tombs and Whyte, 2007: 4). The emphasis here is on 'interrogated', further explored in Chapter 4.

This chapter adds to a biography of harm located within a zemiology that permits and encourages examination of victims of safety crime (Copson, 2016). It recognizes they are victims of violent acts that were largely preventable (Tombs, and Whyte, 2007), as reflected by their family's surprise at their deaths: as Louise Adamson reflected, 'It had never for one minute crossed my mind prior to his death that he might leave for work one morning and not return home. Yes, of course, electricity is dangerous, but it can – and should – be worked with safely ... shouldn't it?' (Adamson, 2016). In accordance with safety crime, this includes consumers and members of the public who are subject to the reach of corporations (Tombs and Whyte, 2007), as well as workers. The victim – the person who suffered the principal physical harm – has died and is represented by their families.

This research emphasizes the experiences of families of victims of safety crime who endure a process that demands their silence and directs them away from the truth and justice. It is an attempt to re-dress the 'continued neglect or indifference' shown by social scientists towards victims, which may 'play a part in denying legitimacy to them and their suffering' (Shover et al, 1994: 96). This chapter documents the experiences of families whose loved ones are victims of safety crime committed by private institutions. Chapter 3 will focus on areas that document the experiences of people whose loved ones are victims of safety crime committed by public institutions.

As detailed in the Introduction, 21 individuals were included in this research, including 11 families whose experiences were documented via in-depth semi-structured interviews. Following the death of their loved ones, the families entered a system where they were processed by various state agencies, which began when the police knocked on their door. As with this first devastating encounter, the families had little choice in whom they came into contact with. As the deaths occurred at different times and locations across the UK, each family was isolated, obscuring their similarities to one another and the commonalities in the operation of power. The inclusion of further examples demonstrates their experiences are not exceptional events but a consistent official response to deaths that involve the comparatively powerful as potential perpetrators. There were similarities between them: first, no matter how they were treated by individuals, the process silenced them; and, second, they left the process without seeing a perpetrator officially identified or punished, as the truth was suppressed. Further, this process was de-humanizing, which is explored in Chapter 5.

To best illustrate their experiences, each case will be split into sections according to the different agencies, with the cases presented in chronological order. The first half will focus on those cases which never entered the criminal justice system and were non-criminalized:

- Michael
- David
- Paul
- Mark
- John

The second half will focus on those individuals whose cases entered the criminal justice system and were criminalized (to a limited extent). These are:

- James
- Andrew
- Robert
- Phillip
- Jason
- Luke

The extent to which the wishes of the family members were met will be reflected upon. Many families shared that they hoped principally, first, to find out what happened in their loved one's final moments and what led up to their deaths – the truth – and, second, to ensure that it would never happen to anyone else.

A victim of safety crime

Most of the people in this research were killed while working in industry using machinery. This included machinery they were operating, such as a tail lift, as well as machinery that was operating around them, for example a grab. Only one person was killed at a static workplace, which they worked at every day. The majority were working at other sites, away from a main office/site and distanced from the headquarters. In all but one case, the individuals died on site as a result of catastrophic injuries and were not taken to hospital; there were no issues relating to the emergency services. Other individuals had previously died in the same circumstances or there had been a 'near miss' that the victim was aware of; one worker had received a note in his wages the previous month detailing the death of a man in the same circumstances that led to his death. Another was working his notice due to concerns about the lack of safety on site. Two members of the public who died did so in the same way. They were among the many who have died in similar circumstances. The importance of 'near misses' cannot be overstated – had definitive action been taken, the people killed in this research would still be alive.

All of the victims were men, ranging between the ages of 16 and 56. Two of the victims were members of the public; the majority were killed at work. Most of those involved were subcontractors working for corporations within other corporations, for example their employer had won a contract to fulfil a part of the work such as installing the sewerage on a house build. This meant their place of death was miles from their home address. One was 'temping', now referred to as a zero-hour contract. One victim was self-employed, and two were working for very large corporations. Two were working in smaller corporations where the families knew the director on a first-name basis. One manager was working alongside the victim at the time of their death and also sustained injuries.

Michael

Michael had little experience of work and still lived at home. His family were proud of him being an apprentice for a reputable and well-known corporation and were close. He was 20 at the time of his death and in the final year of his apprenticeship, which his family had thought was 'a great opportunity to work for a large company'. On the day of his death the factory he was working in had subcontracted one corporation that had then subcontracted in the corporation that paid Michael's wages. He was killed working alone on a large piece of machinery which he had received training on a few weeks before. Michael had described the training to his family as 'a waste of time' because he had not had the opportunity to use the machine. He was working alone in a factory that was over an hour's car journey away from his home; upon visiting after Michael's death, his father reflected that he was shocked by the factory's size, as it was over a kilometre in length. Michael died at the scene. The interview was attended by Michael's parents, Peter and Diane, and sister, Clare.

The police

Michael's family found out about his death via the police, three hours after the incident and 90 minutes after he was due home. They had expected that he would be safe at work and, upon seeing the police at the door, assumed there had been a road traffic incident (RTI). They reflected that the police were 'really, really useless, they had no idea'. The family described the lack of sympathy and were told 'he'd been crushed, and his heart had stopped … they had no compassion on their faces'. Diane immediately demanded to see him: 'I need to see my son; I need to see him now.' The supervisor told them he would try to 'pull strings' for this to happen. They were met at the mortuary but told 'we could only view him through glass'.

Two detectives later visited the family and asked about Michael's 'life, school, college, background for the coroner … a statement to be read out at the inquest as Michael's statement'. The family had not realized how it would be used until they got the list of proceedings. The police took statements that were used in the inquest, which the family reflected were 'the wrong ones – the who, what, where and when'.

The corporation

Representatives from the corporation – a senior manager and an engineer – visited the family late on the night Michael died: '[T]he management's attitude was, "we don't know anything, we have to wait for the health and safety report".' The family were told that those at the top of the corporation were not allowed to contact them directly because Michael had died. They were told management and an engineer had visited the site and had been 'willing' to see them but had been stopped from doing so. A safety environment officer from the corporation later contacted them, but 'all they did was offer their condolences, as is their want'. Most of the correspondence in the first few days related to money, such as offering to pay for the funeral.

Michael's parents said they needed 'to see the site where [he] died', which was facilitated within the first two days. The corporation arranged for a minibus to collect them, permitted them to lay flowers and arranged for the representative they had met on the evening of Michael's death to lay flowers. They provided sandwiches and drinks, and employees lined the site and took off their helmets, which Diane saw 'as a sign of respect, I suppose'. They were told they could not take photographs. The corporation set up a one-off award for the 'Apprentice of the Year' in Michael's name. All contact ceased some time prior to the inquest.

The inquest

The inquest happened two years after Michael's death, which they were told was due to the length of the investigation and because 'various people were on holiday'.

The solicitor advised the family not to read out a statement, which they did not understand and later regretted. Instead, the statement that had been taken by the police was read out; the family had not been told this was going to happen, and 'it came as a bit of a surprise'. They were also shocked that the corporation was able to overrule the statements from the Health and Safety Executive (HSE): they had expected the government body to have more power. No management were present; other employees were called as expert witnesses, including the on-site safety advisor. While the coroner was 'friendly', the family described the inquest as 'very much like "us and them"': for example, the family were sent into another room and had to pass members of the corporation every time they used the loo, which they thought should have been the other way around.

The family recognized that the questions asked by the police, which were included in the inquest, did not attempt to investigate negligence but just the basic facts of what happened. The HSE had wanted a negligent verdict because the machinery had not been booked out, documentation was missing and there were failings following the emergency. These included a missing mobile phone, so there was no way for employees to call for help, no one was trained in first aid on site, Michael was working alone and a key was missing from the machine, which meant he could not be freed. The training he had received on the machinery had a practical element, which the corporation emphasized; the family's statement that he had been nowhere near the machine until he had to use it was seen as irrelevant. The inquest ruled all training was adequate.

The final verdict was 'accidental death'.

The HSE

The HSE shut the site for 48 hours, 'took photographs and spoke to people'. The first the family heard from them was via a letter, which contained a leaflet about the Centre for Corporate Accountability (CCA). The family reached out to the CCA, who visited them before the HSE. The family had to make their own enquiries and reflected 'all I did was try to ring people up … you would tell secretaries why you were ringing, and it was like they didn't care'. The HSE told the family it was paramount they did not speak to anyone about the proceedings 'as it could jeopardize the case' which led them to believe they had uncovered something important. As a result, Michael's mother did not even talk to her own mother about it, out of fear she would say something wrong.

Michael's trade union sent a letter to say they would arrange a solicitor to act on their behalf and with legal aid. A solicitor was appointed, based in a city 90 minutes away from their home. They found her to be skilled but felt only standard questions were asked at the inquest, in accordance with the union, which had had no contact with the family.

Overall, they were impressed by the people they met from the HSE but later felt let down by senior figures who decided not to prosecute, against the guidance of the immediate HSE officer. The family hired a private solicitor at a cost of £250 per hour who told them how to write a letter to appeal. The reply they received emphasized that although seven failings of the corporation had been noted, there were points that lessened each one, including the training that had been provided. They were very upset that there would be no change to any procedure to prevent another similar death because to do so would be 'working to best practice', which is 'not the same as [working to] statutory duties'. The HSE released guidance for corporations which included a demonstration of the way Michael died, which upset the family.

Court

There were no court proceedings, and the family was told there was not enough evidence to proceed with a civil case. They were told that launching a judicial review would be 'foolhardy' because it would cost thousands of pounds. This led them to think the corporation 'would be laughing at us in some way'. They wanted 'to see the firm rapped over the knuckles' and a prosecution that would lead to them putting 'right what was wrong'. Instead, they were left with the 'hope that something would come out' later. They wrote to their local MP but did not receive a reply. The family did not find out what led to Michael's death, and nothing was changed to ensure that a similar incident would not happen again.

David

David was 48 at the time of his death. He was a hard worker who preferred labouring as a ganger; anyone who worked with him was told to 'either work as hard as him or don't work at all'. He worked every day but Sunday each week, travelling around the country, and found it difficult to sit in one place for long. David had briefly been unemployed but had refused to draw any dole. Between that period of unemployment and his death, he had been working for the same corporation for ten years. He was killed on a building site as part of a subcontract to a housing company on a contract that was worth £4.25 million. David was killed when a 24-foot trench gave way; it took four hours to recover his body. The interview was attended by Carole – David's ex-wife, with whom they shared children.

The police

The police did not investigate but brought a person from the HSE to one of their first visits to the family. They said they were 'signing off on it, they didn't feel it was, you know, like anyone else was involved'. The officers gave Carole their card and told her to call if anything came to mind.

The corporation

Carole phoned the corporation to try to find out where David had died because the family wanted to visit. An employee provided directions and added 'of course you realize that all this is David's fault?' This employee had been working 10 miles away at the time of the incident, which Carole did not find out until much later. When the family visited the site two days later, the site was fully operational. Two workers who had been there when David had been killed had refused to continue working, so two other workers had been brought in to speak to the family. They were unprepared for Carole and told them a different account of what happened. Ultimately, they relied upon friends who had worked in the same industry to explain to them how David had died.

Over a week after David's death, one of the owners phoned Carole to say he had left a church service in the hope he could come and see her. She agreed, and he called and dropped off a wage packet – with the day of David's death deducted from the total. A son of one of the workmen later visited; he was apologetic, saying that he had not visited sooner 'because his solicitor had told him he shouldn't'. David's van was passed on to a colleague who lived a few streets away from Carole; it upset her every time she saw it.

Thes HSE

Carole had confidence in HSE at the start and thought they were going to be 'on David's side' but reflected that it did not take long to find out this was not the case. The investigation took a long time, which they were told was because of sickness and to 'maintain continuity'. Carole rang quarterly and found out it had taken 18 months for the boss to be interviewed, and, even then, he was given the choice of whether he wanted to make a statement or not. She reflected that in that time, 'really and truly all we had was two people's [business] cards'.

The HSE officer assigned to the case misrepresented her words, stating 'you said yourself David was reckless', which horrified Carole. When she questioned the continued delay, the HSE officer said, 'you do know we're not working for you?' In response, she contacted Citizens Advice, who gave them a leaflet from the CCA. She contacted the CCA, who assigned a case worker and began a 'paper trail'. Acting on Carole's behalf, the CCA sent letters to the HSE, and the case was passed up the management chain to a supervisor because they were approaching a three-year limit.

After the inquest, the HSE tried to collect statements, but everyone refused. Carole sympathized with this – 'three years down the line … you can understand to a certain extent'. She felt that because the corporation paid 'a decent wage … they don't want to jeopardize their jobs … those blokes have got families and all those to feed'. The HSE said 'they'd tried to get more statements, but without [that] evidence … they didn't feel they could go any further', and the case was closed after the inquest. The family received an apology for the length of time it had taken.

The inquest

The inquest took place a few weeks shy of the three-year anniversary of David's death. Carole remarked that 'you get the feeling that people are allowed to lie all the way through this'. Any statements that questioned the corporation's reputation were disregarded. For example, in the weeks leading up to David's death he had mentioned that he was supposed to be on a training course but that it had been cancelled, whereas the corporation said it had taken place. In another instance, it was presented that David had rung the corporation about the lack of safety; however, when the relevant person was questioned in court, he admitted he had spoken to David on the phone but that he could not remember what had been said. No risk assessment was produced or found on site, but this was accepted; the solicitor said, 'it's the first thing that goes missing on every job'. When Carole had cleared out David's flat, she found a piece of paper in his wages that detailed how another person had been killed in the same way not long before. This was not mentioned at the inquest.

The corporation made statements to say that safety was their priority and that if they had been aware that trees had needed to be dug up to make it safe, they would have done so. Yet Carole recalled David going to court with one of the owners previously because they had taken down a tree without permission. This had led to a lot of additional work and money spent on court costs, something Carole thought the owners of the corporation would want to avoid repeating. On the stand, the owner said he had always told David to take his time on the job and not rush, which left Carole incredulous because the owner's nickname was 'the bull … he'd be there shouting and moaning and groaning'. The last conversation she had with David was about the owner 'ranting and raving on the job … they let him rant and rave, David just walked away from him'.

At the inquest, this was contrasted with David being portrayed as 'a risky person' and as someone who liked to gamble on horses and put himself in danger. One of the owners claimed he had seen David do something unsafe 'a month or so before' and that he'd 'had to call him up on it, but he didn't say what it was'. The inquest emphasized that David had made the choice not to leave the trench as it began to collapse. Colleagues and family believe he reached to save a piece of equipment that cost £2,000. A colleague remarked, 'we've all taken that chance … and what's more, we'll all do it again'.

The family went into debt by at least £6,000 to pay for the funeral and had to pay for the solicitor. Carole referred to it as being 'caught in this trap … you shouldn't have to go to a firm that's relying on charity to run, the system should be there'. She thought the solicitor was 'totally to do with the money … really interested in the purse', when she was 'not really interested in that' but concerned with 'making sure things were done right'. The person from the HSE who had overseen the case left immediately after the inquest because 'he had some kind of breakdown'; they were told they were 'lucky he was at the inquest'. Carole felt the jury were 'confused' about the technical elements and that they nodded when they did not really understand. Of the summing up by the coroner, she said 'I don't understand why there's a jury there because the guy virtually tells them what they've got to bring back.'

The verdict was accidental death, and Carole's solicitor said they would not take it further as a result. The family relied upon people who worked in the job to establish what led up to David's death but without definitive answers. Nothing was changed to ensure this incident did not happen again.

Paul

Paul was 43 at the time of his death, which happened when he was working in a different part of the country. He was 'very astute, he was good, on his last training thing people had said how good he was'. He had worked for the corporation for five years, six days a week. On the day of his death, he was not operating his usual vehicle, which his father described as 'spotless … he had respect for his vehicle'. Instead, he was driving a colleague's vehicle, which was 'a younger vehicle but in worse condition'. Paul was asphyxiated by machinery on the vehicle. He was working alone and could not be freed because no one could reach the controls; people at the scene tried to release him by attempting to lift the machine using a crowbar. The family were told he had died at the scene of his injuries but later found out at the inquest that he had died 30 minutes afterwards of a heart attack, caused by the asphyxiation. The interview was attended by Gary and Liz – Paul's father and his father's wife.

The police

Gary was told his son had died by his ex-wife, Paul's mother. He met the police when he went to formally identify Paul. He reflected that they 'didn't really treat me as people', dismissing him once his ex-wife's partner became involved. He said 'they totally ignored me, the arrogance'. He left several messages with the police, but 'they were never there'.

The place of Paul's death was a public right of way, but the police said it was a building site and noted it down as an industrial accident. For that reason, they did not ask for witnesses, even though members of the public were in the vicinity who had tried to help Paul. One witness had a breakdown when they discovered he had not survived, and another attended the inquest in his own time.

Gary was told there was conflict between the police and the HSE that meant 'none of them were helping each other out'. He was ignored when he called them: 'It was as though, "what do you want me for?"' They said this was in stark contrast to the empathy they received from the nurse at the hospital. They concluded that the police 'don't understand deaths at work'. Gary said he 'got angry' as a result.

The HSE

Similarly, the HSE did not respond to Gary for two months, and only after he contacted the CCA, which began advocating on his behalf. After that, HSE officers provided information explaining what had happened. The investigation took a long time and delayed the inquest. Gary was told this was because the HSE were 'very limited' and 'short staffed'. He appreciated their honesty.

Gary's partner, Liz, reflected that the HSE underestimated them: '[I]t was a bit like they thought we were idiots' until 'we began asking questions … I think it was a bit of a surprise'. At first, the HSE sounded positive, and

Gary got the impression they were building a case against the corporation; he had faith they had 'the truth'. The HSE reported that errors had been made with the vehicle's maintenance and described the lack of a manual as unacceptable. As part of the investigation, they tested the machinery, and it malfunctioned in the same way that led to Paul's death. Yet the case was not taken forward. Gary said, 'the feeling you got from them, "our hands are tied"'.

Gary was 'frustrated' with the HSE and could not understand how they are able to keep 'failing the public, when it comes to death', contrasting this with car incidents, where the police keep control of the scene and go on to prosecute. For him, what happened to Paul was similar to a car incident, yet it was treated differently. As time went on, they warned him, 'you'll never get what you want to hear'.

The corporation

The corporation paid the costs for the funeral via Gary's ex-wife and new partner. At the inquest, the owner of the corporation was 'annoyed with his barrister' and 'called us everything apparently ... outside of the court, everything he could lay his tongue to'. He was angry that 'the coroner had laid some of the blame at his doorstep' and that he was not absolved on responsibility because he had covered the costs of the funeral. One witness attended the inquest and 'had to be held back because he wanted to put one on [the owner]'. Gary reflected: '[T]he company were not all cowboys, but I can see they were run by cowboys, they were cost cutters.'

The inquest

The inquest took place over two years after Paul's death due to the delay from the HSE.

The HSE presented evidence that the machinery had malfunctioned because it had not been maintained correctly. Those representing the corporation defended this with testimony from the colleague who usually operated the vehicle Paul had at the time of his death. At that time, the colleague had overseen maintenance and was also a trainer, who Gary emphasized was 'unqualified'. At the inquest, he was presented as a professional witness, which surprised Gary. In the time between Paul's death and the inquest, he had been promoted to supervisor. The colleague testified that Paul had operated the machine contrary to the training he had provided the day before the incident. However, there was no record of the training. Gary had strong feelings about him – 'his arrogancy, if the other workforce [had been] in there ... he was meant to be a mate'. He said, 'I was disappointed that the coroner had said, "you've heard the professional evidence"', wondering how the facts the HSE presented of 'mechanical fault' with a video of the machine malfunctioning could compare to the testimony of a colleague.

The inquest pursued a narrative of 'operator error'. Gary was confused that the coroner did not give any option other than a verdict of 'accidental death'. Liz said: 'He was dangling the carrot and then pulling it away from you.' Two jurors were crying because 'all they could do was give [that verdict] … they were directed by him [the coroner]'. This led them to wonder why the jury was there – 'it's just a show'.

Gary was frustrated that the HSE was only able to 'present the facts' in a way that could not blame the corporation, and that the CEOs could not be questioned. As Liz put it, 'they come out and say it's the job of another court, well it isn't. This is the time and place to get all the answers to your questions and it shouldn't be left to another court.' She summed up, 'all the time you're led to believe [by the HSE] that they [the corporation] are responsible and then you get the coroner saying one thing – you cannot go accusing them … then you've got the HSE telling me we're not going to prosecute … you sink even lower'. They summarized that throughout the process, 'you're at the mercy of everybody else'.

The verdict was accidental death 'through operator error or poor maintenance'.

The court

Initially, the HSE wrote to the family to say they were going to prosecute, but the family later received another letter to say the senior officers had decided there was not enough evidence for a further court case because there was no 'value of going forward' as it was 'not in the public interest'. Senior HSE officers held a meeting to explain why and concluded that 'the only one that knows the complete truth is Paul, and he's not here to tell us and we're only told what they want us to know, it's on a need-to-know basis'. Gary was frustrated, saying that 'if we were millionaires' they could have taken civil action, but a senior officer at the HSE told them it would have been 'a financial massacre, although you want to do it, you've got the rest of your family to think about it, I live with it but it's all so frustrating'. The HSE had a meeting with the corporation and explained they were close to prosecution but were being put on probation for 12 months. The family were told to 'be grateful they're going to be on probation'. The family were left to surmise what led to Paul's death. There were no assurances or changes made to ensure this would not happen again.

Mark

Mark was 45 at the time of his death. He was an artist and self-employed window cleaner. He died when he fell due to an unsecured rail at the top of a block of flats. Mark was working more than usual because the flats were being renovated in preparation for a grand re-opening. After his death, his friends and ex-partners continued to visit Mark's mother – 'they've been brilliant, they've been the ones who have kept me going really'. She recalled how the church was full, and she struggled to get in; she laughed that five ex-girlfriends attended his funeral because he 'never fell out with [anyone]'. The interview was attended by Margaret, Mark's mother, and Ken, Margaret's husband.

Police

The police visited Margaret three hours after Mark had died and led them to the mortuary for identification. They impounded Mark's car. The police waited outside the mortuary and asked which undertaker they were going to use, which they were unprepared for, saying that it came 'out of nothing, we'd just found out'. The police officer 'plonked all Mark's things in a polythene bag and said, "these are your son's things"; that was it, and we never saw him again'.

The police did not tell them how or why Mark had died, and they instead found out from a report in the local paper. They felt 'blocked at every turn' and that it was 'hard because we hear of other people who have had accidents, and they say the police were wonderful', whereas Margaret described them as 'absolutely no help whatsoever'. She lamented that no one helped or offered to keep them informed.

The corporation

The person who was a joint owner of the flats also lived in the flat; it was their balcony that Mark had fallen from. They were in their flat at the time and heard him fall. Margaret contacted them and asked to see where Mark had died, to which they agreed. However, a relative of the owner called the next day to say they were not welcome and were not to come and that she worked for the police. Representatives from the flat did not contact her directly but sent flowers.

Margaret had to chase up the wages, describing it as 'an insult' that they had not been paid in full. Mark's friends paid for the funeral and collected £400 that Margaret was planning to use to buy a plaque in his name at his favourite football club.

The HSE

Margaret had to write to HSE to ask what was happening. They described the HSE officer as 'horrible: he came here, and we sat at the table, and he started talking about his holiday on a barge and how he'd enjoyed his holiday'. He told them any investigation would be 'a waste of time, he was saying that it was an accident caused by Mark himself because he shouldn't have been doing what he was doing'.

The inquest

The inquest took place seven months after Mark died. It focused on whether the person who owned the flat Mark had fallen from had asked him to clean the window. The owner had changed their statement between speaking to the police and the time of the inquest. In the police statement, the owner said they had asked Mark to clean the window; however, by the time of the inquest, they insisted they had told Mark not to clean the window because it was 'too dangerous'. Margaret was unhappy about this: '[T]o let her off lying, [the coroner] didn't even acknowledge [the] lying, which at the time you're so upset.' This really hurt Margaret: '[T]hey don't know what they do to people when they don't say sorry.'

The coroner warned Margaret not to speak to the owner – 'throughout the inquest … why are you being nasty to this poor [person]'. The coroner presented the owner as someone who needed protection as they had witnessed Mark falling. Margaret 'got the impression that [the coroner] thought it was all Mark's fault; it was his own fault he'd died', and she therefore wanted to 'get it over with as quick as possible' so she could 'go home'. She reflected the coroner 'treated us like we were criminals … treated us so harshly'. When Margaret spoke up in the court, she was told she would be taken out of court if she did it again.

Mark's case was represented by a barrister the CCA provided; the barrister was new, and Margaret thought the 'coroner was horrible to her … every question she asked it was like, "you can't do that, you can't ask that, can you rephrase?"' When the barrister attempted to challenge the change in statement, the coroner said 'she's an old lady, we'll skip that'. Margaret felt camaraderie from the jurors: '[Y]ou get the feeling that the jury knew, two or three days it went on, you got the feeling they were on our side.' The family tried as hard as they could 'to convince everyone that it wasn't his fault'. A juror wrote to them afterwards. Surmising what had happened, which tallied with the thoughts of Margaret, they wrote that this 'was an accident waiting to happen and why the coroner did not pick up on this is beyond me', adding that 'I hope by telling my view to you it will help you a little with the pain of your loss.'

A verdict of accidental death was returned. Margaret summed up, 'at the end of the day, the coroner won, didn't he?'

Misc

The local gazette was kind to the family, for example letting Margaret proofread a report before it was published. They referred to the state of the rail, which had not been permitted as evidence in court. When she wrote a letter to the local newspaper after the inquest to say how disappointed she was, they apologized but said they could not print it due to fears doing so would 'be libel'. Margaret could only surmise what led to Mark's death. Nothing was changed to ensure this incident did not happen again.

John

John died aged 53 from asphyxiation when an unsecured barrier to a car park went through the windscreen of his car. He was volunteering for a large charity at the time as part of an annual event that he ordinarily carried out with his wife, Sarah. She was at home that night because she was heavily pregnant with their third child. After he died, Sarah received many letters from people who had met him telling stories that made her laugh, 'a very funny letter, very him, and it made me laugh'. John was a person who believed in justice, and Sarah wanted to continue that and do what he 'would have thought was right'. The interview was with Sarah – John's wife.

The police

Sarah was asleep at 3 am when the police called her and asked her to go downstairs and let officers in who were waiting outside. Sarah had already had a 'sinking feeling' because John had not come home and had stopped answering his mobile phone. She began screaming and asked whoever was on the phone, 'Is he dead?' They told her she would have to answer the door and that they could not say. Two police officers came into the house. Sarah asked them not to tell her anything about what had happened while she was on her own and to wait until her parents had arrived. She was told they could not wait until then because it would take too long because her parents lived some miles away, so Sarah rung her friend. During the wait, one of the officers walked around the house and commented on the collection of books while repeatedly trying to tell Sarah what had happened, 'you really need to know'. During this time, they asked if John was suicidal and whether he had mental health problems, which led her to ask, 'did he kill himself?' They assured her he had not, but that they had 'to ask these questions'.

When Sarah's friend arrived, Sarah went upstairs because she did not want to hear from them what had happened. Once they had informed her friend, the officer said, 'right, we can go now'. A different officer called the next day to ask questions. She reflected, 'I couldn't stand him … I just found him extremely unhelpful … how he dealt with me.' In the months that followed, she was 'petrified [the] police were going to come to my house'. She did not sleep for weeks and avoided any further contact, for example family members collected John's belongings from the station, and she did not attend any formal identification.

At the time of the interview, Sarah was considering putting in a complaint but decided not to because of the continuing court proceedings. She had moved out of her house, partly because of her experience with the police – 'that night is just imprinted in my brain how awful it was'. She recognized it was a difficult situation but said that it was worsened by their response, which was driven by a desire to get the job done as quickly as possible. Again, she contrasted this with reports in the media of other Family Liaison Officers (FLOs) who had been 'fantastic', whereas she remains 'petrified the police [are] going to come to my house'.

HSE

The case was not investigated as it occurred on private land.

The corporation

The day after John died, the corporation rang everyone who was there on that night and told them not to talk to anybody about what happened. Sarah said the witnesses were 'intimidated' by the corporation. No one from the corporation communicated with the family until Sarah contacted them; she then received a letter and a visit from two elderly women who lived two hours away. One of the women tried to sympathize as her own husband had recently died. A representative attended the funeral, and they were 'gobsmacked' Sarah told them not to wear the uniform. They tried to persuade Sarah to allow this because they were superior in the organization, but she continued to refuse, insisting 'she is just a normal person'.

Inquest

The inquest took place within a year. Sarah secured a solicitor via her own work union. No one who was there on the night John died would talk to her solicitor because they had been told not to by the corporation: '[T]hey all refused … and they are all my friends and John's friends … I found that one the most difficult.' That was one of the main reasons Sarah chose not to attend: 'I knew that they were trying to shaft me … trying to stop the truth from coming out … I felt like I'd go mad if I went there.' Her solicitor was also angry because the corporation could not stop any of the volunteers from being witnesses, yet despite repeated phone calls and letters they did not change their minds. A friend told her on the anniversary of John's death that she would not give a statement to her solicitor because 'I am frightened for the safety of my children.' Sarah said, 'I felt that if it had been one of them, which it easily could have been that was killed that night that me and John would have been stood up there saying, "this is what happened".'

At the inquest, the corporation's solicitors tried to argue that John had failed to clear his windscreen and that it was an accident due to unprecedented 'freak' winds, which the police disputed. A family member relayed to Sarah that 'it was the most frustrating experience he's ever had, sitting there watching them manipulate this ridiculous witness'. Sarah's mother, who attended, was 'so angry over it'. Despite the corporation working with young people and being responsible for their welfare, no risk assessment had been carried out on the activity, which was of great concern to Sarah. She did not attend because 'I did not want the intricacies … I still can't deal with it … I've got my own sanitized version in my head that I am happy with … the outcome is still the same.' Instead, Sarah read about it in the local newspaper so that she knew 'what everyone else knew' and nothing more. She reflected that it was an 'outside hope' that the verdict would be unlawful killing.

The inquest returned a verdict of 'accidental death'.

Legal

There was no court case.

Misc

With the support of the solicitor procured through her workplace union, Sarah began a civil case. She was told whether it was successful or not would depend upon the 'personality' of the judge on the day and whether they like 'personal injury cases' or 'feel sorry for us'. Sarah reflected: 'It has been a real eye opener for me … you think, "my God, this isn't right … it is going in my favour as I appear to be this "right sort of person", what they think is deserving.' When the corporation began making offers, Sarah likened it to 'Deal or No Deal … I have to think about what John would do.' She said John was a 'massive union person' and that she was now the same because they had been 'fantastic'. A similar incident has happened since.

James

James drowned aged 26 when a boat he was on capsized. He had been saving money and had worked many jobs while studying in the evenings. James was 'very caring': he had known the birthdays of all the people he worked with and would make sure each was sent flowers. He would notice when his mum wore a new outfit and would return the following day with something to match. The interview about James was attended by Elizabeth – James' mother.

Police

Elizabeth was alerted to James' absence when his flatmate called to check if he was with her. She had seen the incident on the news and rang the emergency number but could not get through. After finding another number, she was told over the phone that she would have been notified by now if he was involved so she assumed he was either 'alright or injured'. After hearing nothing, Elizabeth drove to James' home address and the place of the incident, going to the local police stations to try to find out information. She went every day, but she was repeatedly told to return the following day. On the fourth day, she was invited into a room in the police station and asked questions such as 'what his name was, where he was born … distinguishing marks or scars'. The officer did not explain why she had to answer these questions: 'I'm of the generation that you just answer; if he'd said "jump", I would have said, "how high?"'

The last question Elizabeth was asked by the officer was 'What funeral directors are you going to use? That was how I found out my son was dead.' Months later, she found out that the survivors had described James

> to a T … they knew he had an SOS bracelet on, they knew what jeans he had on, what boots … even guessed his height and weight … the police have no excuse, I should have been notified from the beginning because [of] those statements they took from those poor survivors.

She left the police station alone and said, 'if I hadn't had my daughters, I would've jumped into the [river]'. Elizabeth returned the next day to identify her son and was dealt with by a police officer who was 'a year younger than my son … didn't have training as Family Liaison'. He did not tell her where the mortuary was and phoned her later that evening to say she wouldn't be able to identify her son and that they would go on description alone.

Elizabeth found out later that by that time, James' body had been recovered and a post-mortem had taken place, which she was not informed about: '[T]his is what made me so angry and hurt later … the people that were supposed to uphold the law, later break it.' She had been unable to eat until she knew James had been found, and being denied access to his body 'had a devastating effect to this day'. Elizabeth tried and had the door shut in her face; an officer 'nearly caught my nose [in the door]'. She was told, 'Now go home, we are extremely busy, he said "I work 16/17 hours a day", [the names of those officers] are ingrained … I will never forget them.'

Inquest

Three months after James was killed, Elizabeth received a letter telling them they would be informed where and when the inquest would take place in due course. She still had not been told a post-mortem had taken place, and when she rung the Coroner's Office, she was wrongly informed she could only speak to them via a solicitor. Elizabeth was not told she could represent herself – 'you've got people in authority all taking advantage of your vulnerability and your emotional state … what should've happened but didn't happen'.

When Elizabeth found out that the funeral director cannot refuse access to family members who want to see their loved one, she 'started being … the woman who was awkward, because I was asking questions … a nuisance, I was interfering, why didn't I let them go and do their job? I mean we had no rights, and it was so wrong of me to be emotionally upset.' The coroner told her and other families, 'I don't understand your obsession to see a dead body'; he was attacked by two different mothers, and Elizabeth intervened to prevent them being charged with assault.

During the inquest, the people who died were referred to with four-digit numbers. Elizabeth asked if they could be referred to by their names, appealing to the coroner, 'I said, "it's hard enough that we're here, you've got no conception of what it's doing to us, inside our heads, and in our hearts … he's got a name … he's my son".' She said the coroner began using his name and towards the end said, 'Well, I've now said your son's name 12 times, I hope that suffices.' Elizabeth decided to 'fight fire with fire'. She paid 'thousands upon thousands' for transcripts of the court, for the barristers and travelling, amounting to '£300,000'. For some time, Elizabeth lived on 'two hours [of sleep] a day, I'd get up in the middle of the night and I'd have a great thumping photocopying machine, and I'd send off letters and documents to everyone and all the family'. It was an 'us and them situation … they were the people in the know and we were all the ones being left with needs'.

The inquest recorded an unlawful killing verdict.

Legal

The Crown Prosecution Service (CPS) set out a case following the inquest to prosecute under maritime laws, which was dropped. The Marine Accident Investigation Branch produced a report which cited faults in marine regulation for over two decades. Two trials ended with acquittals when the juries failed to reach a verdict.

Elizabeth wanted an inquiry to begin but was refused for ten years, which she stated was likely due to links between the board of directors and MPs, 'wheels within wheels'. During that time, she and others lobbied the opposition, who put it in writing that they would launch an inquiry if they were ever elected. When they were elected, they launched the inquiry, which made 30 recommendations. Protocol was altered on this specific stretch of water to reduce the likelihood of a similar incident happening again.

Andrew

Andrew was 37 at the time of his death. He had woken up from a night shift and was killed on his way to collect a birthday present for his wife, Heather. He and Heather shared three children between the ages of two and seven. Andrew was killed when an unsecured 20-foot barrier at the entrance of a car park went through the windscreen of his car, missing his three-year-old who was strapped in her car seat in the back. He died due to asphyxiation at the scene. The interview was with Heather – Andrew's wife.

The police

The police arrived at Heather and Andrew's house less than 40 minutes after he had left. Heather found out about his death via her parents who were told by the police officer while she waited in the kitchen. The police took her to the scene within four hours. Heather's parents identified Andrew; she was able to see his body in the days that followed.

The police took Andrew's car to check for 'mechanical faults' and returned to their home to ask Heather whether he was 'a boy racer, trying to apportion the blame to him'. She interpreted this as the police trying to 'think of the easy way out'. The police investigation was 'basically two minutes', and after eight months Heather received a letter from the local council to say that the police had filed the paperwork and that it would be treated as an RTI. The police had not been in contact with Heather since the initial enquiries. Her father was a retired police officer and helped her compose a letter to argue there should be a full investigation. In response, a team of four police officers and an inspector were assigned to investigate a potential charge of corporate manslaughter. The inspector visited the head office of the store to inform them about the possible charges; he told Heather that '[t]heir face dropped'.

Over the course of months, the team took witness statements, interviewed staff, examined health and safety procedures and requested documents – 'well it went on for nearly two years … it was immense really, over a two-year period'. They found the relevant risk assessment had been completed the day after Andrew's death.

The HSE

The HSE were involved 'from day one'. The HSE officer was 'doing his own investigation as well and obviously he's in liaison with the police'. Heather was involved in the meetings. She described the officer as 'the most thorough and intelligent man … he was like a rat up a drainpipe, he left no stone unturned he was very professional, astute and did everything to the letter'.

The inquest

The inquest took place four years after Andrew's death. It lasted two weeks. Heather was given four hours' notice after waiting four years due to an error, whereas the corporation was given a fortnight's notice. She did not have time to get legal representation: '[H]e [the coroner's clerk] left me in a hell of a position.' It left her with no choice but to represent herself, 'next to this top London barrister, me having no legal experience at all, none at all'. Heather asked questions of every witness: 'I think they were expecting some nervous widow who couldn't compose herself but then it was four years on, and anger will fuel you on, even after all that time you think you're not going to let them get away with it.' Two runners passed questions between the defence barrister and five solicitors in front of 12 representatives from the corporation. The Chief Executive had been flown in from another country on a helicopter.

Heather agreed with a news report from another woman who had been in court:

> [S]he's saying the same thing I saw, they're all out there on their mobile phones, in their suits … ringing somebody and all with their briefcases … they're whispering so you can't hear. They don't look at you, they don't smile at you, it's as though you don't exist, like you're the enemy but they're forgetting why you're there.

Statements that had been taken under the requirements of the Police and Criminal Evidence (PACE) Act had changed between the initial interviews and the inquest. She felt happy the coroner knew one employee 'was a liar'. The person who had failed to secure the barrier was involved in a minor car crash on the way to the court, delaying the session. The coroner said 'can we please go easy on her' as a result, to which Heather responded: 'Unbelievable! Am I supposed to feel sorry for her? Never in a million years.' Heather was the first witness on the stand, and when the defence had no questions for her, she took the opportunity to read out her Victim Impact Statement.

The jury asked questions of those called to the stand. The coroner did not sum up before the jury were sent out, which Heather put down to her being new to the role. They were unable to reach a verdict. That meant 'we had to go all weekend', which was 'hell on earth because you're living on your nerves'. The verdict was not returned until 1 pm on the Monday after the weekend break, which Heather described as 'mental torture'. A verdict of unlawful killing was returned: '[W]e [Heather and her sister] both started to cry.' The corporation had prepared a statement for the press stating they were going to pursue a judicial review, which 'they handed … out to the press before we'd even left the courtroom'. This did not materialize.

The corporation

The store did not close on the day of Andrew's death. A first aider was called but returned to the store, leaving two bystanders to call the emergency services. Heather stated that 'nobody did anything for them, the shocked state they were in, and they weren't offered so much as a cup of tea'. The case made the news, and members of the public came forward to say they had reported the barrier as unsecured to the store previously. The store initially claimed that the car park was not their responsibility because it did not belong to them.

Until the inquest, four years after Andrew's death, the corporation had no contact with Heather, 'not one word of regret, condolence, sorry, we hadn't received a flower, a card, nothing'. Ahead of the inquest, they sent a letter offering to pay for her and her children to go to a local holiday park and pay for accommodation for the duration of the inquest. Heather was unhappy: 'Who in God's name would accept a holiday from a company who killed your husband? Can't they do better than that?' Heather said people assumed the corporation were buying gifts for the children because 'people genuinely believed they were a caring company … my kids can't stand their adverts'.

The inquest was 'the first time I was meeting these faceless individuals who had killed my husband'. On the stand, the Chief Executive said: 'I would personally like to offer my condolences … for the loss of her husband.' Heather responded by saying 'you're four years too late … I dropped him like a stone.' At the court case (discussed subsequently), a director of the corporation approached Heather and her father to offer their condolences.

During the investigation, Heather said the corporation used 'stalling tactics … certain things have been shredded' and, when interviewed, 'people under PACE, they declined to answer questions' on the advice of their legal team: '[T]hey had the top London barrister, they can afford the best, can't they?' During the investigation, they found that there had been no health and safety officer in place for over a year, and emergency doors had been padlocked. The person who had been assigned in the interim also worked in the store on another public-facing role, leaving no time to carry out any other duties.

Court case

Heather met with the CPS with support from the CCA. After a two-year investigation, the CPS contacted Heather via a letter to say they were not going to prosecute due to 'lack of evidence ... because they go on a 60/40-win ratio or something'. Heather recognized the potential issues: '[I]t's too difficult to prove, you've got to prove the controlling mind knew about all the problems and you'd never get that because that person is not even based there.' The 'controlling mind' is based in another country, 'counting his diamonds'. Heather replied with a letter to say they 'should be disbanded'.

After the inquest had concluded, the case returned to court to face charges for breaches of health and safety law. After an hour, the corporation was fined £225,000, which Heather thought was 'absolute rubbish' because the corporation traded 'in billions per annum'. The judge said 'his hands were tied ... but he did want it publicly noted that their health and safety was far below what the public expect'.

Misc

The press took an interest in the case, running articles every day during the inquest. Heather said people in the local area were 'absolutely outraged and disgusted by what had happened'. She waited until the inquest to say anything to the press, on the advice of her father, and took the children to the court to hear the verdict. The case was covered by a national BBC programme on similar incidents across the country. Heather described this as one of the victories of the case.

Robert

Robert was 40 when he died. He had recently returned from a six-month trip to New Zealand and had been awarded a PhD in Chemistry. At the time of his death, he was working as a driver for an agency delivering goods. He had travelled around looking at different corporations to work for as he knew it was potentially a 'dodgy business' and so 'did a wee bit of research'. Robert was crushed when a tail lift on a lorry delivering goods malfunctioned. The interview was with Angela – Robert's wife.

Police

The police called at the house and left when they realized only the children were home. When Angela got home from work that evening, she rang the local police station, who sent officers two hours later. In advance, Angela had called her parents to come over for the sake of the children, as she feared Robert had been hurt on his motorcycle. Close to midnight, 'two very young, frightened looking police officers' arrived. When Angela was told Robert had been killed at work, she immediately asked if it was the tail lift because he had recently spoken about problems with it. The officers stayed for half an hour, gave her the phone number of a family liaison worker and left. No one accompanied Angela to the morgue. She was comforted by a person who worked at the morgue who cried and 'showed an ounce of humanity'. She did not find out how Robert had died for two years beyond a death certificate which stated the cause of death was a head injury.

Angela rang the number of the FLO she had been given to find it was a wrong number. Her eldest daughter rang each station and was 'passed from pillar to post'. They were given the name of an officer who was 'an absolute nightmare, basic humanity, unbelievable … she was phoning up and telling my children about her holidays, making inane conversation'. Angela told her two colleagues of Robert had rung her to say faults on the vehicle were being covered up, and the police officer 'gave me a row and told me not to listen to workplace rumours'. The officer was clear that she thought what happened to Robert was an accident and pressed this to Angela: '[S]he said to me "listen I'm absolutely sure that nothing criminal [happened], this is just an unfortunate accident."'

Angela reflected, 'I don't think I fitted into the box' and that maybe the relationship would have been different if she'd 'been a wee bit more weaker', even though she was 'weak, but if I hadn't asked questions'. As with Margaret, she compared her experience to what she thought other people were experiencing: '[T]here was another part of me thinking, you see things on TV where you see the Family Liaison Officer, they're with the family.' Angela tried to mitigate her poor experience, for example when she went to the police station to collect Robert's belongings, she took a friend who was in the fire brigade and asked him to wear a T-shirt to show he was also part of the services in the hope she would be treated better. However, this was a terrible experience for her as she was asked by officers to wait in the reception at the police station. The officers came out and held up Robert's belongings in a clear plastic bag and asked, 'who is here for [Robert's] stuff?' At this, Angela broke down: 'I just became aware of this screaming … they ushered me into this kind of room.'

Unknowingly, the officers had returned tachographs as part of Robert's belongings. The FLO called Angela repeatedly 'in a panic … she kept phoning me to tell me I was stealing from the driving agency'. The phone calls between the officer and Angela focused on 'asking things of the firm for me', such as facilitating a visit from the boss of the corporation and asking whether they could attend the funeral.

Corporation

The head of the corporation visited Angela within a week of Robert's death, as facilitated by the FLO. She reflected that this had put her in a 'vulnerable position' and felt he was trying 'to find out what I knew'. Throughout the meeting, he kept answering his mobile phone. A friend who was there eventually said 'I think that's enough' and left.

There were a number of corporations involved, which complicated the investigation. Robert worked for an agency who dissolved the corporation after his death. At the Fatal Accident Inquiry (FAI), a witness said they were still working for the same corporation under a different name, so they had to stop the proceedings and forced them to give evidence. Another corporation owned the vehicle Robert was using and another hired them to carry out the work. A parent corporation which owned one of the corporations later put themselves forward for a safety award.

The HSE

Three weeks after Robert's death, Angela received a pack from the HSE saying an investigation was being started. One leaflet had the telephone number of the CCA. The case worker at the CCA started correspondence and what Angela referred to as a 'ripple'. Letters from the HSE followed, and a representative asked her to travel over 400 miles to London for a meeting because they were unable to travel to meet her.

The HSE took statements 15 months after Robert's death. Angela understood they would not amount to much: '[W]ell after people might remember, you're willing to put your job on the line early doors … but after a year, this isn't worth putting my neck on the line.'

FAI

The solicitor the CCA identified for the family at a conference wrote to the Procurator Fiscal (PF) and asked for a meeting. When there was no reply, the solicitor followed this with four or five letters before complaining to the Lord Advocate. Nothing happened quickly, and Angela began to think she was a part of other people's agendas and that Robert had become 'surplus to everyone's requirements'. They rang regularly to ask when anything would be happening. She was told nothing had been decided, but on one occasion when Angela called, she was told 'prosecution starts in a fortnight', which she was incredulous about as 'how can we have prosecution starting in a fortnight when a week ago you didn't know anything?'

Angela described the first hearing as 'like a social club for the lawyers'. Those representing the corporations involved said they were not ready for the hearing and asked for an extension. This happened more than once; the corporation questioned the independent expert and then their own expert report. Angela was warned this would happen and wrote letters to oppose continued extensions.

Initial meetings with the PF said it had been uncovered that there was a 'culture of drivers making do'. A mechanic who worked for the maintenance company testified that he had been told not to fix the defects on the tail lifts because it would mean the lorries were off the road for weeks. This was denied by the managers, who said 'they knew nothing about that and [the mechanic] couldn't remember who said it to him'. Another person had used the same lorry the day before and recorded it had 11 defects. The risk assessment had been filled in by two different people, which to Angela looked like 'after the event somebody panicked and went to the paper and ticked them but that can't even be mentioned'.

One corporation involved pleaded guilty, and no further extensions were granted for the other corporation involved who subsequently also plead guilty. The corporation then spent time in negotiations: '[T]hey were willing to plea certain things, so certain things had been dropped, if they changed the wording.' The PF summed up prior to sentencing, criticizing the corporations for wasting time in the court and claiming the case should have been heard in the High Court but that his 'hands were tied'. The fines were reduced to £14,000 for one corporation and £19,000 for another because of the guilty plea. The solicitors immediately argued there should be a greater discount for the guilty pleas and haggled until they were fined £33,000 between them. As a result of the FAI report with recommendations, the corporation had to remove 50 lorries that were considered at risk of the same defect.

Angela was upset by the proceedings in the court: 'Every time I've been in the court I've thought, who is doing this for the life of Robert? Everyone is trying to get their company's limitation.' She resigned herself to never knowing what happened: 'I know we won't get the absolute truth; I think I'd held on and held on, that I'd get closure, but the truth?' Angela emphasized that it was not about money and that Robert 'had absolutely no chance in that workplace and he [had] no chance in [this] court'. The Sheriff spoke twice to the family, an acknowledgement that Angela said has 'been more assistance than any fine'. Two of the corporations were fined and compelled to recall lorries with the same defect that led to Robert's death. Angela did not get definitive answers as to what led up to Robert's death and no assurances this defect would not be corrected beyond the immediate fleet of lorries.

Phillip

Phillip died aged 24 on a ship working as an (unqualified) stevedore. He was working for a temping agency that had subcontracted his labour to a corporation on the docks. Less than two hours after he arrived on the first day, he was crushed by an excavator. The interview was attended by Jane, Phillip's mother, and Steve, Phillip's father.

The police

The police informed Jane 12 hours after Phillip had died. They were 'brutal' and approached them like 'we had committed a crime'. They interrupted her when she was speaking and 'were just so callous'. They gave her a reference number and the number of the control room. No one returned their calls as it was a Saturday; they had to wait until the week, and 'it was still a struggle the following week'. Jane said the officers who told Phillip's partner about his death had been different and had spent 'a lot of time talking to them … shared roll-ups'.

Once they were given an appointment to see the police, they were met with 'a wall of silence'. Jane was told there was no point in seeing Phillip because there was going to be a post-mortem. They were unaware they could have had their own medical representative, which they wished they had because then they would have known 'he had been killed instantly. We didn't know.' They were not told which corporation was involved until they collected Phillip's ashes and saw it was written on the crematorium's paperwork. They were wrongly told a crane was involved in his death, only finding out months later that this was incorrect.

The police attended the site on the day of Phillip's death but had said, 'oh it's a health and safety thing, nothing to do with us'. They did not seal off the area and allowed people to get on and off the boat. This was reported by the health and safety officer and by a member of the public who developed photographs of Phillip's body. These had been taken by the First Officer of the ship for insurance purposes. The Fire Service attended but would not go into the hold to recover Phillip's body because 'they were afraid … in case it killed one of their people'. No statements were taken or a list of those who could provide statements at a later date. It was three years before the family had a full list of who was there on the day.

After six weeks, the health and safety inspector contacted the police to say that, according to legislation, they should be involved, and a sergeant was assigned to the case. The sergeant had two other members of staff assigned to investigate who worked with the inspector 'trying to unravel this … always in arrears'. Jane said from that point they were 'on board … this is a crime', but that also 'truthfully … they didn't know what the hell they were doing'. In the absence of any training, 'they had no idea where to start'. Jane regularly rang them to find out what was happening, which she said the sergeant was 'fine about'.

A statement was taken from the director two months later, and they went to arrest him but were unable to because he was on holiday abroad. The police arrested the excavator driver on suspicion of manslaughter, but the inspector told Jane it was 'no way his fault'. Nothing was seized, and when they realized items were needed as evidence, such as the chains on the excavator, they were told they had been discarded in the years between Phillip's death and the investigation. Jane summarized: '[S]tatements weren't taken, evidence wasn't kept, measurements weren't taken.' When they tried to interview people immediately after Phillip's death, the director offered permanent contracts to everyone who was employed by the agency. At least one person refused, and another who at 17 years old was legally unable to work there left the site and did not return. Halfway through the investigation, the sergeant was involved in a bad car crash, and the case was handed on to someone new. Jane was not told who that was for another year but was sympathetic that the new person had to 'pick up the threads a couple of years down the line'.

The HSE

Jane contacted the HSE when no one got in touch because of a leaflet in the Coroner's Office that had been produced by Ann Elvin, whose son had died in similar circumstances years before. This was on the same day she collected the ashes from the crematorium. The HSE confirmed during that phone call what she had just discovered on the crematorium paperwork – the name of the corporation. Jane 'did get on very well' with the HSE inspector and had 'sympathy with her dilemma'. The inspector had organized the retrieval of Phillip's body, after the police had left. She had no option but to persuade the driver of the excavator to get back in the vehicle to do so, 'even though he was white and shaking all over'.

Jane became concerned for the welfare of the HSE inspector who had been assigned to the case. She 'was getting leaned on by her superior to the point where she was off work sick … in peril of losing her job'. Jane thought this was because 'she was actually doing the job'. People Jane knew in the media led to direct contact with the head of the HSE. She contacted him to tell him how 'disgusted' she was with the way the inspector was being treated. He responded and 'came on like a ton of bricks [on the office] … had them running in circles', which surprised her.

Legal

The leaflet produced by Ann Elvin that Jane picked up in the Coroner's Office suggested families get legal representation. Friends joined with the family to occupy the premises of the corporation with the aim of stopping work for a day, because they did not stop work on the day that Phillip died. This received coverage in the local press, which led to people contacting the family, some of whom recommended a solicitor. Jane met with her, and she agreed to work pro bono and knew barristers who would ask only for their expenses to be paid.

The solicitor was experienced in prosecuting deaths at work. Jane reflected that this changed things, and that it was 'wonderful having somebody who knows the ropes'. The police prepared the documentation and left it with the CPS in Sussex in August. After six weeks, the sergeant rang Jane to say that when they had followed it up, they realized 'it was still sitting in the envelope on the desk' because 'they didn't realize the seriousness of the case'. It was then sent to London 'with haste', and they were reassured they would hear by Christmas. In January, they were told there would be no prosecution.

The solicitor suggested they launch a judicial review under legal aid, which was possible if it was launched by Phillip's brother, who was earning less than £6,000 per annum. Even then, they were charged what amounted to a few hundred pounds, which they were told they would get back if they won. They carried out fundraising as a form of insurance if the case went against them, benefitting from the charity of three comedians who raised £10,000. When the judicial review was successful, they used the money to cover the barristers' expenses.

Their barrister 'had been diligent, really diligent'. He was bemused that the police were providing the relevant documents, reflecting they 'aren't usually this cooperative with us', as he usually dealt with police misconduct. The person sent to defend the CPS decision 'was shaking and trembling' when he left because he was 'ripped apart' by the judges. This and the decision to overturn the ruling not to prosecute left the family 'on a real high'. The CPS took another six months to review the case. Jane wrote to the Director of Public Prosecutions, who eventually replied and took advice from the QCs, reflecting 'the number of QCs in this area is very small'.

Jane was 'in and out of hospital' with 'stress-related ulcers'. Unable to help with the active elements of the campaign, she wrote letters – 'even if I'm ill I can sit and write letters' – replying to people who had been in contact and to follow up with the CPS and the HSE. She continually contacted people when her solicitor hit dead ends, and, to her surprise, people were helpful: '[I]t was the oddest thing that people really did give me information. The less I said, the more I listened, the more they kept giving me information.' Upon receiving official documents, Jane pulled them apart and could see 'the huge errors'. For example, the director had 'fudged' measurements, writing in both metric and imperial – 3 feet was changed to 3 metres, 'an enormous difference' that Jane was able to correct. When measurements were unavailable or vague, she worked with the HSE inspector to look at the photographs and find them, using other objects in the photo, such as the parked police car, to work out the height of the bags.

When the case was heard in court, Jane felt the 'the judge was partial'. For example, the prosecution delivered their closing remarks, and the defence counsel stood up and said 'he's not ready to do it'. Court could not reconvene for another five days. The judge promised to sum up for the prosecution before the jury were sent out to negate the time in between; however, he did not and instead provided a character reference for the accused, saying 'he has been a good man, he has never been in trouble'. Jane summarized: '[I]t was sure as hell not impartial.' After two days of waiting, the judge said he would accept a majority verdict. Subsequently, the director was cleared of manslaughter and found guilty of two health and safety crimes, receiving a fine of £50,000.

Inquest

There was no inquest because the case went forward for corporate manslaughter. This meant that the temping agency was never under scrutiny, for example for lack of adequate training. Jane wanted this to happen because the agency had failed to visit the premises they sent Phillip to and had been sending workers there for months before the incident.

The corporation

No one from the corporation wrote to the family, and the fact they did not know where Phillip had died meant Jane felt he was treated 'with less respect than a piece of lost property'. Phillip's friends put up photographs in the local pub, and by coincidence, a man who had been working next to Phillip on the day of his death came into the pub. This led to a conversation with Phillip's friends. Until that point, he had not been able to talk to anyone but began to open up and asked if they thought Jane would mind if he spoke to them. He rang Jane and said 'the first thing I want to tell you is that it was quick'. They were unable to speak much more to him as he was 'so terribly drunk. He had been having dreadful nightmares.'

The week before Phillip's death, a health and safety officer had carried out an extensive exercise with the corporations on the dock, but the one Phillip was sent to chose not to take part. They were 'dreadfully short of staff … which was part of the trouble': for example, there was no manager, and the ship's agent was also working as a supervisor. Two crew members who did not speak English had been employed to assist with the job that morning. There are no universal hand signals, and the crew members relied upon those they had used in another country. To reduce the time it took to remove the goods out of the ship, the grab that killed Phillip had been illegally modified. Jane said that the 'whole set up was designed to kill somebody'. The police sergeant was angry, and after he visited the corporation, he reported to Jane that 'they don't give a toss'.

Media

The case was covered in a newspaper by a journalist who was a friend of two of Phillip's friends. The National Union of Journalists 'were rooting for us': they attended the judicial review, and a journalist friend of Phillip's friends published a special article in the *Guardian*. Nothing was altered to ensure this could not happen again.

Jason

Jason was killed with a colleague when a chimney they were dismantling from the inside exploded. He was a steeplejack employed by a corporation away from home, subcontracted to another corporation. He was working his notice and was due to start a new job the following month in a different area that was closer to home. The interview was attended by Yvonne – Jason's mother.

Police

Yvonne was told Jason had died by her ex-partner who knocked on their door at 1 am. They drove to the workplace and were introduced to the Police Liaison Officer (PLO). Yvonne wanted confirmation Jason had died but drove home that same day when she was told it was too dangerous to remove the bodies. The following day, the PLO rang and spoke to Yvonne's sister. Yvonne asked her sister to find out when she could bring Jason home, but 'I don't think she realized the phone was on loudspeaker … and she said, "doesn't she realize there's nothing left to bring home?"' Yvonne did not hear from the Liaison Officer again. The police visited the family a week later and asked who Jason's dentist was and 'did he drink? What was his family life like? It sounded as though they wanted to lay blame at [their] door.' They left after an hour.

The police told the family they were questioning three managers. They visited Yvonne at work and 'told us that there had been evidence that somebody was to blame, and they were looking to bring charges of manslaughter'. Three months later, they were told three people had been charged with corporate manslaughter: '[T]hey wouldn't tell us what and why they were charged.' Yvonne rung and asked questions, without any support, 'no support, victim support, no nothing'.

Legal

The court case began at the Crown Court just over two months after the incident. Yvonne was clear that the court case did not consider her and Jason's brothers, and 'they were not treated as victims'. This was clear from the first day, when the family arrived and found no seats had been reserved and they were turned away because it was full. A police officer gave up their seat so Yvonne could stay, but Jason's brother and father had to wait outside. She found it difficult that the family were sat in the same area as the families of the managers in the days that followed, 'with very little regard to our feelings and suffering, what we were going through'. She found it callous to hear them talking about which shops they were going to go to during the lunch breaks when they had to listen to 'autopsy reports and see photographs, videos of the chimney burning down'.

The Crown Prosecutor said in his opening speech 'that an email had been found in a drawer and that two of the managers had received this email that told them to stop what they were doing' because to continue to take down the chimney from the inside was dangerous and there 'was a great possibility of a fire and explosion'. The managers had sent the email because Jason and his colleague stopped work and left the chimney twice over concerns the material in the chimney was toxic and asked if they needed breathing apparatus. However, 'they ignored the email and put it in a drawer and sent Jason [and his colleague] back into the chimney', stating that the email had 'said nothing about if it was toxic or not'. Jason and his colleague were not told about the contents of the emails and returned to the chimney and continued working.

Despite what seemed like strong evidence, Yvonne said 'we knew straight away, after the first day that the case was going to collapse, you just knew'. Several experiences led them to this belief, which began on the first day when they were approached outside the court room by a barrister who was representing one of the managers. Once he confirmed they were Jason's parents, he said 'this has got no reflection on your son, but it is the way the trial has got to go … we are not blaming your son'. Yvonne reflected: '[H]is words then, we'll never forget.' Yvonne voiced her concerns to the police and CPS, who told her 'their witnesses were lying on the stand' and changing their statements. One of the corporations involved had been given immunity from prosecution – 'we don't know why … we can't find out'. The defence claimed Jason's boss had not considered the welfare of his employees and had said he did a risk assessment and while pointing to his head had said he 'had it up here'.

The prosecutor detailed that the corporation Jason worked for had won the tender to carry out the work because they were more than 50 per cent cheaper than the next cheapest bid. The barrister for the defence stood and said: 'I thought we agreed not to talk about money.' Yvonne said she knew then that 'the whole truth wasn't going to come out'. The family, the police, the prosecutor and the barristers met in a room and were told if the case was dismissed, the corporation would plead guilty of charges under health and safety. The family were advised that it was better to agree to this because if they were to continue with the trial and lose, Jason's daughter would not receive any compensation. The police and the CPS promised to help them with a civil case.

Jason's father agreed, and everyone returned to the court. The jury came back, and 'it was explained that there had been a change in the case and one of them had to stand up and repeat after the judge … that they found the three men not guilty on the manslaughter charge'. This was 'unbelievable'. Yvonne said she would always 'remember … one young lad … he just looked at us and shook his head in disbelief'. At that time, the 'not guilty' verdict meant there was no chance of the case ever being heard again in a criminal court.

The following day, the family were back in court to hear the health and safety charges. Yvonne wrote a letter to the judge detailing how it had affected them as a family, 'but the CPS barrister stopped it getting to the judge'. Instead, he told the judge a police officer would sit with her and help 'draft a letter', which the police officer said he 'felt terrible about'. Yvonne refused and said he could write it but not put her name to it. The corporation was found guilty and fined £14,000 under charges related to both deaths, '£7,000 each per life between three people with time to pay'. When the manslaughter charges were dropped, a manager shook the hand of his barrister in front of the family and said 'thank you for getting us off'. After the health and safety charges were read out the following day, they asked for their costs to be paid. Yvonne summed up: '[W]hen the trial was over, four years on, they killed Jason again.'

Yvonne had a meeting with the CPS after the trial and asked why the trial had 'gone so badly wrong'. When they questioned the accuracy of some of the information presented at court, they 'looked shocked'. The prosecutor asserted that they did not have to speak to Yvonne, 'we don't have to tell you nothing', and only had to communicate with his ex-partner, as they shared a child which made her the next of kin. They attended meetings with the CPS in London to try to find out why managers had been given immunity, but they were dismissed. Reflecting on the experience, Yvonne thought it was a mistake to 'put so much faith in the justice system'. She thought the CPS and the police were 'fighting for Jason … that was so ignorant of me'.

HSE

The family attended meetings with the HSE 'to try and get answers', but once the police charged the managers, they were told 'it's a police case and we had to contact them'.

After the legal proceedings had ended, Yvonne met with the HSE, who said 'the court case went terribly wrong, if there ever was a case of murder, Jason's case was that'. With her permission, they wanted to use the case 'as a training thing to send round as to how things can go badly wrong'. This did not happen in the end.

Inquest

The inquest was opened and shut because of the police charges. The family were not told about this, and a few causes of death were listed on Jason's death certificate because the Coroner's Office 'lost the organs'. After the trial ended, Yvonne wanted the inquest reopened because she thought it might be a chance to find out the truth. She collected all the evidence required to call for one, including the minutes of the court case, the health and safety reports and the police reports, which cost money. She tried to involve local MPs, and the coroner considered the request. The Coroner's Office consulted with Yvonne's ex-partner, the three corporations and three managers to see whether it should take place. She received a letter to say her request had been refused because she was the only one who wanted it to take place.

The corporation

Jason was subcontracted to the job; three corporations were involved. Within a day of Jason's death, Yvonne met with Jason's boss and two other managers, who 'were on the defence all the time, we knew they didn't want us there, you could feel it'. The more questions the family asked, 'the more they became quite distant and abrupt'.

After the trial finished, Jason's brother began to look on the internet for information about the corporation. He found that another worker had been killed at the same site, three months after Jason, contrary to evidence presented in court that stated no other person had ever been killed at that workplace. Nothing was changed to ensure this could not happen again.

Luke

Luke was 18 when he died. He was working as an apprentice at a garage that had been identified by the college as a suitable place to learn. The garage was owned by one person and managed by another. Luke died following an explosion in which he suffered 80 per cent burns. The manager was injured in the same incident. Luke's father, Ian was interviewed.

Police

Luke survived for three days; in that time, the family were at a specialist burns unit at the hospital. Ian described the police as 'brilliant'. On the first day, they were allocated an FLO whom Ian describes as a family friend: 'He helped us with everything, any questions we needed to know, any part of the investigation with the HSE.' He could ring him up any time, and 'he was there'.

A detective sergeant from the Homicide Squad was also involved and worked with the FLO. The police 'backed up the forensic evidence', and their investigation supported the findings of the HSE investigation. The area was sealed off as a crime scene, and within a year the family were in court to hear charges of manslaughter.

HSE

The HSE 'were involved straightaway'. The police called them in before Luke had died. Ian described them 'as excellent, really good'. An inspector visited the family once a week to keep them informed and accompanied them throughout the trial. They provided expert witnesses, and Ian felt both the HSE and the police 'were on our side'.

Inquest

The coroner informed the family there would be no inquest because the case was going to court but said 'any information you need, just phone me up'.

Legal

The trial lasted a fortnight and was a 'rollercoaster ride'. The CPS provided a barrister, which the family did not pay for. Ian thought they were 'going to lose the case', even though 'there was so much evidence', when the judge asked 'why is this case before me? It was an accident at work.' However, it took 'two weeks to switch that judge's mindset from "this man shouldn't be before me" to "[the manager is] guilty of manslaughter"'.

The family were surprised by the operation of the court on a number of occasions. First, Ian thought the judges were 'too friendly with the barristers' and that rather than them 'going against each other … you see then having a cup of tea'. Second, the judge 'didn't seem to take any interest in all these expert witnesses coming up from the HSE' and sought out on his own to find out whether what happened to Luke was standard practice by visiting a business that was local to where he lived. Thankfully, the owner of that business said they would never attempt that, which Ian 'found strange [because] that meant more to [the judge] than the stuff he'd learnt from the HSE'. The police officer helped them to do a Victim Statement, which took 'the best part of three hours … [and] a lot of tears'. However, the judge said he would not read it, 'not in my court'.

Ian said they 'realized that it was all a game' that did not put them or Luke first. For example, the family had to sit in the gallery with the family of the owners of the corporation. The family were making 'snipes'; the FLO argued to the judge that they should be moved. Once they were moved to the press box, '[the accused's] solicitor complained because we were directly opposite the jury', so they had to move again. In another example, the defence asked for the family to be removed from the court 'every chance they got'. On one occasion, they were taken out, and the FLO said to them 'we've got to tell you this, the defence are going to bring up the fact that Luke asked the ambulance driver if he was going to die'. Ian did not know this at the time and was 'upset' but felt 'prepared'; however, they 'went back into court and nobody even mentioned it'. He felt that 'it was just another ploy … to try to demoralize you then bring you back in again'.

The jury returned a guilty verdict of gross negligence manslaughter, and the manager was sentenced to nine months in prison.

Prior to sentencing, the judge asked for a copy of the corporation's bank statements because he said it 'was a serious offence and you will pay dearly'. This led Ian to believe that 'he was going to go to town' on them. However, two days before he went to court, the owner had transferred £25,000 between his accounts, which was permitted, leaving Ian to think it 'was a real farce'. When the manager was sentenced, the barrister for the defence drew on an article in the newspaper and held it up to the judge to say that Luke's mother would 'forgive them, but she didn't say that at all'. Ian was unable to challenge it, even though they were sitting in the court. The owner was fined £10,000 with costs of £15,000.

After the manager had served two months, the family received a letter to say that the case was going to be heard at the Court of Appeal and were reassured by the police that 'it was only one item that was under scrutiny, so it was nothing to worry about'. The FLO took them to London. They sat 'about five hours waiting for [the court to sit]'. As soon as they went in, 'it was just obvious that we weren't going to be listened to'. Rather than looking at one item of the case, the judges reviewed the entire case.

The appeal judges took issue with the inclusion of evidence from a fire fighter in the first trial. The fire fighter had interviewed the manager with the permission of the ambulance crew to find out if there was anything dangerous in the workshop, to ensure the fire brigade were safe to enter. At the appeal, the judge said this evidence was inadmissible as the 'fireman should have realized that it could possibly lead to a court case'. Ian was accompanied by a Chief Inspector, who said: 'I have never heard that before, that's nonsense.' He was surprised because firefighters do not have the power of arrest and would not need to caution anybody to find out what caused the incident.

Despite this, the 'judge was adamant' and 'threw the case out on the grounds … [it] was inadmissible', pointing to the drugs the manager had been given, going against evidence presented in the trial from the doctor who treated him at the scene and 'who said that no one was given enough pain relief that they can't be questioned'. The three judges went out of the room, and Ian checked his watch – 'they were gone for 35 seconds … there was no jury, just these three judges'. They turned to the manager and quashed the charges, telling him: 'You can leave with your reputation intact.' The family's barrister asked for a re-trial but was refused; their 'barrister didn't get a word in edgeways'.

By the end of the process, Ian said his 'faith in British justice went out of the window'. He felt 'cheated. I thought, "this can't be the end of it, they've got away with murder" … it was so obvious it was the old school.'

Corporation

The manager who was also injured visited the hospital when Luke was at the burns unit. He told the family he was with him at the time of the explosion and attended the funeral and cried, hugging Luke's mother 'saying how sorry he was, it was all his fault'. Ian said his 'contempt' for him came not from what happened but from 'the fact he lied afterwards'. They 'put an extra £20 in Luke's wage packet. That's the sort of people we were dealing with.' At the trial, the owner could not remember Luke's name and referred to him as 'the YTS [Youth Training Scheme] boy'.

A college had identified the corporation as a place to send Luke under an apprenticeship. The owner told the court he thought the college taught health and safety and that it was not his job. The college produced the risk assessment and related documents they claimed Luke had signed. However, Ian's wife said it was not Luke's signature, as it differed from that on his provisional driving licence. The police said that they were 'acting as a witness for the prosecution so there was nothing they could do' to question this 'until after the court case'. This was never followed up. Ian took comfort in the fact that local people chose not to use the corporation due to local press coverage.

Summary

There were common experiences the secondary victims shared following the death of their loved ones, including responses which led to their cases leaving any official process and being pushed to invisibility, whether it was at the earliest opportunity or in a reversal of the verdict following punishment. These can be summarized under the following headings.

No investigation

The lack of investigation was frequently cited as a reason for the cases to be halted. The police did not investigate some of the cases at all, because they occurred on private land or because it was assumed to be an RTI. On other occasions, they quickly passed the cases to the HSE. Even if the families had the funds and successfully navigated a private prosecution, sufficient evidence had been lost. Without the power of the police, the corporations were able to view the death as accidental, and any potential crime scene was quickly restored to a workplace or right of way; witnesses returned to being employees or members of the public. While the police had extensive resources compared to the HSE and should have been guided by existing protocol, they failed to use their immediate powers to investigate and gather the kind of evidence required by a court of law.

Delay

Delays were frequent and unexpected by the families. An under-funded agency, under staffed and without the power of the police, the HSE took months and years to interview witnesses and staff. Obstacles put in place by the corporations were accepted by the HSE, which stalled the cases and chose consistency in its own staffing over prompt investigation. These delays meant employees had left and led judges to doubt the witnesses' recollection of events. In more than one case, it was only the involvement of a charity which pushed the investigations on.

No victim, no criminal

The police and senior figures at the HSE stated cases were 'not in the public interest', and that although the death could have been avoided, it remained an accident rather than a crime. Workers were blamed for their own deaths due to being reckless or making poor choices, which contrasted with corporations that were able to portray themselves as innocent despite evidence other people had died in similar circumstances. When the families as secondary victims resisted the blame directed at their loved ones and attempted to demonstrate that corporations might not be innocent, they were viewed as trouble makers and as causing unnecessary fuss in what was otherwise a straightforward accident. The Police Liaison Officers did not always represent the family members but aligned themselves with the potential perpetrator, impressing upon the bereaved what they believed had happened, mirroring the thoughts of police officers who attended the scene in the immediate aftermath, in the absence of any investigation. Coroners continued this, relying upon their own knowledge and 'expert' evidence selected by the corporation, which was confusing even to the jurors.

Suppressed truth

The family members did not always find out what led to the death of their loved ones and were not reassured it would not happen again. They had to rely on others, for example colleagues or friends, to find out exactly how or why their loved ones had died. This left many of them 'filling in the gaps' and being unable to find out definitive answers. This is the case even though the answers were available and could have been provided to the bereaved. However, this was suppressed because it might have increased the chances of the corporations being held accountable. All of this meant the cases did not end with any individual being held responsible. Further, it harmed the bereaved as secondary victims.

Conclusion

This chapter has explored the experiences of families as they were forced to navigate the official response following the death of their loved one – a victim of safety crime. It includes five families whose loved one's deaths were not considered as potentially criminal and exited the process prematurely followed by six families whose loved one's death ended with a fine. These families did not know each other, isolated as they were across the country. However, all the families shared a common official response, which led them away from the legal process and away from the truth about what led to their loved one's death.

Of the families discussed in this chapter, 18 per cent proceeded straight to court, where the corporations either faced corporate manslaughter charges or were prosecuted for health and safety offences; 36 per cent brought charges of manslaughter against the corporations to court. Of those, all but one case ended in acquittal. One director was convicted of corporate manslaughter before the charge was overturned upon appeal. Forty-five per cent of the cases resulted in a fine for the corporations, which involved ten corporations across five cases, the average fine being £34,000, which is £18,847[1] less than the average. The families were not reassured that similar incidents would not happen again. Indeed, some found out that other people had died in similar circumstances, either after or before the death of their loved one.

How the families were treated depended upon the individuals randomly assigned to them (if anyone was assigned at all), but even in the best-case scenarios, all of them suffered three major blows, as detailed in the comment at the end of each case. First, the police largely left the scene as soon as possible, and the lack of investigation scuppered any subsequent legal process. Whose evidence was presented in the court was difficult to predict or ascertain, and cases relied upon the thoughts and direction of the judge/coroner, irrespective of the wishes of the jury. This can be summarized as an active suppression of the truth since the evidence was available but had to be collected by official bodies within a small window of time. The families' reasonable questions led to mistreatment. Had the families done nothing, they would have had similar outcomes, but in speaking up and challenging the common response, they were silenced in a way that was de-humanizing. Second, the HSE led from the top and stopped cases from continuing; even when officers were supportive and worked for the families, they were ultimately directed by their superiors to abandon the cases as 'not in the public interest'. The existing regulations proved inadequate in keeping their loved ones safe and then failed to ensure no one else would be killed in the same way in the near future. Finally, each case shared a comparatively powerful perpetrator who was not perceived as potentially criminal. When the perpetrator(s) are powerful, the victim must be either invisible or complicit in their own death. Almost every victim was blamed for causing their own death, either explicitly or implicitly. This was enabled by the lack of evidence, unanswered questions from the family, delays in gathering evidence and evidence that was selected to pursue this narrative. This leads to further harm, as explored in Chapter 5.

Chapter 3 focuses on the experiences of people whose loved ones are victims of safety crime committed by public institutions in relatively well-known cases that have been the subject of research. It continues to explore the process that the families experience and the ways in which the truth is suppressed and their silence demanded with a common comparatively powerful offender who benefits from the official response.

Note

1 In 2008/9 (Freedom of Information request reference no: 2010020046, cited in Snell and Tombs, 2011).

3

A Common Response: Deaths by Public Institutions

Chapter 2 documented the experiences of families whose loved ones had died as a result of safety crime by private institutions. It identified when each case left the legal process and the ways in which all were silenced and the truth suppressed. This chapter focuses on victims of state/corporate crime who are better known compared to the victims in Chapter 2. Many feared the institutions prior to the event, as Pauline Campbell states,: 'I was panic-stricken and terrified that she was going to die – and she did, the next day … I still feel overwhelmed with anger at the way she was treated' (Allison, 2006). The public is generally aware of the specific cases discussed in this chapter or, in the context of deaths in custody, as part of the broader issue. All of the victims' families have received support from charities and advocacy groups, and many are part of campaigns.

The examples from these areas illustrate the official responses to such cases and allows parallels to be drawn between them and the experiences of the families detailed in Chapter 2. Like the families in Chapter 2, the cases left the legal process prematurely or ended with a fine or an unlawful killing verdict. There are similarities in their treatment and how the truth was suppressed and how they were pushed to silence. This chapter draws from these areas to demonstrate how the powerful harm and the consistent official responses to such harms under the common responses identified and summarized in Chapter 2.

The following cases are included:

- The Hillsborough Disaster
- State killing
  - Christopher Alder
  - Gareth Myatt

  - Sean Rigg
  - Ian Tomlinson
  - Jimmy Mubenga
  - Seni Lewis
  - Adrian McDonald
  - Aisha Cleary
- The Grenfell Fire

The Hillsborough Disaster

The first case is the Hillsborough Disaster, which has been written about extensively and painstakingly by academics, journalists and those involved (Scraton, 1999, 2016; Sampson, 2017; Conn, 2010, 2014, 2021). What follows relies on those accounts.

Events on the 15 April 1989 led to the death of 97 spectators at a football match between Liverpool FC and Nottingham Forest FC. The 2016 inquest found the cause of death for 97 per cent of the victims was compression asphyxia, directly attributable to being crushed in the Hillsborough Stadium. Most of those who died had been directed into Leppings Lane, located behind the goal in the 'away' stand; 94 people died on the day, the majority at the stadium (86 per cent). Few received any medical intervention; 12 were taken to hospital but pronounced dead on arrival. One person died six years after the match, and another died 32 years later.

Those who died in the Hillsborough Disaster were members of the public who were watching football in their leisure time. Most of the victims were male (93 per cent) and aged between ten and 29 (80 per cent); 3 per cent of those killed lived in Sheffield, but most had travelled from elsewhere, mainly from Liverpool. Nobody who was working at the FA Cup semi-final was killed.

Following the results of the Taylor Inquiry in 1989, the Chief Constable of South Yorkshire police offered his resignation, but it was refused. He retired a year later (Jones, 2017). The Police Complaints Authority decided not to continue with disciplinary action against two of the officers for 'neglect of duty' because the most senior officer (Duckenfield) drew his pension early, retiring on medical grounds following a diagnosis of 'severe depression and post-traumatic stress disorder' (Scraton, 2013).

Prior to 1990, the families were advised by legal representatives to take £3,500 each as compensation (Sampson, 2017). A bereaved mother was offered £1,200 compensation and 'had no choice to accept it' to use for the inquest (Jones, 2017: 42).

In 2016, a new inquest reached an unlawful killing verdict, overturning the original 1991 accidental death verdict. In 2019, Duckenfield went on trial for manslaughter. This ended with a hung jury and acquittal. The then safety officer of Sheffield Wednesday Stadium was fined £6,500 under the Health and Safety at Work Act 1974 and ordered to pay £5,000 prosecution costs (Conn, 2019). It was judged that he had failed to take reasonable care of the Liverpool supporters because there was an inadequate number of turnstiles at the Leppings Lane end. When setting the fine, the judge considered his good character, the view of South Yorkshire police, who said he was diligent, that Hillsborough was safe and that he had been vilified on social media (Conn, 2019).

No victim, no criminal

The victims in Hillsborough were treated like criminals prior to their death. The police were preoccupied with containment to the extent that as fans began to pass out and die, calls for help to the police were met with contempt; superiors in the police refused to give the order to open the gates on to the pitch, and when fans did make it to the pitch, the police formed a line between them and the Forest fans.

In the immediate aftermath, the stadium was treated as a crime scene, pursuing a narrative that treated those who had been killed and survivors as criminal. Evidence they had been drunk, or behaved anti socially, was actively sought – for example the taking of blood from all victims. A daughter was asked by South Yorkshire police officer if the man who identified her mum was 'shagging' her (Jones, 2017: 11). In an apology in the House of Commons, Prime Minister Cameron shared, the 'police officers carried out Police National Computer checks on those who had died … to impugn the reputations of the deceased' (Cameron, 2012). Families were denied the opportunity to hold their loved ones in the hours after their death (Scraton, 2016); parents who asked to spend time with their dead son were refused and told they were there for identification purposes only. One father was able to hug his son because he pushed a sergeant who tried to pull him away, and another 'kicked up a fuss' to spend longer with his brother (Sampson, 2017: 151).

In 2025, the deputy director of the Independent Office for Police Conduct (IOPC) continued to support what had been presented by survivors and family members since 1989, namely that there was 'no evidence to support claims that the behaviour of supporters was a contributing factor' (Conn, 2025). This admission was made when no one would be held responsible nor accountable within the police force, representative of the entire process the families and those affected by the Hillsborough Disaster endured in the previous 36 years.

Selected evidence

Evidence that implicated the police, such as CCTV footage, was lost. Prior to the Hillsborough Independent Report in 2012, a bereaved father received a telephone call from a Chief Constable who told him he was 'under no obligation to disclose anything' and that the papers relating to the disaster belonged to him. He pushed: 'If I wanted to, I could take them into the yard and have a bonfire with them' (Jones, 2017: 2).

In the Taylor Inquiry in 1989, experts were selected using the criteria laid down by those in charge. John Ashton recalls his eyewitness account was discredited – he was referred to as not credible because he was no longer practising but worked in a university, and because he spoke to the media, which meant he was 'seeking attention' (Sampson, 2017: 190).

In summing up at the inquest in 1990, the coroner steered the jury away from a verdict of unlawful killing, assuring them that an accidental death verdict would not mean absolution 'from all and every measure of blame', that being 'incompetent is not the same as saying that a person is being reckless' and that 'someone would have to make compensation payments in civil litigation' (Scraton, 1999: 20). A bereaved mother concluded: 'The coroner had his own agenda. A law unto himself' (Jones, 2017: 44).

Handwritten accounts by police officers on the day of the disaster were submitted and alterations had been made by police solicitors and a senior officer. The alterations included 'criticisms of the police response' and 'deletion of references to "chaos", "fear", or "panic" or "confusion" among officers' (Scraton, 2013: 22). This process, which dramatically altered the tone and substance of 71 per cent of the statements describing the events on that day, went unquestioned by Lord Justice Taylor. The same evidence had been presented to the inquiry by Stuart-Smith, who concluded in 1998 that in a few cases 'it would have been better' not to have made alterations; at worst, it constituted an 'error of judgement' but not 'unprofessional conduct' (Scraton, 2004: 27, 190).

Suppression of the truth

The coroner declared that any evidence after 3.15 pm of the disaster was inadmissible because of the similarities between the deaths and the irrevocable damage he considered would have been done by then, which was supported by pathologists who claimed that following initial injuries 'death due to asphyxia was inevitable within four to six minutes' (Scraton, 2013: 19). This was contrary to what family members had been told, including Anne Williams, who was informed by a police officer that her son had asked for her ('Mum') as she held him at 4 pm. However, at the mini inquest she was told by medical staff that this could not and did not happen.

Powerful figures lied about what happened and told the truth only when forced to do so, thanks to the gargantuan efforts of family members and survivors. Even with the campaigns, and after a private prosecution, two inquiries, government scrutiny, a police inquiry and two trials, the unlawful killing verdict in 2016 was the closest the families and survivors got to justice. As a bereaved mother stated: 'You cannot have 96 unlawfully killed and no one held accountable for it' (Jones, 2017: 86).

State killing

Deaths in custody are included in the remit of the charity INQUEST. What follows draws gratefully from their work, including the document 'I can't breathe: Race, death & British policing' written by Prasad and published in 2023, together with other reports.

Christopher Alder, a 37-year-old father of two and former paratrooper, died in 1998 from positional asphyxia on the floor of a police station after struggling to breathe. Officers had placed him face down on the floor of the custody suite, his hands cuffed behind his back with his trousers and boxer shorts around his ankles. Monkey noises and his final rattles of breath could be heard on an audio tape (Inquest, 2000).

This case ended with an unlawful killing verdict, offered to the jury against the calls of those involved. Full representation was funded, and Janet had early support from INQUEST.

In 2003, a judge at the Independent Police Complaints Commission (IPCC) (now IOPC) disciplinary hearing decided a disciplinary tribunal was unnecessary because 'the officer had been suspended for four years and had been through a coroner's inquest and trial', and it was 'not in the public interest' (IPCC, 2006: 26) – the officers 'had suffered enough' (IPCC, 2006: 27). Instead, the officers were told to attend training courses. In 2004, four of the five officers were granted retirement on medical grounds related to stress on full pensions with payments of compensation.

No investigation

There was no scene of crime, and evidence was discarded. In the immediate aftermath and in the weeks that followed, evidence was destroyed by West Yorkshire police, who investigated the death, including the clothes Christopher wore. They did not test the clothing of the officers or analyse blood samples in the van. It was not a potential homicide: '[T]he Custody Suite never sealed and investigated as a crime scene' (INQUEST, 2004: 3).

The officers involved were not challenged, and 'the questioning of them in interview was weak', with facts being gathered that sought to support the officers (INQUEST, 2004: 3). The officers involved 'have never answered any questions about the incident' (INQUEST, 2004: 4) in court because they were suspended from duty awaiting a trial of misconduct in public office and therefore had the right not to incriminate themselves and refuse to answer any questions at the inquest under the Coroners Rules (Inquest, 2000).

No victim, no criminal

The police investigations pursued a narrative that supported their early conclusion that Christopher was 'difficult'. Two police officers who were called to the hospital where he was being treated after being punched outside a nightclub made unfounded assumptions about his behaviour, indicating they thought his confusion arose from alcohol and drugs rather than his head injury or a fear of hospitals. The officer contacted the control room and remarked he was 'being a wee bit troublesome. Probably the reason why he got smacked in the first place' (Hardwick, 2006: 95).

Despite no formal punishment, the officers involved were viewed as having suffered, gaining victim status, unlike Christopher's sister, who was told by a Detective Superintendent that they would not answer her questions if she was representing organizations such as INQUEST and told her: 'If you are going to be like that you can leave now.' The Detective Superintendent said he would not deal with any solicitors and would deal with another member of the family he could talk to. He advanced 'Janet was very difficult … aggressive, abusive. She kept throwing the race card in right from the off … Suddenly Janet was on a platform … saw Christopher as a vehicle' (Hardwick, 2006: 312).

Suppressed truth

Following an inquiry, the family did get partial truth as to what happened in the events that led up to Alder's death. But they did not see any justice or assurances that this would not happen again. One person who was charged with the assault of Christopher was the man who punched him outside the nightclub. Initially, he was arrested for murder, which was reduced a month later, three weeks after it was apparent it was not the punch that killed Christopher. This was later judged to be an unlawful arrest designed to divert attention away from the behaviour of the police (Hardwick, 2006).

At the trial in 2002, the Crown was 'generous' to the defence, for example calling all medical experts rather than only those who were 'clear, credible and certain' (INQUEST, 2004: 5). However, in 2002, the trial collapsed when the judge said the officers could not be convicted due to 'insufficient evidence of recklessness' and ordered the jury to find the officers not guilty (Hardwick, 2006: 24). The jury were 'alarmed and incredulous at being asked to return a not guilty verdict' (INQUEST, 2004: 5).

Gareth Myatt died aged 15 in 2004 after being restrained at Rainsbrook Secure Training Centre. He was three days into serving a 12-month detention sentence when he was 'subjected to a "seated double embrace" restraint technique' (INQUEST, 2005).

MP Sally Keeble called for an inquiry in 2007 as she expected Gareth's death to be an individual failure but realized it was a 'complete systematic collective failure' with 'a complete lack of any sense of horror on the part of officialdom at what happened' (Hansard, 2007).

No person or organization was held responsible or punished. In 2008, a joint committee on human rights recommended changes to the use of restraint and abolished the technique Gareth was subjected to.

No victim, no criminal

Gareth and children like him were perceived as 'faking it' by those more powerful in charge of their care. At the inquest in 2007, it was heard that Gareth had told the officers that he could not breathe and was told 'if you're shouting, you can breathe'. Gareth warned the officers that he was losing control of his bowels before defecating and being sick.

Suppressed truth

Slight recognition of the harmful use of restraint came from an MP, and then the procedure was altered four years after Gareth's death. However, a Ministry of Justice report published in 2016 suggested children were continuing to suffer following restraints, with an average of one child per week 'struggling to breathe or losing consciousness whilst being restrained' (Allison and Grierson, 2016).

Sean Rigg died aged 40 in 2008. He had been a professional footballer before turning to music production. He died after he was restrained in handcuffs and the prone position by four police officers for seven to eight minutes. At the entrance to the custody suite, he was unconscious; officers can be heard on the CCTV saying 'he was "faking" or "feigning" unconsciousness'. He died of cardiac arrest because of being held in a prone position.

The inquest returned a narrative verdict. It concluded the police had acted disproportionately, and 'officers failed to uphold his basic rights', which 'contributed to his death' (Prasad, 2023: 65). The coroner issued a report that called for joint protocols between the police and the NHS trust to carry out risk assessments for those in custody. Three of the officers involved in Sean's restraint received compensation following a civil claim for the delay in the investigation and the failings of the first Independent Police Complaints Commission investigation (Casale et al, 2013).

No investigation

The place of Sean's death was not treated as a potential crime scene. Evidence presented by the police supported their summary that his death was unrelated to their actions, countered only by CCTV and a retrospective investigation. There was no investigation immediately after his death, which was criticized by a later Independent Office for Police Conduct investigation. It took eight months for the relevant police officers to be interviewed, and it was nine months before anyone spoke to the emergency services at the control centre (Prasad, 2023). The investigation concluded the police had acted appropriately and 'there was no evidence of neglect or wrongdoing' (Prasad, 2023: 65). The lack of evidence was given as a reason for not taking the case any further.

No victim, no criminal

Sean was seen as 'faking it' prior to his death and not treated as a victim, even when unconscious. All charges were dismissed as unproven allegations, and two police members on the hearing concluded 'seven minutes [of restraint] would not in itself necessarily be regarded as being for an excessive time' (Prasad, 2023: 65: 7).

Suppressed truth

The inquest called on 60 witnesses. A police officer testified that he had carried out a risk assessment on Sean while he was in the police van, which was corroborated by another police officer. This was contrary to CCTV footage, which proved the officer had not entered the van (Prasad, 2023). A review in 2013 found evidence of restraint on a witness's mobile with timings that was not requested and therefore not put to the officers involved ((Prasad, 2023).

The family of Sean Rigg waited eight years to hear that no-one would receive any punishment following his death and received apologies from the IOPC. The family found out the partial truth because of the presence of CCTV cameras; nothing was changed to ensure this would not happen again.

Ian Tomlinson died aged 47 during protests in London in 2009. Described as a 'much loved father, grandfather and husband … whose alcohol problems' had driven 'him away from home' although he 'remained committed and loving to his family', he had been walking home when an 'officer in a riot helmet' raised his baton and struck him before 'violently pushing him to the ground' (INQUEST, 2009: 11). He died an hour later.

The pathologist involved in the first post-mortem was struck off following an investigation by the General Medical Council (BBC, 2012). Previously, he had been suspended for four months for omitting 29 autopsy findings in another case, concluding a woman had died of natural causes when she was murdered by a perpetrator who went on to kill two more women (Israel, 2011).

Despite a verdict of unlawful killing, no one was held accountable for his death. The family received an official apology from the police in 2012. Changes were made related to police response to protests.

No investigation

There was no scene of crime, and important evidence in the inquest was submitted by bystanders who had recorded the incident.

No victim, no criminal

The police painted a picture that supported their view that Ian was a victim of his own making – the family were told he had 'run out of batteries' (Lewis, 2010). The IPCC told the press that the family were not surprised by what happened because of concerns about his health (Ian Tomlinson Family Campaign, nd). After photos and witness reports released by the *Guardian* showed Ian being struck by an officer from the Territorial Support Group, the family were told by the police that the person who struck Ian may have been a member of the public wearing a police uniform (Lewis, 2009b).

The police claimed they had valiantly tried to save Ian while being attacked by protestors, releasing an IPCC-approved statement within four hours of his death stating that they had been prevented from giving Ian first aid because protestors had thrown objects at them (INQUEST, 2009). This was successfully countered by information gathered by bystanders and tourists.

Suppressed truth

The coroner tried to prevent the involvement of the IPCC and did not inform the family of the post-mortem (INQUEST, 2009). It later emerged that the police force had previously expressed concerns about the pathologist chosen by the coroner, and he did not have a contract with the police (Lewis, 2010). The family were refused access to his body for a further two days (INQUEST, 2009). Photographs of Ian taken after his death show bruising to the head, contradicting the results of the post-mortem; this led to the suspension of the coroner, who omitted these injuries (INQUEST, 2009). The IPCC and police advised the family 'not to say anything' because they could 'jeopardise the case' (Lewis, 2009a).

At the inquest in 2011, the officer was questioned and admitted he had filled out his notebook incorrectly by recording that he had a lost a baton during the protests and had been hit by a protester (Israel, 2011). In 2012, the officer concerned was sacked for gross misconduct at a disciplinary panel.

Jimmy Mubenga, a 46-year-old described as a husband and caring father of five, died in 2010 on board a British Airways flight following restraint by a G4S guard, which led him to suffer a cardiac arrest (INQUEST, 2011). Jimmy moved to Britain from Angola in 1994. Following a conviction for actual bodily harm in 2006, he served two years in prison before receiving notice of his deportation, after which he was taken from an immigration centre to Heathrow Airport. A struggle occurred on board the flight, and Jimmy was handcuffed 'in the rear stack position' and restrained for between 30 and 40 minutes; during this time, fellow passengers heard him shouting that he could not breathe, 'they're killing me' and appeals that he had a family (Monaghan, 2015: 5).

In 2013, this case secured an unlawful killing verdict, yet despite the high burden of proof required to achieve this, it was not matched in a criminal court, and no person or corporation has been held responsible for Jimmy's death. The coroner's report included a 'Report to prevent future deaths', which raised concern about racism, untrained guards, incentives to suppress those detained and no training for confined spaces.

No investigation

There was no potential scene of crime following Jimmy's death. It was claimed there were no witnesses on the plane who had a clear enough view of what happened (BBC, 2014).

No victim, no criminal

Jimmy was judged as 'faking it', and those involved removed themselves from responsibility for his conduct. At the inquest in 2013, the coroner viewed racist content on the phones of guards involved in Jimmy's death (BBC, 2014). This included Facebook posts and messages sent after Jimmy's death suggesting pervasive and 'casual widespread racism' in G4S (Monaghan, 2015: 17). The defence suggested Jimmy was 'too big, strong and vociferous and helped to bring about his own demise', successfully arguing that if they were responsible in any way, it was 'because of a lack of training', and they were therefore not to blame (Webber, 2014).

Suppressed truth

In 2011, whistle blowers from within G4S told a parliamentary committee that their senior management had previously been warned about the use of restraints on deportees on more than one occasion and that staff referred to the practice of forcing a deportee's head down so they did not disturb other passengers as 'carpet karaoke' (Webber, 2014).

At the trial in 2014, the judge chose to exclude evidence of the racist texts and jokes sent between the guards and agreed with the defence that 'homophobia, misogyny and anti-Liverpudlian prejudice mixed in with the racism' might offend the jury and unfairly discriminate against the guards (Webber, 2014). Accordingly, the media were restricted from reporting the coroner's findings and the previous inquest verdict.

Seni Lewis died aged 23 in 2010. Described by his mother as someone who 'had loads of good friends … he stood up for', he died of a hypoxic brain injury after being starved of oxygen when he was restrained by 11 Metropolitan Police officers at different times over 45 minutes (Gayle, 2017). This occurred in a hospital his parents had taken him to after he had experienced an episode of sudden mental ill health (Gayle, 2017).

Despite condemnation and various panels that judged Seni to have been subjected to unreasonable force, no one was punished or held accountable for his death. The coroner ruled out the possibility of unlawful killing, recording a narrative verdict. In 2018, 'Seni's law' was enacted via a private member's bill. This law requires police who respond to calls at mental hospitals to wear body cameras in order to standardize how events are reported in the future (Sabbagh, 2018).

No investigation

There was no investigation following Seni's death. Over two years, police officers were interviewed and invoked their right to silence (Prasad, 2023).

No victim, no criminal

Seni was judged as 'faking it', and his behaviour was seen as caused by his own actions. It took seven years for the inquest to be held because there is no statutory requirement following a death in a mental hospital (Sabbagh, 2018).

Suppressed truth

In a hearing that was closed to the press and public, the IPCC recommended six of the officers involved in Seni's death face a police misconduct panel to answer charges of gross misconduct. In 2017, the panel dismissed all charges because 'the failings were outside the remit of the panel' (Prasad, 2023: 74).

Adrian McDonald died in 2014 aged 34. He was the father of two children. Described by his brother as someone who loved his family, he died after 'being restrained, bitten by a police dog, Tasered, and then placed in the van where he lost consciousness' (Prasad, 2023: 84). Adrian could be heard on a police recording saying 'I can't breathe' and 'please' (Parker, 2020). Officers could be heard telling him he could breathe because he was talking (Prasad, 2023). An ambulance was called after nine minutes; he was pronounced dead at the scene.

Officers received written warnings which were then revoked after appeals. Nothing was changed to ensure a similar death in the future would not be repeated.

No victim, no criminal

Adrian was judged to be 'faking it', and his behaviour was judged to be a key factor in his death.

Suppressed truth

A jury heard Adrian had suffered muscle-level wounds from the dog bites; they concluded Adrian died due to 'cocaine induced paranoia' and that 'the level of force may have increased his stress levels' (Prasad, 2023). Bodycam footage showed the police failed to call an ambulance and reassured Adrian he was safe (INQUEST, 2018).

Aisha Cleary died either hours before or just after her birth in 2019 in HMP Bronzefield from catastrophic hypoxic insult. The coroner stated she 'arrived into the world in the most harrowing of circumstances', born to her 18-year-old mother, Rianna, who was on remand, 'alone and without any clinical or other care and assistance' (Travers, 2023: 1).

No one was held accountable for Aisha's death, and the main officer involved remained employed within the prison. Other cases have followed in the years since, including the delivery of a stillborn baby in HMP Styal by a mother whose cries for an ambulance were ignored by staff (Razzell, 2021).

A Prisons and Probation Ombudsman report in 2022 stated what happened was a result of the absence of policies for pregnant women held in custody and made recommendations such as improved training for staff. Prior to the inquest, the deputy director of the prison wrote to Rianna to say they were sorry she gave birth alone and admitted during the inquest that the prison's response to her calls for help were 'wholly and completely inadequate' (INQUEST, 2023).

No victim, no criminal

Rianna was viewed as untrustworthy and difficult and treated with contempt by those with the power to care for her. She did not receive any prenatal scans, and the staff speculated as to her due date and wrongly wrote down she was at least five weeks before her due date when she was full term. On the night of Aisha's birth, Rianna pressed the buzzer in her cell at 8.07 pm and asked for a nurse, who was not called by the officer on duty. When Rianna was 'holding on to the wall' 25 minutes later and 'there was blood on the bed', she managed to ring the buzzer, but no one answered (Travers, 2023: 41). Her daughter's life was contested by the institutions and corporations involved to pursue a narrative that they were not responsible for a stillbirth.

Suppressed truth

Sodexo (the corporation that ran HMP Bronzefield), the Ministry of Justice and Ashford and St Peter's NHS Foundation Trust called for the coroner to treat Aisha's death as a stillbirth and stated that the coroner 'had no jurisdiction to make … critical conclusions' (INQUEST, 2023).

The Grenfell Fire

On 14 June, a fire in Grenfell Tower spread and burnt for 24 hours. A total of 72 people died, the majority at the scene. Most of those who were killed died in their own homes. Others were found in the lobbies or on the stairs trying to escape, and three 'fell from the tower' (Moore-Bick et al, 2024: 9). Two victims died at hospital: one stillborn baby and a resident who died in 2018 after her health 'deteriorated in the months that followed her escape' (Moore-Bick et al, 2024: 101) when she was carried out of the tower by a firefighter.

The fire destroyed elements of the tower to the extent that a full post-mortem was not possible for every victim. That said, the inquiry judged the principal cause of death was 'inhalation of asphyxiant gases' (Moore-Bick et al, 2024: 16) and 'asphyxia from asphyxiant gases' (Moore-Bick et al, 2024: 17). The smoke was caused by the burning of materials from 'the external cladding and insulation and the window infill panels, the window surrounds and the contents of the flats' (Moore-Bick et al, 2024: 18). The fire spread rapidly because the panels that clad the outside of the tower 'acted as a source of fuel' and spread the fire both 'horizontally and downwards' (Moore-Bick et al, 2019: 4). The cladding had been changed in a refurbishment of Grenfell Tower that took place in 2016 when the council chose to cover the exterior with zinc cladding instead of aluminium panels in order to save £293,368 at a time when they had £274 million in reserves (Forster, 2017).

Those who died were members of the public, and all but four called Grenfell Tower their home. The victims ranged from an unborn baby to an 84-year-old; 85 per cent were of Black, Asian or minority ethnic origin, and 21 per cent of those who died had a disability (Booth, 2024a). Nobody who was working that night was killed, although many people who were exposed to the smoke, including firefighters, are suffering from long-term health disorders (Stec et al, 2019).

There have been several convictions related to the fire; however, the majority were for fraud against people who, in the aftermath, pretended they had been residents of the tower and falsely claimed for costs of accommodation and travel (Tombs, 2019). Additionally, a man who lived next door to the tower was sentenced to three months in prison for taking and sharing photographs of a dead victim from the fire, and another resident did 200 hours of unpaid work, 40 days of rehabilitation and paid £205 in fines after police found 'cuttings, butane gas canisters and an oven in his flat' used to cultivate cannabis (Tombs, 2019).

In 2019, the Fire Commissioner 'was forced to retire early' (BBC, 2019). In 2024, 114 firefighters won up to £1.1 million each in compensation after they 'sued construction corporations, the landlord of the council block and the London fire commissioner' (Booth, 2024b) for resultant trauma and personal injuries suffered because of their attendance at the Grenfell Tower Fire. Fault was principally found because of the lack of training on fires in high-rise buildings and the 'stay-put' policy. The London Fire Brigade spent £15 million on participating in each of the inquiries (Booth, 2024a).

The Chief Executive of Royal Borough of Kensington Council was required to resign by the Communities Secretary in the week following the fire. It was reported that between 2019 and 2024, the corporations involved had received about £250 million in public contracts. Kingspan achieved pre-tax profits of £794 million in 2023, and Arconic made £706 million in 2022. Rydon made a £15 million pre-tax loss, and Studio E went into liquidation in 2020 (Booth, 2024a).

Delay

Since the Grenfell Fire, and following an extensive and costly inquiry, there have been no arrests or punishment for the deaths of the 72 residents of the tower. The police investigation delayed sending any results to the Crown Prosecution Service (CPS) due to the inquiry.

In March 2019, the police said any charges would have to wait until after the conclusion of the inquiry, estimating this would be in 2021. In 2024, the Met's deputy assistant commissioner said it would take 12 to 18 months to look carefully at the results of the inquiry ahead of sending files to the CPS (Sinmaz and Booth, 2024). When questioned over the delays, the deputy assistant commissioner warned that if the investigation was rushed, there could be repercussions at the criminal trial (Riding, 2024). The deputy assistant commissioner wrote to the families of the victims and to survivors informing them they would not meet their original deadline and that charging files would now not be submitted to the CPS until September 2026 (Fire Protection Association, 2025). He blamed a lack of investment in police resources for the delay. This meant the CPS would not make a judgement on whether there would be a case to answer until late 2026 or early 2027 (Fire Protection Association, 2025).

Between the incident and 31 March 2023, £88.5 million had been spent on policing related to the Grenfell Tower Fire. The inquiry cost over £200 million (Booth, 2024a). Taken together with the rehousing of residents and legal fees, the cost rises to £1.2 billion (Booth, 2023).

No victim, no criminal

The relationship between Kensington and Chelsea Tenants Management Organisation (KCTMO) and the tower's residents was 'characterised as an attitude of contempt' (Tombs, 2020: 126) and 'distrust, dislike, personal antagonism and anger' (Moore-Bick et al, 2024: 15). This is perhaps best evidenced by the fact residents had created action groups in 2010 that attempted to represent their concerns, concerns which included the lack of fire safety encapsulated on a web page titled 'KCTMO – Playing with Fire!' (Tombs, 2020: 126). Such 'vocal activists' were regarded as 'militant troublemakers' (Moore-Bick et al, 2024: 15). In addition to KCTMO and RBKC, around 700 different corporations are connected to the refurbishment of Grenfell, with evidence gathered from 36 per cent of them (Symonds, 2022).

In September 2024, the inquiry presented its findings of phase two. It concluded the fire 'was the culmination of decades of failure by central government and other bodies in positions of responsibility' (Moore-Bick et al, 2024: 7). In closing submissions, the lead counsel Richard Millett KC accused corporations of a 'merry-go-round of buck-passing' in order to protect their own interests. The inquiry concluded that '[c]ertain aspects of the response demonstrated a marked lack of respect for human decency and dignity' (2024: 24). The Chief Executive was 'unduly concerned for RBKC's reputation' (Moore-Bick et al, 2024: 26) and did not respond to the disaster in a way that met the needs of the survivors, showing 'no regard for their cultural and religious needs' (Moore-Bick et al, 2024: 26). While the inquiry published the truth and confirmed the fears of the residents, the chair was not able to follow this up with arrests of any of the corporations implicated in the fire. Indeed, many of the corporations continued to win public contracts.

Suppressed truth

The inquiry criticized regulators for 'a lack of scientific rigour … lack of analysis [and] unprofessional behaviour' (Moore-Bick et al, 2024: 9). Arconic exploited 'weak regulatory regimes' and 'deliberately concealed' the danger of using materials that did not meet European or UK standards (Moore-Bick et al, 2024: 10). The corporation lied on several occasions, giving 'false and misleading' statements (Moore-Bick et al, 2024: 8). Similarly, Celotex 'embarked on a dishonest scheme to mislead its customers' (Moore-Bick et al, 2024: 11) and worked with the Building Research Establishment to produce inadequate reports and hide key information. Kingspan made false claims, and despite carrying out tests that were 'disastrous', it continued to promote its product (Moore-Bick et al, 2024: 12).

The inquiry confirmed the concerns of residents were dismissed by the local authority and their landlord, concluding that the corporations involved 'engaged in deliberate and sustained strategies to … mislead the market' (Moore-Bick et al, 2024, cited in Sinmaz and Booth, 2024).

Conclusion

This chapter explored the experiences of families and survivors as they navigated the official processes following the deaths of their loved ones in well-known cases, including the Hillsborough Disaster, seven deaths in custody and the Grenfell Tower Fire. In doing so, the chapter demonstrates the ways in which the truth is controlled and suppressed rather than revealed. In this, the families are at best silenced and at worst disregarded and discredited. Whether it was a fine under Health and Safety at Work Act 30 years later or a withdrawn written warning on a police officer's file, the survivors and family members did not see punishment of their more powerful perpetrator. In the case of the Grenfell Tower, this is still ongoing at the time of writing, but the process is following a similar overall pattern to many other similar incidents.

The number of agencies the families in this chapter experienced was greater than in Chapter 2. As family members of victims of state corporate crime, they were subject to a lengthier process involving legal challenges, inquiries and disciplinary hearings, which meant they were subject to greater questioning and further delays. An additional burden was that officials were investigated later for their initial responses to the death rather than, or in addition to, the actual death of the victim. For example, responses by the police were investigated decades later yet this also failed to end with punishment. The public nature of the cases did not always engender support but exposed the families and survivors to wider condemnation.

This chapter established several similarities the families encountered, including delay, a lack of immediate investigation, an inadequate official sanction and the refusal to identify a victim or a criminal. Chapter 4 examines the similarities between the cases detailed in the two chapters and highlights these as obstacles families encounter, which they can ultimately do nothing to overcome. Instead, the powerful have a number of tools at their disposal that enable the truth to be suppressed and secure silence. Chapter 5 demonstrates how this causes further harm to the victims and survivors to the benefit of those in power, demonstrating that 'when justice suffers, so do we all' (Box, 1983: 223).

4

How Victims and Secondary Victims Are Pushed to Invisibility

Chapters 2 and 3 explored the experiences of bereaved families whose loved ones were victims of safety and corporate/state crime. The chapter aims to add to a biography of harm that goes beyond the 'snapshot of social life' that the 'lens of crime all too often restricts us to' (Tombs, 2020: 128). This chapter records the experiences of families as an indicator of how the powerful respond, connecting the personal to the public state (Carson, 1982). This chapter argues that despite their differences, all left the criminal justice system because of obstacles that were ultimately insurmountable. Whether each would be considered criminal without these obstacles is not the subject of this book, but what the cases have established is that these were 'acts and omissions ... which have not been interrogated' (Tombs and Whyte, 2007: 4), and, as such, the truth was suppressed at the expense of the families.

Louise Adamson recalled how the defence 'asked the Sheriff to make a direction that we, the family, should not smile at the jury! Let's face it, there was nothing for us to smile about' (FACK, nd). This chapter examines the processes the families had to endure that filtered any potential powerful perpetrator out of the criminal justice system and the effect this had on them as secondary victims who endure the official and unofficial responses. It discusses the common social and political obstacles that silence the families and suppress the truth about what happened to the victim. In doing so, this secures the innocence of the powerful perpetrator.

It begins by identifying the obstacles that enable corporations/the state to remain invisible, which supports Box's assertion that there are 'differential benefits ... accrued by the powerful, privileged and wealthy' (Box, 1983: 223). The persistence of these obstacles demonstrates how, when threatened, principles of justice are sacrificed by those with power, rather than realized (Scraton, 1999). Combining these experiences aims to counter the isolated experiences of families who may believe they have been 'unlucky', or that they are to blame for this treatment. Through a collective examination of 'the processes, structure and policies which produce' and enable these responses, it becomes apparent they are not random but an operation of power (Canning and Tombs, 2021: 109). The common responses will be detailed in the following sections, which as in Chapters 2 and 3, are examined in chronological order to highlight the process the families endure. These include the lack of crime scene and evidence, delay, the selection of evidence, coroner direction, a law designed not to work and the 'benefit of clergy' (Sutherland, 1983: 9).

The rest of the chapter explores the common finding that in each case there was 'no victim, no criminal'. This can be analysed through the existence of the blameworthy victim, a construct used to discredit those harmed in their death and exonerate any potential perpetrator. If those who are harmed are not going to be invisible, then their function is to take the blame. From the police to the court, the appearance of the blameworthy victim is a consistent feature impressed upon the families by people whom they had no choice to deal with, as Janet Alder sums up, describing how, during the inquest, 'I found myself just looking around at all the people that had been brought into my life against my will' (Alder and Glazebrook, 2024: 130). In positions of power and influence, the notion of a victim who was complicit in their own death was both pervasive and harmful. Chapter 5 will examine the effects of this.

The police

The focus of the criminal justice system is on less powerful perpetrators and common crime; the actions and inactions of powerful perpetrators are rarely seen as criminal by those in a position to apply the label. A narrow version of violence is easily recognized, one that is legitimate and opposes the state, requiring the rule of law and a strong police response (Scraton and Chadwick, 2009), whereas the violence of the powerful requires the 'short arm of the law' (Punch, 1996: 253) and a light touch, unless compelled retrospectively to fulfil its function. The law was continually interpreted by officials in the criminal justice system (Snider, 2003b) and in the absence of training and awareness, many relied upon 'common sense' notions and immediately framed the deaths as accidental. The first to do this was the police, who, in doing so, created the largest obstacle for the families to overcome.

No crime scene, no evidence

As the first people called to the scene, the police have immense power in the 'golden hour' after they arrive. They have the power to take control, yet in many cases the police officers did not approach the scene of death as they might when faced with a regular homicide. Instead, following each death, they approached the scene to investigate whether there had been 'foul play', which was their sole criterion of criminality. In the words of Bergman (1991: 18), 'foul play' is 'whether the deceased worker was pushed from scaffolding or into dangerous machinery by an angry workmate'. Once the police had eliminated this, they initially withdrew from every case but two in this research, and without any further investigation they labelled the fatal incidents as accidents (Slapper, 1999).

In managing the site as an 'accident' or a matter for the Health and Safety Executive (HSE) – a regulatory body – the police blocked opportunities for the deaths to ever be framed as criminal. This reflects a propensity for officers to view deaths at work as accidents and confusion over the boundary between themselves and the HSE (Slapper, 1999). The police have guidance which applies to 'cases where the victim suffers injuries in such an incident that are so serious that there is a clear indication … of a strong likelihood of death' and are compelled to treat '[e]ach fatality … individually' (HSE, 1998: 5). Enacted in 1998, the Protocol for Liaison was in operation in all but one of the cases; it determined that the police should take a central role and 'assume primacy for an investigation and work jointly with other relevant enforcing authorities' (HSE, 1998: 5). The view that only foul play equated to criminality was so persistently held by police officers that they overrode their own protocol. It is impossible to know how many other cases of safety crime have been filed as something else, as happened following the death of Andrew. Initially filed as a road traffic incident (RTI), it eventually became one of the most successful cases, ending with an unlawful killing verdict and the highest fine of all the deaths in this research. The police investigated retrospectively because of the actions of Heather, and ironically evidence was available because it had been investigated as an RTI. Had the death not happened on a public highway, it is likely the police would have left shortly after they arrived, as they did in the other cases.

Where the police were the potential perpetrators, they were able to pursue a narrative of events that exonerated them, which was a '"literal denial" of their collective or individual culpability' (Scraton, 1999: 16). Investigations were carried out by their colleagues in neighbouring forces. For example, following the Hillsborough Disaster, the West Midlands police force conducted the first investigation of South Yorkshire police. Janet Alder questioned the independence of 'the police investigating themselves – surely that wasn't right?' (Alder and Glazebrook, 2024: 43). West Yorkshire police investigated her brother's death in East Yorkshire. Evidence went missing, such as CCTV footage within the Hillsborough Stadium, with the QC for Sheffield Wednesday claiming that the cameras had been 'accidentally turned off by somebody's knee' (Conn, 2014). Similarly, Christopher Alder's clothes were burned before any testing could take place (Alder and Glazebrook, 2024). The victims' families, though not part of the profession, could see basic measures were not being taken, such as the sister of Sean Rigg, who was 'flabbergasted' the police 'didn't cordon off the area … they weren't doing basic things' (Prasad, 2023: 70).

Failure to treat the scene as potentially criminal meant that the evidence required for a successful court case was missed, discarded or destroyed. In this research, access to the scene was not restricted in three of the cases, and individuals were able to enter and leave. In the absence of police power, no one protected the victim, and the scene was open to manipulation. As secondary victims, they were not able to demand that the police apply policies rationally (Sanders and Young, 2000), and any power they later had to compel the police to investigate was rendered somewhat redundant in the absence of proof. They could never have controlled this, least of all because protocol deemed there was no problem requiring a resolution.

Delay

Though holding great power, officers do not 'investigate [safety crimes] with any rigour', which explains why there are 'almost no prosecutions for manslaughter' (Slapper, 1999: 127). The lack of immediate involvement of the police and protracted investigations meant the required proof became more elusive (Croall, 1992). This is not unique to smaller cases but also applies to those that are under public scrutiny. For example, following the capsizing of *The Herald of Free Enterprise*, the police did not investigate the company until three months after the inquiry and following an inquest verdict of 'unlawful killing' (Slapper, 1999). They had to be compelled to do so by the Director of Public Prosecutions, who was instructed by the High Court after the Crown refused to act (Slapper, 1999), which suggests that urgent investigations following mundane safety crimes are likely to be even rarer. This is supported by the findings of this research, where there was an immediate police investigation in only two cases: one that led to the sentence of a director and another that reached an unlawful killing verdict. In the only two other cases to benefit from a police investigation, the police were compelled to do so retrospectively and neither ended with a guilty verdict against director or manager.

Retrospective investigations that happened months and years after the death meant evidence that could have been crucial in court was not seized and had been 'lost'. This included machinery involved in the deaths that had been used since and equipment which had been repurposed or dumped. In most cases, risk assessments were not found – one ex-partner of a victim was told by her solicitor that this is the first thing that goes missing. Many of the families expressed doubts about either the location of the lost risk assessment or whether it had been completed or seen by their loved one at all. The judgement of risk was assessed in the court by the presentation of risk assessments, a low threshold that proved adherence to health and safety regulations, checked after the deaths but not interrogated (Tombs and Whyte, 2013). This paper-based proof had little impact on the court and was easily circumvented, rendering it a tool only for the corporations. For example, training was said to have taken place which family members were sure had not, and it was acceptable for Jason's manager to say that he noted the risk assessment in his head. The benefit of time also meant documents could have been changed – many of the families felt that documents had been completed after their loved one's death as the signatures were unrecognizable, but they were unable to challenge this in court.

Sean Rigg's sister said she noticed 'systemic patterns in other [deaths in custody] cases', including delays in sharing information, not interviewing key witnesses and giving those involved time to speak to each other (Prasad, 2023: 71). The officers involved in Sean's death were not interviewed for nine months. A key witness in the Christopher Alder death was not interviewed until nine weeks after the event, leading the family to wonder whether this was 'to give the officers time to "lean on" him' (Alder and Glazebrook, 2024: 129). Official documents such as the 'Use of Force' reports went missing (Alder and Glazebrook, 2024). Survivors and family members affected by the Grenfell Disaster are currently waiting for the outcome of a police investigation. The deputy commissioner of the Metropolitan Police has warned this delay is necessary because 'we have one chance to get this right' (Fire Protection Association, 2025). The results were first promised in 2021, four years after the fire.

The experiences of the families demonstrated that the principal role the police played was to notify the family of their loved one's death. It was not to conduct a thorough investigation; indeed, any investigation focused on the basic facts and failed to investigate the possibility of negligence or criminality. Each case became officially perceived as it had initially been viewed: an accident. Without an urgent investigation, the truth was suppressed. In approaching the deaths as 'accidents' with no clear perpetrator, the police failed to treat the victims as legitimate. The families had no power to investigate and were forced to wait for the next stage of the process.

Summary

The police had the potential to make a real difference in each of the cases. However, this opportunity was lost as in many of the cases in this research they failed to secure the scene of death, delayed taking statements, did not uphold the family's rights and began investigations that blamed the victim (explored in the second half of this chapter). Against protocol, they did not approach what had happened as potentially criminal or treat each case individually. Without relevant evidence or witnesses, a successful future prosecution was severely hampered. Most of the deaths of the victims in this research were not investigated by the police; all of those that were not investigated ended with an accidental verdict at the next stage, supporting Slapper's (1999: 125) assertion that '[i]f the police fail to get the necessary witness evidence during the initial investigation, then the matter is very often effectively closed'. The delays and lack of a potential crime scene had a knock-on effect, the consequences of which the families felt at each of the following stages.

The inquest

The victims in this research died suddenly and unexpectedly. Unless the cases went straight to the Crown Court, the facts of their deaths were explored in the Coroner's Court, an inquisitorial process that does not seek to apportion blame. Reaching this stage did not rely upon evidence to proceed, and all but two families spent time in the Coroner's Court. The two families that did not have an inquest proceeded straight to court to hear charges for corporate manslaughter. For most families, the inquest was the only process that attempted to establish the facts about how and why their loved one had died. Their experiences of the police in the previous section largely continued into the Coroner's Court, indicative of the 'professional outlook and assumptions of coroners [being] largely isomorphic with those of experienced police officers' (Slapper, 1999: 90).

Delay and the selection of evidence

The delay in the police investigation continued to the coronial system, and by the time of the inquest, families were desperate to hear officially what had happened. Many did not understand the impact of the delays or that no blame could be apportioned at the Coroner's Court, which was continually emphasized to them. On average, the families waited two years and three months for the inquest; the shortest time was seven months, and the longest wait was four years, hastened only when external agencies became involved. Such protracted delays did not prioritize the families, who felt forgotten.

The coroner became an important part in the quest for the truth, but for many families they left a harmful impression. Most families did not see the coroner as protecting their interests or as neutral and believed the coroner was 'not on their side'. This is supported by Slapper (1999: 136), who found a pervasive outlook shared by coroners, whose approach was influenced by their previous experience, 'social and political opinions' and shared background 'predominantly [as] male, white, middle-class lawyers'. During an interview with a coroner, he found the following view typical of safety crimes: 'It's all nonsense … A company can't really kill people. The reason they [lawyers] will argue for that verdict is to assist in the claim. That's all they're interested in.' This was representative of the families' experiences.

Many coroners accepted the lack of evidence as indicative of no fault, worked within the self-determined limits of the corporation (accepting that witnesses were unavailable, for example) and refused to summon witnesses if they believed lawyers were trying to get evidence to bolster a civil claim (Slapper, 1999). Coroners rubber stamped the 'accident' label which the police first applied, selecting information and witnesses to support this presupposition and, in doing so, presented an insurmountable obstacle to the families. This was aided in both the selection of evidence and those who were called upon as experts. Companies sought an 'accidental verdict' and selected witnesses carefully, calling ex-colleagues of the victims as experts because they had been promoted in the time it had taken for the inquest to take place. This was confusing for the families, who questioned their expertise.

Families were bewildered as to how the managers were able to overrule evidence presented by the HSE. They found the coroner viewed both of equal importance despite the work that some HSE officers carried out. Managers who made unsubstantiated claims went unchallenged at the inquest, and individuals representing the corporations were permitted to change their version of events, which surprised the families. They had waited for the truth to be heard yet had to bear witness to it being intentionally complicated. The families had no power to counter or question this but had to listen and remain silent. Margaret found this too difficult, yet when she spoke up, the coroner threatened to have her removed from the court. In the face of the truth being complicated, the inquest became a site of more pain and confusion for the families. There was one exception: at David's inquest, his wife, Heather, was forced to represent herself. She questioned everyone on the stand, informed by a retrospective police investigation; this will be detailed in the following section.

Similarly, families and survivors of the Hillsborough Disaster were forced to silently observe the suppression of truth in the first inquests. Witness statements were disqualified, and questions from the families were unanswered (Scraton, 2004). The decision to disregard events that occurred after 3.15 pm ensured a partial reading of the day would take place, selecting evidence that rendered it unnecessary to examine the emergency response and supporting a verdict of accidental death. Solicitors representing both the police and the ambulance service successfully 'sought to establish at every opportunity that an earlier emergency response could have made no difference' (Jones, 2017: 54). Facts that family members such as Anne Jones uncovered were discredited and discounted from being heard. It took another 16 years for this evidence to be judged as significant, demonstrating the power of the coroner in dismissing the truth. Echoing this, families whose loved ones had died in custody thought information was being withheld in favour of state bodies

(INQUEST, 2023). Notably, Prasad's (2023) INQUEST report criticizes the erasure of the role of racism and wider discrimination that protects the police. During inquests following deaths in custody, race remains 'the elephant in the room' (Prasad, 2023: 72), a situation the coroner perpetuates when they refuse to allow officers to be questioned over the role of racism in the deaths. The disallowance and deliberate selection of evidence was empowered by delay and forced silence on to the families, manipulating the truth into something the family members did not recognize or find helpful.

Coroner direction

All inquests following suspected safety crimes must have a jury that reaches a verdict. In this research, juries either returned a verdict of 'accidental death' or 'unlawful killing'. The former (often used interchangeably with the verdict of death by misadventure) is self-explanatory; the latter is appropriate following homicide, indicating a corporation may be liable. Prior to the jury reaching a verdict, the coroner sums up and describes the verdicts that can be reached by the jury based on the evidence that has been presented. An unlawful killing verdict will be offered 'to the jury at an inquest into a death at work where there is believable evidence (no more) that the deceased died as a result of the employer's gross negligence' (Slapper, 1999: 42). In most of the cases in this research, the coroner removed this option from the jury.

While sitting in a Coroner's Court, Slapper (1999) observed coroners removing the possibility of unlawful killing as a verdict and acting in ways to support this, which included not calling on witnesses, focusing on events after the death and failing to show any interest in missing evidence. The experiences of the families in this research supported this observation, notably in the summing up, where they had expected the jury to have a choice but were confused when the verdict of unlawful killing was removed, frequently wondering what the point of the jury was.

Unlawful killing

The two cases to secure an unlawful killing verdict were different in the following ways. The first case was unique because it had a full police investigation, after Heather appealed the original decision. At the inquest, Heather represented herself and was able to question every witness. Unusually, the coroner did not sum up prior to the jury's decision, which Heather reflected was because the coroner was newly appointed. In the other case to secure an unlawful killing verdict, Elizabeth used the fact that jury members shared toilet facilities with the people in the gallery. Although strictly prohibited from doing so, she used this as an opportunity to ensure they were aware of the rules, which led jury members to assert their rights to the coroner. She decided to do this because she had previous experience of the coroner, whom she saw as an adversary; in this, she was prepared. Both of the cases that secured an unlawful verdict relied upon acts that would be difficult to reproduce, supporting the sense that the result of the inquest was 'the luck of the draw' (INQUEST, 2023: 16).

The coroner in the first inquest following the Hillsborough Disaster directed the jury towards an accidental death verdict. In the original inquest, the coroner had directed the jury that negligence could be incorporated within a verdict of accidental death (Scraton, 2002). He pointed to compensation that would follow and asserted that an accidental death verdict would not mean no one was to blame (Scraton, 2004). The wide discretion directed to him by the Coroners' Rules had a real effect on the verdict, which was overturned a decade later. The coroner at Jimmy Mubenga's inquest allowed the racism of the guards involved in his death to be examined, which led to an unlawful killing verdict (Prasad, 2023). However, it was later disallowed by the judge in the hearing at the Crown Court.

The difference between the coroner and judge in Jimmy Mubenga's case demonstrates the power coroners and judges have, irrespective of the jury. Between the evidence and a jury composed of members of the public, the arbiter is another obstacle the families must circumvent. It is unsurprising that families echo the sentiments expressed by a mother whose son had been killed after being electrocuted: 'Why are the jury here? You are telling them what verdict to return' (Slapper, 1999: 99).

Summary

The coroner had a huge impact on each of the families in this research, and most families left the court process without answers and feeling worse than when they entered. The truth had been suppressed through delay, evidence had been selected and the coroners directed the juries away from an unlawful killing verdict. Families were confused over the purpose of the court and the evidence that was heard. For most, this was the only court they entered. A minority did not see a coroner but a judge in a Crown Court, the problems of which echo the experiences previously mentioned.

The Crown Court

A small minority of families reached the Crown Court, which is reflective of the small numbers of corporations and directors who are convicted of manslaughter. In the 1990s, Bergman (1994, cited in Slapper, 1999) estimated that fewer than ten cases per year were referred to the Crown Court. This rose to 40 cases between 2011 and 2023, an average of just over three per year (Freedom of Information Request, 2024). This does not reflect the total number of those killed or the potential perpetrators. Two families who reached the Crown Court had not experienced the Coroner's Court; this was their chance to see the potential perpetrators and hear the truth in a court which, unlike the coronial court, did seek to apportion blame. However, this was still close to an impossibility. The cases that reached the Crown Court to hear manslaughter charges were not heard because of the complicated law created to respond to safety crime, the suppression of evidence and the presumption that the director was innocent of criminality.

Designed not to work – lex imperfecta

This research supports Punch's (2009: 66) assertion that the laws relating to safety crime are 'lex imperfecta': designed not to work. The law exists in theory but is not meant to work effectively, so few corporations are ever punished or prosecuted. The law has not developed to overcome the necessity of establishing *mens rea* in the case of safety crime. Charges of corporate manslaughter rely on it being proven that the individuals implicated have the required intent and ability to commit crime by their own hands and with a guilty mind (*mens rea*). A corporation does not have a will, guilty or otherwise, and so therefore cannot be guilty of a crime (Slapper, 1993). Corporations do not speak as a whole and do not give consent or make commands, such that prosecutions of corporations struggle to succeed (Wells, 2009).

The proof required to establish *mens rea* was absent in all but one of the cases in this research, even though half of the cases involved small businesses, which are historically far more likely to be successful at identifying *mens rea* than large corporations. The one case that met the criteria in court, before being quashed, involved the manager being onsite and working alongside the victim on the job that killed him. The common law of corporate manslaughter rarely establishes the *mens rea* of a corporation. It is less likely when subcontracting is involved, which it was in five of the cases in this research. At least three of these corporations were multinational corporations where the director was based outside of the UK, far away from the scene of death. With the emphasis on locating *mens rea*, these victims of safety crime were never going to be regarded as victims of real crime by the law (Wells, 2009).

This was set as a precedent by Lord Bingham following the failed prosecution in the case of the *Herald of Free Enterprise*. After 193 passengers were killed when the ship sank off the coast of Zeebrugge, the Sheen Inquiry (1987), an official investigation which pre-dated any legal response, found that the practices of the owners were 'infected with the disease of sloppiness' (Report of the Court, cited in Slapper and Tombs, 1999: 151). Townsend Thoresen (which had become P&O) was found to be at fault, and in a preliminary ruling the court accepted that corporate homicide could be proven (Slapper and Tombs, 1999). In the court case, the prosecution used the 'doctrine of identification' and attempted to prove a 'controlling officer' was guilty of manslaughter in order to convict the corporation (Slapper, 1999: 55). As the Sheen Inquiry concluded, it was the faults of many in the corporation that ultimately led the *Herald of Free Enterprise* to sink. The prosecution attempted to combine the mistakes of the employees to prove that P&O was guilty of reckless manslaughter (Wells, 2001).

This was referred to as the 'aggregation principle', which attempted to establish the required *mens rea* to combine the actions and guilt of those identified. However, Lord Justice Bingham – as he was to become – dispensed with the 'aggregation principle' and the existence of the corporate mind. He stated that '[a] case against a personal defendant cannot be fortified by evidence against another defendant' (R v HM Coroner for East Kent ex parte Spooner [1989] 88 Cr App R 10 at 17). Consequently, the Director for Public Prosecutions withdrew the charges against the remaining individuals (Slapper and Tombs, 1999). By rejecting the 'aggregation principle', Lord Bingham ensured that few corporations would ever make it to court in the future (Tombs and Whyte, 2007).

The cases bore out that the law is about 'deniability' (Punch, 2009: 51), which is easier to achieve for corporations. With the hidden and selected evidence, corporations were able to publicly deny their responsibility. Relevant details that illustrated the context that led up to the death of the families' loved ones and connected the deaths to the wider context of profit and gaining a competitive edge were suppressed (Pearce, 1990). To reach an official judgment of innocence, the truth of the deaths had to be manipulated by the corporations, which was enabled through state processes, including in the Crown Court. As secondary victims, they saw the truth denied, altered and suppressed to suit the needs of the corporations (Punch, 2009), which were able to control and shape past events in a rush to frame them as non-criminal in the eyes of the law and official accounts (Box, 1983).

The potential for criminality is dispersed through a structure of corporations and subcontractors that enables profit over life and complicates accountability. The number of subcontractors involved in the refurbishment of the Grenfell Tower encouraged 'a "race to the bottom": enabling private corporations to reap immense profits … while evading the scrutiny of local democratic control' (Chakrabortty, 2017; Foster, 2017b; Tucker, 2017, cited in MacLeod, 2018). Ironically, it also increases the risk that no one will be held accountable for the 72 people who died in the refurbished tower.

No/selective evidence and delays

Since the burden of proof required to prosecute corporations is high (Punch, 2009), it is imperative that the police collect sufficient evidence. The failure to do this coupled with delay fatally affected the cases. According to the Crown Prosecution Service (CPS), it was insufficient evidence that stopped most from getting to the Crown Court. This was even the case for the family who secured an unlawful killing verdict (the equivalent of homicide) at the inquest. Heather wanted it to be given a chance, but the CPS dropped the case. The case ended, and Heather wrote to them to say they should be disbanded. Slapper (1999: 76) noted a case in which the CPS dropped charges of manslaughter against a director because of 'want of evidence against him' even though 'there were several witnesses in court that day ready to testify against him', a breach of their own guidelines.

The families whose cases reached the Crown Court had similar experiences to those who attended the inquest in that evidence was selected and suffered from delays. Yvonne and her family believed the delays they experienced were due to the CPS working hard preparing to defend their loved one. They discovered this was untrue during the court case, but by then it was too late. Instead, they listened to the corporation refer to how no other employee had been killed. When they later returned home, a web search demonstrated this was false, yet the CPS failed to challenge it in court. In another instance in the same case, the defence attempted to argue Jason had been killed by a bang to the head prior to the explosion. The family were incredulous that the company was trying to argue this but were unable to counter the claim because the victim's organs had been lost. Similarly, those affected by the Grenfell Fire had to listen to Whirlpool claim that a lit cigarette had started the fire, which was dismissed by the inquiry as 'fanciful' (Moore-Bick et al, 2019: 515). Like any other member of the public, the family could not have foreseen this malpractice, nor did they have any control over it. Even if they had foreseen it, they had no option but to put their trust in the official bodies that ultimately failed them.

The difficulties of proving *mens rea* years after the offence proved too large an obstacle to overcome in the final case. This was a case that according to the CPS was not initially deemed strong enough to get to Crown Court. The Simon Jones Memorial Campaign (SJMC) successfully won a judicial review to overturn a decision by the Crown Prosecution Service not to prosecute. They reflected they 'were on a high' and began to gather evidence retrospectively in the six months they had prior to the court case. Once again, delays were crucial – evidence had been discarded, and witnesses had moved on. Further to this, the delay was mentioned in the director's favour in the judge's summing up:

> Remember the events were a long time ago. There may be danger of real prejudice to the defendant. Memories fade, and people can't remember with crystal clarity the events of years ago … The delay of three and a half years may affect some witnesses' memory. Are they lies,

> or are they genuine mistakes? Remember the time lapse ... If there are innocent reasons for lies, then you must ignore the lies. (SJMC, nd: 145)

There was nothing the family could have done to prevent this – the delay was not what they wanted, nor within their control, yet it was used by the judge in favour of the defendant.

Luke's case reached the Crown Court and built a solid case, with the assistance of a thorough police team and the CPS, and the owner of the company was convicted and sent to prison. However, on appeal three judges acquitted and subsequently released him because firefighters at the scene failed to caution him. The appeal judges told the director that he could leave with his reputation intact. Since Jason's and Luke's deaths were dealt with in court, neither of the families had any right to an inquest, although Yvonne desperately wanted this to happen in the hope the truth would be heard.

Following the Hillsborough Disaster, families reflected that those with power defended their interests in opposition to the truth. As the son of one of the victims put it, 'selective revealing of information also results in the delay of justice to the point of which it cannot be served' (Jones, 2017: 65). The truth is guarded by those in a position to do so, who complicate events and release information slowly. Charges of common assault could not be made in the Ian Tomlinson case as it had passed the six-month time limit before it reached trial (Parliament, 2010). At the trial of officers following the death of Christopher Alder, several medical experts were called who produced conflicting information that confused their own prosecution (Alder and Glazebrook, 2024). In the trial brought against the guards following Jimmy Mubenga's death, the judge chose to exclude evidence of the racist texts sent between the guards that had been uncovered at the inquest in case it led the jury to discriminate against them. Jimmy Mubenga was the only case of a death in custody from Chapter 3 that was heard in Crown Court. None of the cases from Chapters 2 or 3 were successful.

Benefit of clergy

Sutherland (1983) compared the treatment of corporations to medieval society, when the most powerful secured immunity due to the 'benefit of clergy'. He remarked that those with the power to influence laws are unwilling to see members of corporations as criminals. Tombs and Whyte (2007) agree that corporations have been morally elevated to a position where they can define their own status. When those involved in the courts believe that the offences committed are not really crimes, it affects subsequent sentencing decisions (Croall, 1992).

The cases that appeared in the Crown Court had to successfully pass the test of the CPS, which most of the cases did not. Slapper (1999) examined cases that had comparative levels of blameworthiness present in the successful prosecution of OLL Ltd for the manslaughter of four teenagers who drowned while on a canoe trip, better known as the Lyme Regis canoe tragedy. However, the cases he examined were dropped by the CPS. He explains this is partly because the Crown Prosecutor must consider what a reasonable jury 'ought to decide' (Slapper, 1999: 149), which is likely to benefit those in positions of power. This same benefit, which the families suspected of the coroner, was extended to the judges, who sat between the families and the jury. Punch observed that judges have more in common with the directors in terms of class in that they benefit from 'social capital' (Punch, 2009: 51). This was observed by the three families who made it past the CPS to the Crown Court.

Those with power were able to protect themselves, using the law rather than being prosecuted by it. For example, in Jason's case, three witnesses from three different corporations who were involved were granted immunity from prosecution. When the family asked why this was, they were told it was necessary to 'get them on side'. On more than one occasion, the family believed there was something else going on that accounted for the warm reception that the owners, as the accused, received within the court. Elizabeth described it as 'wheels within wheels'. Many families commented that they were part of an unfair game, one which they could not win.

The problem of the circumstances of the death being seen as incapable of being manslaughter was a notion that followed the families through each stage of the official response, from the police officers to judges and coroners. In one case, the judge openly asked: 'Why is this case before me? It is a death at work' (Luke). Though part of normal practice in court, one family described how they were shocked the judge gave the director a character reference when he was unable to provide one himself. This was detailed in the judge's summing up: 'You have heard that the defendant is of good character, is 59 years old, and has never been in trouble. This is evidence which you should consider in his favour. He has given evidence himself. His good character may mean that he is less likely to commit offences' (Phillip). The good character outlined by the judge was linked to his propensity to offend. In addition, the judge distanced the director from the traditional criminal (Punch, 2009), describing how he had found the police interview frightening.

The corporation's appearance in court did not reduce their power, which was wielded in the court. For example, one corporation threatened a family by stating that if they pursued the court case, they would lose civil claims for compensation for the victim's young daughter. Such bargaining tools are unavailable to conventional accused parties. The court case was not only stopped but, to the horror of the family, the company returned to the court to be officially judged as 'not guilty', and the case was duly dismissed from court. The company left the court as an innocent party, and for that family, despite protestations after they realized the implications, that was the end of the process. The company had successfully negotiated its innocence, and the family felt manipulated. In this, as secondary victims, they had a minimal role in the proceedings, and as such they were 'not always silenced, but … how they are allowed to speak, and how their experience is turned into something the law can digest and process, is a demonstration of the power of law to disqualify alternative accounts' (Smart, 1990, cited in Ballinger, 2016: 41).

Families and survivors of the Hillsborough Disaster were confused by their treatment by the judge compared to the treatment of the police. In the private prosecution, the judge reassured the defendants that whatever the outcome, they would not have to go to prison because of the worry it would cause them. In contrast, as bereaved family members, they received a ban that prohibited them from campaigning for the duration of the trial. Ahead of the trial in the Christopher Alder case, it was claimed the CPS promised the police they would not be prosecuted for manslaughter (Alder and Glazebrook, 2024). At a point when the families, after a long wait, were in a court that had the power to provide a punishment, they were thwarted. Further, the powerful defendants were protected ahead of any verdict or sentencing, with the trial itself deemed as too worrying for them to endure.

Summary

Many families commented that they could not win, and all cases but one ended with the public proclamation of the innocence of the company following appeal. Not readily positioned as criminal, powerful 'defendants' were not interrogated by the law or its agents. Problems of delay and the selection of evidence were greater obstacles for the families at this stage. Judges continued to view safety and state crime as not the business of the court, and the corporations left without viewing themselves as criminals (Gobert and Punch, 2003). All resisted legal criminalization and continued to operate as businesses and as employers. They could continue to operate and remain unaffected by their actions, for example, the people who make up the corporations do not come face to face with secondary victims nor do they have to confront the consequences of their actions/inactions. The dissonance between the corporations and the death of the victim was perpetuated (Gobert and Punch, 2003). The corporations left 'with their reputation intact', in contrast to the families, who left with a huge distrust for systems they had imagined would protect their loved ones.

Independent bodies: the Independent Office for Police Conduct (IOPC), inquiries, committees and the HSE

Once the cases had failed in the Crown Court and received a verdict from the coroner, some cases moved to scrutiny from an independent body. Following safety crime, this meant facing prosecution for offences raised by the HSE. Following deaths in custody involving the police, cases moved to disciplinary proceedings raised by the IOPC. Both bodies are funded by the state (the Department for Work and Pensions and the Home Office) and claim independence in the name of protecting the public. Although not a general feature of safety crime, inquiries have also been launched following corporate and state crime.

As seen in the previous sub-section, a small proportion of cases in this research reached Crown Court, but all cases failed (in the long term) to secure justice there. The alternative and most common route for justice for those harmed and killed at work was to see employers face prosecution for health and safety offences. Despite this being the most well-worn route, families continued to experience insurmountable obstacles, and for those who overcame these, they received what felt like a consolation prize. These independent bodies are not considered a part of the criminal justice system, and the people they deal with are rarely assumed to have acted in ways that are potentially criminal. However, outside of the criminal justice system, these bodies offer limited hope that those involved will be held responsible and their lives changed because of what they did (or did not do) which led to the death of their loved one.

Delay and selected evidence

Under-resourced, under-funded and publicly mocked (Pearce, 2008), the HSE was the final stage for many families and the last hope they had of justice. Companies were able to thwart investigations (Croall, 1992) with the continued delays, which the HSE reassured families was in the name of continuity, indicating the cases would be weaker without the delay; Michael's family were told this directly. Statements were not gathered promptly by the HSE, and the involved parties later refused to answer questions when they were approached 18 months after the victims' death. Families, with grace, considered that old work colleagues would have nothing to gain from giving statements that may implicate their employers. Potential witnesses had been promoted within corporations, and key employees had resigned. Contrary to promises made to the families, the delay had not strengthened the case but halted it, and the continual reassurance that equated delay with future success misled the families that a case was being built. Anniversaries,

Christmases and birthdays passed without any contact from formal agencies. Carole's experience was typical: she was told by the HSE that although they had tried to get more statements, without additional evidence from the corporation, 'they didn't feel they could go any further'. The HSE officer offered his apologies.

Delays facilitated the non-response of the IOPC in the allegations against the officer involved in Hillsborough and the deaths in custody. The officers involved in the Hillsborough Disaster were not disciplined by the IOPC, because they had left the police by the time of the IOPC investigation. The officers in the Christopher Alder case had been suspended, and it was felt that it was 'not in the public interest' for them to be disciplined. The officers involved in the death of Sean Rigg were investigated twice by the Independent Police Complaints Commission (IPCC) and then the IOPC, with the later investigation finding fault with the first. However, all charges were ultimately dismissed. Two investigations were also launched in the case of Ian Tomlinson: the first exonerated the police officer, while the second sacked him. The most common response of the IPCC or IOPC was to recommend more training and to apologize.

Inadequate response

The inadequate responses from the HSE continued in the sanctions that were delivered, and for some of the families, recommendations made were mitigated further and produced confusing messages. In adhering to regulations, the corporations worked within the limits that were set for them (Box, 1983). In one example of this, a family was told the company did not and would not alter their working practices because of their son's death because that would mean they were working to 'best practice', and 'best practice' was beyond the statutory duties that were required of them. Two families were wrongly promised that their cases would be heard on health and safety offences. One of these was Paul's case. Years after Paul's death, Gary was told the HSE had dropped the case after placing the company on probation. Gary hoped it made them realize 'how close they came to prosecution'. However, he reflected 'but I have no idea' because the HSE never got back in touch.

The family who secured an unlawful killing verdict at the inquest returned to court to hear charges for health and safety. As detailed earlier, the CPS had refused to take the case forward to the Crown Court for manslaughter charges. The hearing for health and safety charges took an hour with no jury. The HSE had high expectations the fine would be substantial – Angela recalled how 'even [the] health and safety [executive] thought three quarters of a million [pounds]'. When the judge returned, the company was fined £225,000. That year, the company in question returned pre-tax profits of

£520.4 million (Thompson, 2009). Upon sentencing, the judge said 'his hands were tied … but he did want it publicly noted that their health and safety was far below what the public should expect'. Fines reflected the sentencing guidelines and were low, and therefore one family was offered apologies by the judge. The Sheriff turned to the family and said 'this should have been in the high court'. Angela recalled he 'apologized' before explaining the fines were 'the top fines I can give out'. The process and official guidance had restricted the punishment, and the Sheriff was only able to informally console the family of the victim.

Of the 11 cases, five ended with fines under the Health and Safety at Work Act 1974. Due to the nature of subcontracts, across these five cases, ten corporations were involved. Following bargaining for a reduction in sentencing, for example after corporations had been shown leniency for pleading guilty to health and safety charges, the average fine across these ten corporations was £34,000. The extent to which the fines reflected the seriousness of the death or reduced future risk taking is debatable. For example, one company that was prosecuted under health and safety offences received a fine that was 0.000432 per cent of its reported turnover for 2015 (the company was fined a few years earlier). This is the equivalent of a person who earns £26,500 per annum being fined 11 pence. This was still considered an unprecedented 'win'.

A restricted agency

The 'war on crime' has never included families or victims of safety crime (Whyte, 2007). The unthinking war imagery that is waged on criminals where rationality can be dispensed with, and anyone who opposes it are seen as enemies (Best, 1999) has, however, been declared on red tape:

> Conservatives in government are winning the war on red tape … like the Red Tape Challenge, which has now seen over 1,000 regulations scrapped, we've saved firms £1.5 billion a year … we've freed thousands of businesses from unnecessary health and safety inspections, prevented responsible employers from being held liable for those workplace accidents that are outside of their control. (Hancock, 2014: para 1)

It is clear what a war on red tape entails: it is the arbitrary reduction of regulation that saves businesses money, fewer inspections and the assurance employers will not be held liable for their failings. The rhetoric of regulation and 'red tape' has a reinforcing effect. Regulation has not been prioritized by governments but continually reduced.

By choosing to respond to safety crimes with regulation and policing via regulators, there is an acceptance that these crimes require a different, lesser approach (Slapper and Tombs, 1999). Regulatory responses play a clear part in failing to recognize those killed as victims of crime. A regulation has been breached, and although the consequences are grave, they are far removed from the cause and the actions of an offender. The metaphysical gap is a significant feature of regulation – the corporations might have made a mistake, but it was just that, an oversight and not a crime (Wells, 2001). Regulation has been reduced to a symbolic gesture offered to the families, a lesser sanction that acknowledges harm has, but should not have, taken place (Carson, 1974).

Families received apologies and statements that acknowledged something wrong had happened, such as Prime Minister David Cameron's public apology for Hillsborough. The IPCC concluded in the Christopher Alder case that the force 'must show they accept several simple truths of the case: The acquittal of the officers in the trial and disciplinary hearings did not amount to an endorsement of their actions' IPCC, 2006: 12). They are typical of the results at this stage: after all formal justice options had ended, the families were left with apologies and confusing admissions that had few consequences for the officially innocent implicated in the deaths of their loved ones.

Families mentioned taking comfort from the jury members who appeared to disagree with the process. This was significant to the family and authenticated their own thoughts in ways that had been suppressed by the court. Gary recalled two jury members were crying 'because all they could do was give a verdict of accidental death', and Yvonne recalled how 'I will always remember looking at that jury and there was one young lad who I would say was about 26, the age of my lads and he just looked at us and shook his head in disbelief'. A jury member wrote to Margaret, which was a great comfort to her. The following is an excerpt from the letter:

> I feel you are right this to me was an accident waiting to happen and why the coroner did not pick up on this is beyond me … Myself and the rest of the jury felt the old lady was too scared and felt she would be blamed … At the inquest nobody can apportion blame on anybody else but in my eyes the poor condition of the balcony rail has been the major factor in the death of [your son] … I hope by telling my view to you it will help you a little with the pain of your loss.

The reaction of the juries, in both courts, reaffirmed to the families that the whole process was a sham.

For the families in this research, formal justice in the Crown Court failed in all the cases, and fines were a consolation prize. The final obstacle was fines that are high enough to punish the corporations. However, the fines were so low as to insult the families further, which more than one judge recognized. Judges apologized that the fines they handed out to the corporations were determined by factors outside of their control. The symbolic gesture was inadequate to show public disapproval, and its lack of rigour in either deterring or punishing the corporations harmed the families of the victims who had died. They felt wronged, and without any public show of disapproval or agreement, many felt isolated further, compounding bereavement and increasing distrust.

Summary

These independent agencies were a final stage for the families. The HSE is an agency designed to hear the cases of deaths at work and has the power to hold corporations accountable. The reality is that the HSE as a body offers regulation that is restricted and constrained by outside factors such as funding, and the sanctions it offers are inadequate. The HSE saw raising awareness as the best solution rather than shutting down the corporations or imprisoning the directors, similar to the response of the IOPC. The truth was suppressed, and potential perpetrators were able to 'bow out of the scene', their responsibility fading as the victims were implicated in their own deaths. While inquiries may receive press attention, their aim, as Snider (2003) states, is to establish truths, what went wrong and how to avoid it in the future, often focusing on science rather than seeking to apportion blame. Punishment does not follow.

The blameworthy victim

No criminal, no victim

Tombs (1991) explores the notion of the 'accident-prone' victim, describing it as a myth that enables the employer to claim there is nothing they can do to prevent accidents. It is 'a functional *misrepresentation* of the causes and nature of such accidents' (Tombs, 1991: 72, emphasis in original). Tombs and Whyte (2007) expand upon the concept, describing the accident-prone victim as an individual who due to their personality, lifestyle and internal qualities is prone to accidents, irrespective of the workplace. Just as poverty does not inevitably make someone a criminal, because not all poor people steal, similarly it is not the fault of the workplace when a 'lazy, stupid, careless' person has an accident (Tombs and Whyte, 2007: 75). The widely held view that health and safety is a joke makes it easier to view all injured and dead workers as accident-prone victims. Harm is inevitable – it is an acceptable by-product of work and not within the remit of the legal process other than in exceptional circumstances (Smart, 1995). This idea was pervasive throughout this research: secondary victims were either non-existent and invisible or visible but immediately blameworthy and implicated in their own death. Further, this was encouraged by a 'general lack of a search for "fundamental" causes following "day to day" incidents' (Tombs and Whyte, 2007: 77), enabled by the failure of the police to consider the scene a potential site of evidence.

The response of police officers set the tone for the rest of the investigation. In Slapper's (1999) conversations with police officers, he characterized the dominant thinking as:

> The employee goes to work voluntarily, and in exchange for pay. He is not legally obliged to take risks with his life and limb. If he chooses to expose himself to known perils then, although his dependents may be able to sue for negligence, and although the HSE may prosecute for a regulatory offence, the fatality is not really a crime. (Slapper, 1999: 128)

Whether or not the worker was presumed 'accident prone', they were at least assumed to have made a choice to be in that situation in exchange for commensurate wages, ignoring the inferior relationship of workers who are rarely able to negotiate how or where they work or how much they are paid (Whyte, 2007). The pervasive notion of the accident-prone worker, the blameworthy victim and the informed actor meant the police were unlikely to believe any such death they were called to was potentially a crime.

Families were confused as to why their experiences with the police and the Family Liaison Officers (FLOs) were so different from the positive experiences they had heard of from the media; most were not kept informed. They were not treated as legitimate families of victims, which became evident in the first encounters. The routine questioning led families to question whether the victim might have caused their own death: Jason's mother was asked about his mental health when he had died in an explosion, and John's widow was asked similar questions when he had been killed by a barrier extreme winds had blown into his car windscreen. This arbitrary response redirects potential causes away from the corporation and back to the victim, which had consequences for the families. The outcome of this process and line of questioning immediately placed the victim in a position of mistrust. Evidence that did not exist was sought, yet existing evidence in the workplace was discarded. The victim was under suspicion; this began a process to establish a narrative of 'accident', which only made it more likely the death of the victim would be viewed similarly at the subsequent stages of the process.

Some of the officials involved in the cases were brazen and insensitive. For example, a health and safety inspector visited the home of Margaret and told her that the death of her son was an accident that was self-inflicted because 'he shouldn't have been doing what he was doing'. This was immediately devastating for her and diverted all attention away from the scene of his death or the reasons that led up to it (Tombs, 1991). It was common for the victim to be branded as a risk taker (David), for doing something no one was aware of (Paul) and for not being conscientious enough (John). The person who died was treated as the main source of risk (Pearce and Tombs, 1989; Tombs, 1991) after their death when they were not there to defend themselves.

At the Coroner's Court, the victims became culpable and were positioned at the centre of an 'accident' (Bittle and Snider, 2006). The powerful narrative that a person who is killed at work is the victim of misfortune or has died as a result of their own risk taking led to victims being blamed for their own deaths using far-fetched explanations, which were considered and not refuted by the court. In the case where a victim was killed in an explosion because he had been told the use of cutting gear to dismantle the chimney was safe, the defence tried to argue he had not been killed by the explosion. They contested the cause of his death by claiming to have found a plastic lighter at the bottom of the chimney, which they suggested the victims had been using. This was despite the fact plastic would not have survived the fire and the victims had already left the chimney to question the safety of using cutting gear at all. It is beyond the limits of possibility that two trained steeplejacks would attempt to dismantle a chimney with one plastic lighter between them. As Mathiesen notes: '[Q]uestions to which ordinary people appear as obvious totalities, are unravelled into their individual conceptual components, and decisions which from a popular point of view appear quite unreasonable, are made reasonable by the emphasis on the precise legal content of the words' (1980: 107). The families had to hear and watch this and sit in silence.

The belief that all deaths at work are accidents was pervasive, and it was far easier to blame the victim than to meet the high burden of proof required to publicly blame the company. When summing up Phillip's case, which reached the Crown Court, the judge outlined that the director had 'concluded that [the victim] must have put himself in danger', and that the director '[relies] upon people being sensible'. The judge went on: 'He [the director] says, "How could I know this was going to happen? There was a freakish combination of circumstances."' This was a case that had passed the CPS, was an inherently dangerous job, and prohibited. Yvonne was approached by a barrister for the defence outside the court: '[H]e said, "This has got no reflection on your son, but it is the way the trial has got to go … we are not blaming your son." We were taken aback for his barrister to say this … we'll never forget it.' As implied by the barrister, for the company to be blame free, the blame had to be attributed to the victim.

The lives of the victims were interrogated as far as was necessary to support their blameworthiness. As a victim, they were ideal in the sense that they were carrying out a legitimate activity (Christie, 1986). Instead the notion of risk was emphasized. The father of one victim reflected that '[t]hey made it sound at the inquest that he worked in an unsafe way, but in actual fact … he wasn't a risky person, he worked hard, very hard' (Gary). For the court, its officers and the company and its interested parties, it was convenient for the victim to be portrayed as risky and careless. Similarly, in Matthews et al's (2012: 482) research, a family member shared: '[T]hey'll do everything they can … as a means of eliminating their responsibility', which they found 'a really, really difficult thing to have to contend with'. The families were forgotten and sidelined in the process, and while this was positive for the company in the short term, the impact of blaming the victim had long-term consequences for them as secondary victims. As a mother summed up when she screamed at the coroner: 'You are saying my son killed himself. He took his own life. This is just a sham' (Slapper, 1999: 99).

Following the Hillsborough Disaster, families were similarly asked questions that implicated the victims in their own deaths, pursuing a narrative of drunkenness and hooliganism; neither the inaccuracy nor callousness of the accusations prevented these questions being asked minutes after the families had identified their loved ones. The infamous *Sun* headline firmly placed blame on to the survivors and victims as the cause of the disaster. Blood was taken from every victim of the Hillsborough Disaster, and if there was no measure of alcohol, the police used the National Computer to find out if any of them had criminal records, which Sheila Coleman described as 'another shameful attempt at victim-blaming' (Sampson, 2017: 306). The reluctance to place the potential perpetrator under suspicion was set against the willingness of the police to doubt the innocence of the victim and implicate them in their own deaths. Victims were blamed – if not due to 'their aggression and refusal to conform' as per deaths in custody, then it was 'their character weakness and failure to adjust' which explained their death (Scraton, 2002: 112). The effect of this was to make 'criminals of survivors and victimised the bereaved. It was an exercise in the use of crude, unsophisticated institutional powers' (Scraton, 2016: 155).

As in the case of deaths at work, families told INQUEST they were 'often left with conclusions that … effectively blame their loved ones for their own deaths' (Prasad, 2023: 59). Unlike people killed at work or during leisure activities, those who died in custody were easier to implicate in their own deaths. Their background was interrogated and employed at the earliest point to build a strong case they were blameworthy. Families had to hear police refer to their loved one's aggressive behaviour and them being treated as a perpetrator (Alder and Glazebrook, 2024) and a focus on their behaviour to justify the disproportionate use of force. After his death, Christopher Alder's and his family's social services case records had been requested by the police, and his home was searched and sealed for two weeks on the basis that it 'may reveal drugs and/or steroids … which may be of assistance to the pathologist in establishing course [sic] of death' (Alder and Glazebrook,

2024: 91). The police had enquired about his record in the Army. His sister reflected: 'I dread to think how the police would have used his history [had he not been decorated for his service in Northern Ireland]' (Alder and Glazebrook, 2024: 149). There was a clear attempt to discredit the victim after his death, using the power the police had over the families and putting them under scrutiny.

The families were left to defend their loved ones from the negative media reporting and the defensive police response (Alder and Glazebrook, 2024: 149), which they were effectively powerless to refute. Immediately following Adrian's death, the media wrongly reported that he was a 'suspected burglar', which led to condemnation from the public, who wrote in online comments that he deserved to die (Prasad, 2023: 87). His family had to actively protect his two children from the consequences of this misinformation and tried as individuals to undo the damage caused by ringing up local radio stations (Prasad, 2023). However, this continued to be a part of police and IPCC statements and was not officially refuted because 'doing so would "jeopardise the case"' (Prasad, 2023: 87). This was a part of the manipulation and management of the media, including purposeful misinformation (Scraton, 2013). Blaming the victim depended on their dehumanization (Pemberton, 2008b). Family members understandably drew on their own knowledge of their loved one to either disregard or accept the findings at the inquest (Matthews et al, 2019). Yet this still publicly sullied their name.

The police pushed an alternative narrative in the immediate visit to the families, for example that the victim was a member of a gang, and persisted to do so even when this had been refuted (Prasad, 2023). This meant pursuing any stereotypes that conveniently prop up dominant discourses. In the case of deaths of Black men in custody, this meant focusing on the police fearing '[a] big, strong, Black man' (Prasad, 2023: 86). The families reported having to defend not only their loved one but themselves against racialized stereotypes from the outset. Several described how they faced negative media reporting and inaccurate police statements that started in the immediate hours after the death. Families told INQUEST they encountered a pattern of defensiveness by officers that focused on condemning the person who had died. In their view, the IOPC and inquests inadequately challenged the police's version of events. Secondary victims are often left with conclusions that, they say, effectively blame their loved ones for their own deaths.

Those killed at work were also judged on whether they were 'inadequate', 'mentally ill' or made a poor decision (Scraton and Chadwick, 1987, cited in Scraton, 2002: 111) that was unconnected to the context within which they died. Those around them – whether colleagues, members of the public or the police – were almost unfortunate to be there as witnesses. This idea permeated to the extent that the more powerful potential perpetrators saw themselves as victims. In response to clear CCTV footage, the officer who struck Ian Tomlinson told the court that Tomlinson was 'almost inviting physical confrontation' (Walker, 2012). Actions are scrutinized, focused on the victim, such as was the case after Grenfell when the Leader of the House of Commons commented he would leave a burning building, ignoring the fire brigade, because 'it just seems the common sense thing to do' (BBC, 2019). The notion that people who were utterly powerless are still somehow responsible for their deaths is pervasive.

One-off, random events

The notion of terrorism or robbery draws together events spread across time and distance into a monolithic threat. Deaths by the powerful have no such common term. In this research, it was the families who suffered in isolation, their loved ones taken due to something that was unforeseen and random. In both, the context is absent, and the events appear isolated: we recognize that harm has happened, but it is a one-off event. This disregards the similarities between these deaths and fails to counter the idea we are over protected and far from a golden past when there was common sense rather than health and safety.

It is widely claimed that health and safety culture has 'gone way beyond what was intended' (Grimsby Telegraph, 2014: para 1). The government actively mocks what it describes as 'elf and safety' ideology by decrying a lack of 'common sense' that negatively affects responsible employers (James et al, 2012). In support of enterprise, successive governments have encouraged the use of compliance, and an increasing number of prosecutions are viewed as unnecessary. The regulation of buildings and football stadiums and measures to protect those in custody are assumed to be excessive. Therefore, when a tower is engulfed in flames, fans are crushed in a stadium and people die in custody, they are viewed as aberrations.

Yet this idea of one-off, unforeseen events was counter to the findings of this research. In each case, there were very clear examples of similar or identical incidents that had happened in the recent past. Families might not have feared that harm would come to their loved ones at work, but after their deaths they realized what happened was predictable. For example, prior to his death, David had brought home a piece of paper in his wages which detailed the death of another employee in an incident that was almost identical to the one that ultimately killed him. The two men who were killed as members of the public were involved in an incident that had happened many times before and since. The two youngest victims had been at work for mere hours or days in a job they had no prior experience of nor training for. For both, the act that killed them was not within their control and could only have been avoided had they refused to work. Their deaths were not 'acts of God' nor accidental but were caused by decisions that could have been avoided (Gottfredson and Hirschi, 1990). Neither should have been placed in the obviously risky situation that killed them.

The Hillsborough Stadium had experienced 'near misses' in the past. It had been withdrawn from the list of potential venues for the FA Cup in 1981 after 38 fans were injured in Leppings Lane; the perimeter fence was opened to avoid serious harm (UK Parliament, 2012; Rigg, 2019). In 1989, despite this near miss, Sheffield City Council inaccurately listed the capacity of the Leppings End Terrace on the stadium safety certificate (Rigg, 2019). The year before, fans had shared their terrifying experiences of being held in the pens (Sampson, 2017), including Andy Burnham, who recalls his feet being 'lifted off the floor'; he wondered how his father and brother were coping when he was struggling to breathe (Burnham, 2012). People expressed that the stadium had a reputation: 'Everyone knew the Leppings Lane was a bad end' (Hooton cited in Sampson, 2017: 19), and immediately after hearing about Hillsborough, fans understood exactly what happened. The previous police commander had put measures in place to reduce this risk, foreshadowing the event.

The Grenfell Inquiry demonstrated the significance of the Lakanal House fire in 2009, in which six people died. The inquest that followed those deaths highlighted that one victim was wrongly 'urged to remain in her flat … based on the theory of compartmentalisation', but the 'blaze moved unusually quickly and in unexpected ways' (Walker, 2013). The verdict noted that the council did not carry out fire risk assessments with any urgency and there was a failure of them and their contractors (Walker, 2013). Moore-Bick et al (2019) stated in the Grenfell Inquiry that the recommendations made by the coroner in the Lakanal House fire inquest were not treated with any sense of urgency, and concerns were dismissed by officials and ministers. Instead, the government followed a deregulatory agenda so that 'matters affecting the safety of life were ignored, delayed or disregarded' (Moore-Bick et al, 2019: 11). Clear indications of risk went back to 1999, with numerous recommendations and warnings failing to be heard or acted upon (Moore-Bick et al, 2019: 11). Tombs (2020) details multiple examples of fires in England caused by fridge freezers, including one that led to the death of two men in October 2014. It is impossible to argue Grenfell, eight years after Lakanal, was unforeseen or a one off.

No victim, no criminal

In the cases in this research, the actions of the corporations in committing the crime and then distancing themselves from the event afterwards were enabled by official processes. A failure to restrict access to the scene of the death or collect evidence for further investigation indicated to any potential perpetrator that the police had not placed them under suspicion. Most of the officers left the scene and began working in cooperation with the potential perpetrators rather than approaching them with suspicion or neutrality. This included FLOs, who posed questions to the families on behalf of the corporations as well as impressing upon them that what happened was accidental prior to any investigation/evidence or official judgment.

The police often perceived the victims as unlucky and failed to see a potential perpetrator or a possible crime. According to Slapper (1999), this is because there is an 'invisible man' who 'is a company director' and all the significant 'behind the scene role in the events which culminated in death will not be appreciated as significant … it is nearly always omission rather than an act … Thus, both the possible offender and the possible offence are invisible' (Slapper, 1999: 126). The deaths of the people in this research were caused by acts or omissions prioritizing the interests of the employers rather than the employees (Gottfredson and Hirschi, 1990). The reasons for the deaths could be attributed to a number of decisions taken to create shortcuts and to maximize profit that reflect the company's desire to make a profit with a 'dehumanising structure of irresponsibility' that is a 'necessarily a-moral, calculative rationality' (Tombs and Whyte, 2015: 158). This is neither seen nor appreciated by the police officers.

The criminal justice system relies upon evidence and the actions of several employees who take forward the case on behalf of the victims and the state. The framing of the deaths as accidental and not potentially criminal had continued consequences throughout the process and posed a major obstacle to any justice. None of this was within the control of the families, many of whom believed the 'justice system [would] fight' on behalf of their loved one (Yvonne). They had no option but to turn to the state for justice, presenting itself as it does as 'independent, free and detached from the material conditions to which it actually adjusts' in order to maintain its 'matter-of-course authority or prominence' (Mathiesen, 1980: 92). They were unaware, or unable to identify, that the state and the company were inexplicably linked, and that the potential perpetrator was able to avoid accountability, enabled by the process of the state.

The corporations and the actions of the powerful were not perceived as potentially criminal. Yet, consideration of the behind-the-scenes role and the context demonstrates a disregard of safety. For example, in one case the company had successfully won a bid to complete the work for half the price of competitors. They were able to slash the bid by using a cheaper process that risked the safety of the workers. This was not discussed at the court. Yvonne recalled that when it was raised, 'their barrister stood up and said, "I thought we had agreed not to talk money."' The selection of this evidence was disallowed, agreed in advance to never be heard. In another case, the director had modified the grab himself to make it more 'efficient' despite warnings displayed on the cab by the company that created the machine. Such decisions or omissions were not viewed as criminal by the corporations themselves, and the offence remained invisible. This was further reflected in the state's failure to punish and hold them accountable.

Further, in a 'society that embraces … the increasing commodification of all human relationships', the distance the court creates increases the likelihood of future occurrences of safety crime (Wright and Hill, 2004: 117). Snider (2003a: 66) note that 'corporate executives are unlikely to shame themselves for corporate crime or to experience shaming through their peers'. The intervention of the process and the professionalism of the court (Christie, 1977) appeared to increase 'cognitive dissonance' (Gobert and Punch, 2003: 29). For example, a director who was injured in the incident expressed remorse in the immediate aftermath. He had cried and hugged the mother of Luke, expressing it was his fault and apologizing. This changed by the time of the court case, when he claimed to have been unaware of what Luke had been doing and that his own injuries had been caused by trying to save him. There was little evidence of a corporate conscience that prioritized the well-being of employees over the need to make a profit. When faced with the option of helping the families by telling the truth or avoiding the threat of liability, the corporations chose the latter (Sinclair and Haines, 1993, cited in Matthews et al, 2020).

Summary

Law is a powerful discourse, and in the case of safety crime, it reproduces power (Bittle and Snider, 2006). The pervasive notion that the victim had caused their own death in a random accident was enabled by the law and encouraged by those with the power to influence it (Tombs, 1991). The victim was dead and unable to defend their actions, and while they were de-humanized in court by the process that sought to blame them for their death, they were not personally harmed by it. Instead, it was the families, as secondary victims, who bore witness and were de-humanized by the official process. Any victim who has died can be blamed for their death (Rock, 1998) and be de-humanized in the court.

Official recommendations were not heeded but ignored and dismissed with terrifying consequences for the people who found themselves in the same situation in the years that followed. Those who knew about the risk were similarly dismissed and had no power to compel those in a position to do something about it to act. The assumption of being over protected by those with power, burdened as they are by 'red tape' and regulations, increased the vulnerability of people put into those situations. When the bereaved families found out what happened was foreseen and preventable, they were the ones who suffered. By separating and judging these events in isolation, the risk of future harm increases. The corporations and powerful were not viewed with suspicion – this ran throughout the research. The unlikely nature of a powerful perpetrator was supported by a blameworthy victim.

Conclusion

This chapter has focused on the obstacles the families in both Chapters 2 and 3 experienced when they were thrust into the official process following the sudden deaths of their loved ones. Despite being very different cases, an examination of their experiences highlights commonalities that enable any potential perpetrator to avoid being treated as criminal. From contact with the police to the independent bodies, the families found the truth was suppressed and they were silenced through the lack of a crime scene and evidence, delay, the selection of evidence, coroner direction, a law designed not to work and the 'benefit of clergy' (Sutherland, 1940: 9).

Those who find themselves like the families in this research have little to no chance of seeing a perpetrator punished in court. The discourse that such deaths are accidents prevails. It affects those working in the legal system, from the police to the judges who are reluctant to re-frame the perpetrator as potentially criminal rather than victims of misfortune. This research argues that these judgements are not reflections of the truth but instead demonstrate that when faced with a powerful perpetrator, the source and cause of the harm is rarely interrogated. There are several obstacles that stand between the truth being heard and acknowledged publicly and the punishment of any potential perpetrator.

Families who progressed the furthest through the criminal justice system asserted their rights to the coroner via the jury (Margaret and Heather) or benefitted from unequivocal evidence, notably CCTV footage, text messages and evidence that had not been destroyed (Tomlinson, Alder, Mubenga, Hillsborough). The only case that ended with a prison sentence was quashed, but it should be noted that it met the test of *mens rea* because it was a small business rather than a corporation, and the manager was directly involved in the incident. Most victims of safety crime in this research worked as subcontractors and would never pass this test.

The way the victims and families of the victims of safety crime were treated at every stage of the criminal justice system slowly and incrementally filtered them away from justice. As Tombs and Whyte note: '[N]one of the various mechanisms whereby safety crimes are rendered relatively invisible are particularly remarkable in isolation. What is crucial, however, *is their mutually reinforcing nature* – that is, they work in the same direction and to the same effect, removing these crimes from "crime, law and order" agendas'

(Tombs and Whyte, 2007: 69, emphasis in original). The suppression of the evidence relied upon the families either being invisible or for their loved one to be blamed, which came at a great cost to those who were already suffering the most. Seeing this played out in the public arena further harmed the families. This, and its effects, will be detailed in Chapter 5.

5

Harmful Effects on Secondary Victims

Chapter 4 examined what happened to victims of safety crime which enabled the suppression of the truth. What seemed extraordinary to the families in Chapter 2, who were largely alone and isolated, was also experienced by families, often collectively, in Chapter 3. The small moments such as long-term sickness that led to delays or coroners who directed the jury were repeated as each was moved out of the criminal justice process (Tombs and Whyte, 2007). Chapters 2, 3 and 4 focused on illustrating the experiences of secondary victims as they bore the consequences of being removed from the criminal justice process. The suppression of the truth demanded the invisibility or blaming of the loved one who died, and, in turn, the responses were the same.

The effects of this will be detailed in this chapter using a social harm framework, in part to redress this under-researched, invisible crime (Davies et al, 2014). It is entirely the point that I cannot call what happened to the victims in Chapters 2 and 3 criminal, but what I can say is that their deaths could have been prevented had 'lessons been learnt'. It is also true that their families suffered from preventable harms, caused by the process they had to endure. It is vital to recognize these harms and what 'the legal system fails or refuses to acknowledge' (West, 1998, cited in Smart, 1995: 181). This is unapologetically a 'value laden notion' (Pemberton, 2016: 32). This process demanded a further response from the families, which compounded their grief and relationship with society, and whose victimization mirrored 'wider social inequalities' along 'class, gender, race' and economic and cultural lines (Croall, 2016: 72).

Hillyard and Tombs (2005) outlined an approach to examine how people are harmed and affected throughout their life; this was broken down into five harms: physical, financial/economic, emotional and psychological, sexual and cultural safety (Alvesalo, 1999). Pemberton (2016) expanded upon this to examine physical/mental health harms, autonomy and relational harms. In doing so, he collapsed three of the harms and expanded cultural safety into two. Canning and Tombs (2021) incorporated and expanded these categories, adding 'harms of recognition', out of Pemberton's (2016) relational harm and Yar's (2012) considerations of misrecognition, building upon Fraser's (2000) work.

From this early conception of harms, this chapter will examine the following harms:

- physical, psychological and emotional harms
- financial harms
- harms of misrecognition
- autonomy harms

First, physical, psychological and emotional harms will be examined. The decision to look at them in one section is due to a natural overlap between the categories and the recognition that a clear link was made by the families between physical and emotional health. For example, it is difficult to refer to mothers admitted to hospital for gastro problems without acknowledging this as an effect of devastating grief coupled with their inhumane treatment. Further, the grief was a consequence of the very physical act of the sudden and unexpected death of her son, all of which she was forced to deal with. Second, financial harms will be discussed as a barrier to justice, principally in relation to the lack of legal advice.

Third, harms of recognition are examined, understood as a manifestation of cultural harm (Copson and Boukli, 2020). For Fraser (2000: 109), being denied recognition/misrecognized is a 'distortion of one's relation to one's self and an injury to one's identity'. This can be resolved by replacing the value patterns of the dominant group and undoing the 'institutionalized patterns of cultural value that constitute one as comparatively unworthy of respect or esteem' (Fraser, 2000: 114). Both the harms of demeaning representations and the struggle for recognition are crucial to this research. The identity of the families is challenged by those with power: their position as people who have been harmed is minimized, experienced as double victimization (Shover et al, 1994), and their attempts to question the process and alter the outcome are dismissed. They are treated as nuisances who are posing unnecessary questions, not in pursuit of the truth but because they want personal recognition, or they are unwilling to 'move on' and so on. They are misrecognized as the powerful refuse to acknowledge their responsibility for their actions, 'a defining characteristic between the powerful and the powerless' (Tombs, 2020: 131).

This is organized abandonment, 'an amalgam of racist ideologies and class spite' that for Bhandar (2018) was manifested in the Grenfell Fire as a 'callous disregard for the value of human life, the calculated indifference towards working class and racialised people that characterise the actions of politicians, policy makers, and corporate lobbyists who have pursued a de-regulation and privatisation agenda at any cost'.

The notion that the victims in this research had a choice to live and work somewhere else overrides the decisions made by powerful actors that neglected to keep them safe (Gilmore, 2007). The targeted neglect and structural forces that operate behind the deaths is felt by those who question the invisibility of those who cause the harm in the first place.

Finally, autonomy harms will be examined. These can result from role deprivation and the 'performance of roles that remain largely unrecognised and unrewarded' (Pemberton, 2016: 29). While for Pemberton (2016: 29) this refers to contributions to society that are unrecognized, here it relates to secondary victims whose actions are invalidated, affecting their 'self-worth and self-esteem'. Crucially, it relates to 'the ability to *control* the circumstances that have a direct impact upon people's lives' and 'remain powerless in significant decision-making processes' (Pemberton, 2016: 30, emphasis in original). Autonomy harms examine the consequences of secondary victims being prevented from flourishing and controlling their own lives (Canning and Tombs, 2021). In response, they blame themselves for the lack of justice, turning the focus on to their behaviour.

Physical, emotional and psychological harm

Chapters 2 and 3 detail the aftermath of a total of 188 deaths, the gravest of physical harm. Most of the people were pronounced dead at the scene after violent deaths that should be of interest to the media, according to the principle that 'if it bleeds, it leads'. However, most of those whose deaths are detailed in Chapter 2 barely made the local newspapers and did not evoke outrage among the general public. Details of how each person died should not be catalogued as a gratuitous record, but the context of what happened, and the individual at the heart of it, is crucial. Behind the machinery was the manager, the chief executive officer (CEO) and the corporation (Dorling, 2005), and a consideration of this is crucial to corporate and safety crime. Whatever 'render[ed] them vulnerable to premature death' (Bhandar, 2018) is integral to the physical harm they experienced. The physical harm was the most serious, yet how the person died reflected their treatment in life in relation to the powerful.

In life, as in death

The treatment of the victim prior to death relies upon the 'devaluation of human lives, the lives of those without social-cultural and economic capital'

(Bhandar, 2018). This does not only appear at the time of their death but is evident during their life and in the immediate aftermath of their death.

The victims who were killed at work were manual workers at the lower end of the hierarchy. Most were working as subcontractors on jobs that relied upon physical work located away from home. Following their deaths, the corporation largely dispensed of them. Those who died did not have relationships with their employees that stretched beyond the exchange of a wage, and once they had died, this relationship was either immediately abandoned or ended shortly thereafter. For example, corporations sent wages to the families of their loved ones, omitting to pay the victim for the day of their death. Though seemingly shocking, it was a common occurrence. Others facilitated visits to the site or set up an award in the name of the victim; however, this did not last. There were more examples of callousness, such as the director who compelled workers to wash the blood of the victim off the sacks of product so work could continue around his body. Despite being someone who 'worked fucking hard' (Carole) and '[w]hatever you asked him to do, he would get on and do it' (Ian), little care was extended or guaranteed to the family after their sudden death.

The same men who were being killed in unsafe industries made up most of the spectators at football matches in the 20th century and took 'resulting fatalistic attitudes with them into their leisure' (Johnes, 2004: 142) – while the football ground was unsafe, it was good enough for the average football fan. A survivor of the Hillsborough Disaster summarized, saying football stadiums were 'reminiscent of Dickensian England or a Russian gulag, where supporters were treated like animals being herded to the slaughter' (Ashton, 2012). Held in pens and forcefully searched in exchange for being a spectator at a football match, fans were not supported by any legislation. Instead, the police sought compliance from clubs, who resisted pressure for intervention from the local authorities out of fear it would lead to disproportionate spending (Johnes, 2004). Measures put in place prioritized fans as hooligans over and above keeping them safe which led to the deaths of fans as demonstrated in the Popplewell Inquiry, which found that ahead of the Bradford fire in 1985, fire extinguishers had been removed out of fear that fans would use them as missiles. Fire exits had been locked in the name of crowd control (Johnes, 2004). In death, too, evidence was sought to pursue a narrative of drunk and hooligan Liverpudlian fans. Dorothy Griffiths, the sister of a victim of Hillsborough, commented that seeing the details of the blood results from victims in the paper during her lunch break, including children, led her to think fans were seen as 'sub-human in some way' (Jones, 2017: 43). Treated like animals in life, there was a similar disregard in death. The dehumanization of those with less power increases the likelihood of mistreatment and lack of prosecution against such treatment.

For those killed in custody, a 'racist culture' de-personalizes those detained, which results 'in a lack of empathy and respect' that puts their 'safety at risk' (Monaghan, 2015: 18). This is pertinent for people under the control of guards who are legislated to use force, such as Jimmy Mubenga. Webber (2014) writes that as a foreign national offender with a record, Jimmy Mubenga was 'as far down the social pecking order as it is possible to be', dehumanized not only by the guards but by 'other politicians and media', making any support of prosecution even less likely. The reference to the use of force as 'carpet karaoke' speaks to the routine nature of legislated violence and casual disregard for others. Christopher Alder came to the attention of the police as a victim who had been knocked unconscious, yet 'right from the start they treated him more as a perpetrator' (Alder and Glazebrook, 2024: 123). Rather than viewing him as an injured party, the Independent Office for Police Conduct (IOPC) report said officers had a 'readiness … to assume the worst' (Hardwick, 2006: 331). It continued: 'The grim conclusion I have reached is not that Mr Alder mattered enough to those who dealt with him – but that he did not matter enough for them to do all they could to save him' (Hardwick, 2006: 31). Adrian McDonald's brother referred to the 'horrific injuries' he suffered in the hours before his death because he was bitten by a dog and tasered – 'he asked for help, nobody thought he needed medical assistance' (INQUEST, 2018). Both were disregarded in the final minutes of their lives and suffered physically, under the care of those with more power, whom they had no control over. This is a 'general disdain for all [the executive's] fellow human beings', specifically related to race, that is 'no less evil than one who kills for passion' (Reiman, 1998: 68).

Gareth Myatt had suffered from racist bullying and lived in care for five years prior to his imprisonment (Willow, 2014). His experience was typical of those children in care who Mr Justice Munby said had 'suffered abuse or neglect … permanently excluded … [with] a history of mental health problems … no educational qualifications … homeless' (2015 cited in Janes, 2018: 43). His mother recalled that he was confident as a child, which changed when he started school and came home upset; people would wait outside his house and shout racist slurs (Smith, 2007). After his death, an MP said the following about Gareth Myatt: '[H]e often came to my advice surgery. He was an extremely difficult child, but he was tiny … he was a shrimp of a young man. *He was so small that he hardly existed*, and he was frenetic. He was like an eel' (Hansard, 2007, emphasis added). In life and in death, Gareth was de-humanized by those with power over him. The ease with which labels can be applied to those with less power serves those with power. The mother of Aisha was racially stereotyped before she was pregnant and after the death of her daughter. Referred to as a gangster by her offender manager during the inquest, she 'was viewed not as someone in need of care and compassion but as a discipline and control problem. Her calls for help went unanswered, and her pain was ignored' (Race Equality Foundation, 2023). More than just a label applied, it contributed to extreme harm.

Of the continual de-regulation leading up to the Grenfell Fire, Bhandar (2018) highlights the 'glaring absence' of those people who would be affected, the 'racialised, migrant, working class, those living with disabilities, single mothers – in their manifold intersections, are rendered absent, invisible and worthless in the minds of those making the decisions'. This reproach, both before and after the fire, was summarized by a resident of Grenfell when speaking to the leader of the council: '[T]he culture that you promote is the same culture that brought Grenfell into being. Because you don't listen, you don't care' (C4 News, 4 November 2017, cited in Tombs, 2020: 127). '[C]olonial relations' were 'variously renewed in the twenty-first century' (Wright, 2023: 139) in both the existence of Grenfell Tower and the subsequent fire.

This silencing and dehumanization continued after death – those who matter so little that there is a chance the circumstances of their death will not be investigated at all (Tombs, 2005). And if their subsequent death is subject to a full investigation, it is highly unlikely that anyone will be held accountable. The existence of any legal process is enough to defend 'accusations of institutional injustice' (Webber, 2014). The treatment of those killed in their final moments affected those who loved (and love) them.

Secondary victims

More men are affected by safety crime because of their dominance in manufacturing occupations (Tombs and Whyte, 2007 cited in Croall, 2010); up to 90 per cent of victims are men (Matthews et al, 2012). After their death, it is women who are most likely to suffer the short- and long-term effects of a sudden death as widows and mothers of children. In all but one case, women were interviewed in this research.

The effects of sudden and violent bereavement were life changing. The families spoke of their lives as two distinct periods: before their loved one died and after. Friendships were lost – they referred to people crossing the road to avoid having to pass or talk to them, for example. Those bereaved found solace in unusual places and with people whom they were not close to before, as illustrated by Sarah, who referred to her child's reception teacher – a 'lovely woman' who attended to her son's feelings around the cremation, for example holding a burial for a class goldfish when it died, as well as texting Sarah every day and leaving tea on the doorstep. Sarah reflected: '[S]he has got me through it really. She is the one that has spent the night here on three anniversaries.' This may be true of any bereavement following a sudden and violent death; however, there are two points crucial to this research. First, these were avoidable deaths, and, second, the official response to these avoidable deaths was suppression, which caused further harm to those who were already suffering.

The way the families were treated in response to a safety crime and the death of the loved one had huge effects that exacerbated long-term behavioural and emotional consequences characterized by anger and injustice (Matthews et al, 2012). This was at a time they had experienced a sudden and traumatic death and were vulnerable to depression, post-traumatic stress and cancer (Matthews et al, 2012). Being treated poorly by the criminal justice system is an injustice that compounds this suffering (Scraton, 2009). Any sudden death is traumatic, and any additional exceptional circumstances only add to this pain.

'Theatre of law'

As in the case of Scraton's (2009) research, the families of victims were tortured by an official process they had no choice but to enter. The law did not deliver the truth or justice but additional pain and humiliation. The families' expectations of the legal system were crushed by the 'theatre of law' (Scraton, 2009: 246). This supports Yvonne's recollection of the court:

> The [defence] barristers just ran rings around them and the witnesses; they said that the witnesses lied on the stand so why weren't they held in contempt? … [N]othing was done … not so much to me but two of Jason's brothers [who] were in that court … [T]hey were given no consideration, the way they watched me being treated.

As with Robert's parents, who, Angela vividly describes, 'brought him into this world, he was a late baby, she had him when she was 40 odd that they don't have to right to know what took him, or what could have been done to avoid taking him out?' The victims had families who were not only personally hurt but also watched other loved ones in pain.

There were occasions when the families felt the process was trying to 'demoralize' them, as Ian recalled:

> We stayed in because we weren't part of the jury so we could hear the legal argument. Then [we] had to be taken out … The Family Liaison Officer [FLO] said:
>
> 'We've got to tell you this, the defence is going to bring up the fact that [your son] asked the ambulance driver if he was going to die.' We didn't know that at the time. We were upset but were told

> to be prepared for it when it [came] up. We went back into court, and nobody even mentioned it. It was just another ploy. Something to get you out of the room, try and demoralize you then bring you back in again.

The families felt manipulated, their emotions controlled by those who did not love the victim.

Families referred to it as a game in which they were used. Gary and his family were moved around the court, and people from the corporations made 'snipes' at them and their FLO. To see their loved one forgotten in the legal process wounded them as secondary victims. Angela claimed the main victim was

> treated as though they were unimportant: It matters that there was a man in the middle of this … [At] every stage of the proceedings the person and the families are forgotten, absolutely forgotten, the prosecution has got nothing to do with the fact that somebody had died [and it] became apparent every day.

She made her feelings clear when she concluded her partner 'had absolutely no chance in that workplace and he [had] no chance in that court'. Aside from the failure of the process to deliver justice, a number of families pointed to the mistreatment they suffered when the victim, their loved one, was treated inhumanely after their death.

Callousness

In the courts, the corporations focused on establishing their innocence, with little regard for the families. Ruggiero observed that '[p]owerful offenders develop their own collective super-ego informing their practices, their views, expectations and interactions with others' (2015: 53). This 'super ego' was empowered by time and the treatment of officials; the powerful offenders in this research were emboldened by the court procedures to pursue profit. For example, it is standard practice for fines to be reduced following a guilty plea and for plea bargaining to take place. When Angela witnessed this, she was disgusted and insulted, partly because the fine already seemed paltry and to argue over it was a further insult. Yet any decision taken by the company not to enter negotiations in the court would have been outside of the realms of what the law encourages and expects. Had the individuals in the corporations chosen not to attempt to reduce the fine imposed by the court, they would actively have forgone profit, against the central goal of any company. Through their legal representation, the corporations were expected to be at their worst, which the family had to witness. For example,

Jason's family witnessed legal representatives being thanked for 'getting them off' as everyone left the court. No one considered how she might feel seeing and hearing this, and no one had to.

In the same court, Yvonne described her own frustrations, believing the official she dealt with had 'no conception of what it's doing to us inside in our heads, in our hearts'. Attempts to redress the imbalance were not warmly received. Elizabeth described how, when she became upset that the coroner was referring to her son as a number throughout the inquest, he 'kept saying [my son's name] then … he said [addressing me], "well I've now said your son's name 12 times, I hope that suffices"'. Elizabeth had to express it was 'hard enough that we're here', yet her appeals for her son to be humanized were met with clever replies.

Margaret expressed that she wished she had been treated better by the head of the court: 'Just that would've helped, I think if the coroner hadn't treated us like we were criminals … and not treated us so harshly, which they did, it was harsh.' Yvonne became increasingly upset by the proceedings and how her son had been forgotten in the process. She retaliated by printing out photographs of her son with his daughter and taking them into the court because 'that was my way of saying, this is a person … they have got a face because in the court the person who has been killed is not treated as a person … he is a person, can you remember him? I will never let you forget what you have done.' The victim was not at the heart of the process, and the families suffered as they bore witness to this; when they attempted to alter it and compel humane treatment, they were rebuffed.

As was reflected in Rock's (1998) findings following homicide, the families in this research were manipulated with little regard for their emotions or how this might have a long-term effect on the relatives. They were not considered by the court, for example they were given nowhere to sit in the court after waiting years to hear the cases (Yvonne). Their loved one had already been killed, yet the court, in the words of a bereaved father, 'assassinated' them (Gary). It was the family who left the process still bereaved, without justice and further wounded.

Janet Alder reflected that the trial victimized her and made a 'total mockery of my brother's life' – 'having to watch it felt like abuse' (Alder and Glazebrook, 2024: 107, 200). Throughout, she heard 'sniggering' and 'giggling' from other police officers (Alder and Glazebrook, 2024: 183) and felt pressure from those who 'so patently resented me and wished I would just go away' (Alder and Glazebrook, 2024: 141). She was not treated as a family member of a victim, as demonstrated by the barristers for the defence looking at post-mortem photographs in view of the gallery: 'It didn't matter what the truth was, they did and said what they wanted with no shame, and we as a family couldn't do anything about it' (Alder and Glazebrook, 2024: 143). Family members of those who had died had no choice or power in the court, and the legal proceedings caused them short- and long-term harm.

Ripple effect

The absence of their loved one altered the lives of wider family members, which, in every case but one, involved young children. For the mothers in this research who were grieving themselves, they also had to respond to their children who were at increased risk of consequences that could disadvantage them for many years to come (Matthews et al, 2012). Partners were open about the problems they had experienced and how they coped with the case:

> I had to teach myself how to face every day … I could see my teenage daughter was self-harming … because she had fallen out with Robert the night before, I also went back to work after six weeks because we needed a wage so I was kind of … off my face. (Angela)

This research generally spoke to one family member, but it can be supposed that as in Matthews et al's (2012: 651) research, people changed irrevocably: '[W]hen he died, Mum went with him.'

Children who had otherwise been well behaved changed character. This was the case for Sarah, who had to respond to this as well as having another child and a newborn baby:

> Then I had [my son] playing up at school, terrible, questioning your authority all the time. He's the oldest and the one affected by it, very affected by it. So, I have got him getting into fights at school, not doing what the teachers are telling him to do which is all out of character. So, you are trying to deal with that and the new baby. It is just very, very difficult.

They had to cope with their own bereavement as well as the reactions of other family members and friends. This made any fight even more difficult. The corporations did not help with any of these consequences, as Heather noted when describing how her daughter had been in the car when her father had been killed: '[T]hey didn't care my daughter was screaming every night, having nightmares.'

Delayed – pushed to insignificance

Grief was exacerbated by the huge delays. The families waited on average over two years for the inquest, and in that time, they had to deal with a lack of information. Research in Matthews et al (2012: 657) described it as 'like one person crying in the wilderness'. A survivor of the Grenfell Fire described the wait as 'torturous', keeping them on a 'carousel of waiting, waiting for justice' (Symonds, 2022). Louise Brooks, whose brother was killed in the Hillsborough Disaster, described the delay, sacrificing decades of her life, 'as hell' (Jones, 2017: 78). The father of Seni Lewis described it as being 'drawn out and it has effects on us every day – especially when people are trying to delay the issue' (Justice for Seni, 2016). This pain could not be expressed anywhere publicly and certainly not at court. The families were not expected to show emotion; Carole was given the impression by officers that 'it was so wrong of me to be emotionally upset'. A daughter of someone who was killed at Hillsborough recalls: 'For years we have been ignored … we were told that we had to leave the courtroom if we felt anger and if we couldn't control our crying … that was one of the most difficult parts' (Jones, 2017: 50). Something highly emotional was tightly controlled by those who were unaffected, and sometimes directly, as was the case when the coroner said to a victim's stepfather, 'I don't know why you are upset he wasn't even your son' (Jones, 2017: 44). Others guarded their emotion to avoid letting the 'bastards see what they've done to you again. Don't let them see what they've reduced you to' (Sampson, 2017: 195). The family of Ian Tomlinson expressed similar frustration: '[W]e haven't been able to talk, we just want to let people know how we feel. We are grieving' (Lewis, 2009b). Emotion was tightly controlled, and the expression of it was used against family members, as Brenda Weinberg, whose son, Brian Douglas, had died after being struck by police, warned Janet Alder: '[I]f we become emotional that is used as evidence of a negative characteristic of Black people' (Alder and Glazebrook, 2024: 68). Their actions were scrutinized, just as their loved ones were – they were 'damned if they did, damned if they didn't'. Grief, frustration and horror at what they had to witness was prohibited and judged, in addition to bereavement.

Sudden and violent deaths are more likely to lead to mental health problems in women, those recently bereaved and in cases where the person who has died is young and a close loved one (Kristensen et al, 2012, cited in Matthews et al, 2019). In addition to mental illness, physical illness was a common side effect, and many of the families were in and out of hospital with diseases ranging from stomach problems to cancer, which led to premature death. Family members who had campaigned for years became ill and died prematurely, including one person interviewed in this research. Jane was hospitalized after her son's death with 'nasty stomach bleeds' and spent her time in hospital writing letters to various people asking for information. Sheila Coleman commented at one of the Hillsborough appeals, 'I remember looking across to Anne Williams in her wheelchair and thinking, "This is what you've done to this woman"' (Sampson, 2017: 317). Janet Alder was taken to hospital for asthma attacks throughout the trial (Alder and Glazebrook, 2024), an additional harm to respond to on top of grief and emotional turmoil.

For those affected by the Grenfell Fire, the effects are devastating – harms that result from grief, reliving escape, witnessing others who did not and survivors' guilt as well as navigating an uprooted life (Tombs, 2020). In addition to this, those affected had this trauma intensified by the complete disregard of their lives and those they cared about, as Lowkey (2018, cited in Charles, 2019: 185) puts it:

> How can you expect youth that saw their friends, that saw the expendability of their lives directly demonstrated to them to not become nihilistic, it's, it's an inevitability; not everyone. Some people use it to motivate them to bigger and better things, moving forward and enjoying and appreciating the good in life but other people, you know, especially in the first year and a half have got nihilistic about things, they don't see any possibility of accountability.

The 'violation of trust that creates distrust' (Sutherland, 1940: 5) has widespread effects that the families must suffer. Sarah moved house to get away from memories of the night she was treated inappropriately by the officer, forced to relive an additional trauma that could have been avoided. Gareth Myatt's mother, who expected her son to be supported at Rainsbrook, lamented: 'What I have heard has deeply upset, angered and shocked me. I loved Gareth so much and my life will never be the same' (INQUEST, 2007). The families of the victims and survivors of Hillsborough were tormented by 'serious questions about the institutional, structural and embedded deficiencies in the law and its administration' (Scraton, 2009: 246). While emotional and psychological harm are 'difficult to measure' (Hillyard and Tombs, 2005: 20), families involved in corporate and state crime reported a multitude of problems that go beyond loss, supporting Sutherland's belief that white-collar crime is more likely to 'tear at the core of a social system' (Geis and Goff, 1983: x).

Financial and economic harms

The affordability of justice

Many families had lost the main breadwinner and therefore had to pay for a funeral and a wake with little or no compensation. They then faced the legal process and found they were in the difficult position of not being able to afford legal representation, access to court documents (which strengthened their ability to fight) and simple practical requirements such as the ability to pay to travel at peak times during their working day. This was juxtaposed against the company, who had comparatively little difficulty in hiring legal representation secured from insurance, getting access to photocopies of court documents and being able to appear in court without fearing for their own economic livelihood. Justice appears possible, it appears fair, but in practice there is an imbalance that is felt by the families, as Mathiesen notes: 'The freedom which exists is in principle open to everyone. The point is, however, that in practice only those who in fact have the resources required to use it can take advantage of it … [T]he freedom which exists formally is reduced to a freedom *for dominant interests*' (Mathiesen, 1980: 113, emphasis in original).

The support of legal advice was crucial in interpreting the procedure of the court and rebalancing 'unequal interactions' (INQUEST, 2023: 10), and without it, the rights were another obstacle – for example, the families were not aware they could have their own medical representative at the inquest and were not informed or found out too late to use this right. Their needs were disregarded. The right existed and could be pointed to as evidence of fairness; however, as in the Protocol of Liaison, their rights existed only on paper, useless to the people who needed it in what were to become life-changing moments.

Families were surprised that they needed legal representation at the inquest. They wondered how it was going to be paid for, and it was an additional debt after the loss of the breadwinner. Most families relied upon money from unions, either via their membership or the victim's. One found a person to represent them pro bono, and two benefitted from a now defunct charity that provided legal representation. Heather intended to secure legal representation but had to represent herself because she was given less than 24 hours' notice of the date of the inquest. This was contrasted with the corporation, which was given notice and had arranged to fly the CEO over via helicopter. The Coroner's Office did not offer to move the date of the inquest and instead offered their apologies.

In the absence of money, the families had to get into debt just to participate in the process and meet the minimum requirements of the court. Carole paid £3,800 for representation at the inquest, describing it as a 'trap … they should have legal aid … appoint a solicitor to represent the person that died'. In response to the decision of the Crown Prosecution Service not to prosecute, the families were told they could launch a judicial review, but this relied upon money. Jane launched a judicial review and applied for legal aid but was not aware that this meant any assets she had were at risk, including life insurance, saving schemes and her house. Even after the judicial review had been won, she was responsible for covering the solicitor's costs, which amounted to £8,500. This would have cost her even more had she not asked for the receipts from the opposition's solicitor who had claimed for taxis when he cycled everywhere. She compared her own position to that of the wealthy: 'I'm absolutely broke, really have no money … and yet

Maxwells and the Guinness' have it.' This was a case that benefitted from donations, including from a union that donated funds even though Phillip wasn't a member of any union.

Other families wanted to launch a judicial review to hold the corporations to account but could not take the risk; all were advised against this, including Diane, who paid a solicitor £250 per hour to tell the family it would be 'foolhardy'. No one could find out how much it would cost so they could even consider it. Like many others, Carole did not have access to money to push the case further and reflected: 'To be honest, would we have gone any further? I think we would have if we'd had a bottomless purse.' Whereas families knew they would have to find the money for a judicial review from somewhere, for example re-mortgaging their house, Heather reflected that it would be easier for large corporations, which could 'just put an extra penny on the beans' to challenge the coroner's verdict. Those affected by relatively small, less-profitable corporations still felt they were financially disadvantaged because they had more assets than the families and were in a better position financially to bring about justice.

Money was linked directly to power and class. One of the owners of a corporation paid for the costs of Paul's funeral. Yet when the prosecution attempted to prove at the inquest that the victim had died because of a mechanical and not operational fault, the owner referred to the money he had spent. Gary recalled that in court the owner shouted: 'I've done everything for them, I've paid.' For him, his ability and willingness to pay for the funeral led to outrage when his company was questioned in court. Paradoxically, wider family members assumed the next of kin had received a large compensation pay-out and were hiding it (David). This draws parallels with Spalek's (2006) research.

The inequity between the families and the potential perpetrators continued following the Hillsborough Disaster and the deaths in custody. Even though the defence was a public body, many were shocked that the police force and other bodies had access to public funds whereas the prosecution did not. One barrister represented 43 families, which contrasted with the police, who had access to public money for their defence. Information was released to the police four weeks before the families saw it (Jones, 2017). At Christopher Alder's inquest, the coroner had funded a barrister for the family, which was 'unprecedented' and for which they were elated; however, the police benefitted from a barrister for each of the five officers involved in the death as well as one each for the health authority and ambulance trust (Alder and Glazebrook, 2024: 88). A woman whose loved one had died in custody reflected how access to legal advice had allowed her to exercise her rights, and that without it, the autopsy would have been carried out without family representation (INQUEST, 2023). Good legal advice was crucial, yet families were often told that legal representation was 'either unnecessary, or "up to you"' (INQUEST, 2023: 9).

None of the families had the luxury of not worrying about finances when faced with the death of their loved ones. The potential to secure justice seemed to be available, yet the lack of funds for the defence, which contrasted with the wealth of the defendants, was another obstacle that one family in this research and the survivors and families of Hillsborough overcame. To find the money for a judicial review and private prosecutions, they had to fundraise and rely on the charity of others. The unequal access to justice reflects the lack of recognition that safety crime has received in the law. What exists is symbolic; 'Even if the law is broken, it is clear whose law it was' (Gusfield, 1967: 178). As secondary victims, they were doubly disadvantaged. Not only did they not have the finances that the corporations had but they were also emotionally connected to the victim and faced with a corporation whose 'corporate personhood is actually to depersonalise the human consequences of the corporation: to remove its human content' (Tombs and Whyte, 2015: 85).

Harms of recognition as a manifestation of cultural harm

Nuisance when not invisible

The de-humanization the families endured served to deny them victim status and push them to invisibility. The families were stereotyped or stigmatized, and what they thought they knew to be true about their loved one was questioned and erased, replaced with the dominant values of the corporation, legitimizing the power held over them (Pemberton, 2016). Focusing on legal definitions of crime rather than harm permitted this (Pemberton, 2016) – for example, the truth was silenced and evidence dismissed as inappropriate at the different stages the families had to navigate (Smart, 1995). Their status as family members of a person who had been killed was invalidated: for example, they were no longer a mother with the sympathy and rights this entails but seen as a nuisance, not permitting professionals to do their job out of their own self-interests.

The families expected their needs would be met or at least protected in the legal process, but instead many left the process distraught. One wife asked: 'Who represents the person who died? Nobody does, absolutely nobody' (Angela). The families had a minimal role in the proceedings, and as such they were 'not always silenced, but … how they are allowed to speak, and how their experience is turned into something the law can digest and process, is a demonstration of the power of law to disqualify alternative accounts' (Smart, 1989, cited in Ballinger, 2003: 221). When the families expressed their confusion and sought answers, at any stage, they were seen as problematic.

Police officers initially approached the families as they had the crime scene: keen to leave, viewing what happened as nothing to do with them. When the police were questioned, the families were met with dismissal – for example, officers impressed upon them how busy they were (Elizabeth) or ignored them (Gary). Denied status as secondary victims, when the families attempted to influence the process in some way, for example by challenging officials to ask relevant questions, the professionals involved responded defensively and without concern for their welfare:

> [T]he Crown Prosecutor took us to this room and got really nasty … I asked questions … I … said somebody was killed on their site three months after Jason, 'why wasn't this mentioned?' They looked shocked; the Crown Prosecutor … he asked, 'Where did you get it from?' So [my son] piped up and said, 'Off the internet last night.' [The Crown Prosecutor] then turned to me and said, 'We don't really have to speak to you because you are nothing, you are only his mother and you are nothing, we don't have to tell you anything.' (Yvonne)

Their questions were met with contempt, while state agencies put their priorities ahead of the needs of the victims and their families (Scraton, 2009), including protracted delays. If the families asked questions, they were unnecessarily interfering in areas they had no business in:

> I started being … the woman who was 'awkward', because I was asking questions … I was a nuisance, I was interfering, why didn't I let them go and do their job? I mean we had no rights … There is still that brick wall there … obviously there's more questions because I keep saying why and [the police] say, I shouldn't ask why. (Carole)

Elizabeth's grief and dogged pursuit of the truth while challenging the coroner was interpreted as pathological: '[H]e [the coroner] told them that I was unhinged and in need of hospitalization … they should completely disregard what I was saying, that I was not sane.' Pathologized, she was no longer valid as a grieving mother but seen as abnormal.

Those considered as the 'defence' may not think about the decisions they made once that day is over, whereas the families were left to mull them over. When called to account for those decisions, officials showed their lack of understanding further, unapologetically placing additional blame on to the relatives and discrediting their needs. For example, for wanting to touch and see her son, James, after his death, Elizabeth was described as 'obsessed' by the coroner, and the basic needs of a mother wanting to see her son were disregarded. A brother of the victim said he would never return to England after the court made his brother 'nothing' (Jason). This compounded the problems that came with bereavement and sudden death.

Pressure and frustration

As secondary victims, the families were vulnerable and had their own lives to continue with, lives that had been irrevocably changed. The future was challenging due to their bereavement without the additional de-humanizing process they found themselves a part of. Heather was angry about the work she had had to do to pursue her case:

> [N]obody knows what pressures are on you and the frustration and anger of it all that are on you, nobody knows, as far as I'm concerned, me as a widow shouldn't have to do that, it should be automatic, the system is in place that when somebody dies, a company has killed them it should be automatic that it's thoroughly investigated, you as a widow shouldn't have to research corporate manslaughter, you shouldn't have to seek the people out and say, 'hang about now, I don't agree with this, it should be this, this and this'.

Families who fought for information to alter the trajectory of justice were seen as an obstacle to the process of the court. Those who refused to be silent were punished, not only by officials but by their peers. The memories the families had in the long aftermath were stark, despite any time that passed, as this family member articulated: '[T]here's no justice for a life … I still cry over the way we were treated and the way the dead were treated. They had no rights, so don't talk to me about justice' (Scraton, 2013: 16).

The families who continued to pursue the truth after years had passed were criticized for refusing to 'move on', purposefully halting grief and refusing to accept 'reality'. Dorothy Griffiths described how she and others affected by Hillsborough were 'dismissed' as 'moaning. I have heard this said many times – it was time to let go and grieve for our relatives rather than just going on about it' (Jones, 2017: 22). The anger and hurt they expressed was seen as being a show, an indulgence that was both performative and self-serving, as summed up by Boris Johnson, who declared in the *Spectator* in 2004 that 'Liverpudlians self-defined "as victims"' which they 'resent' yet 'wallow in it' (Scraton, 2019). Observers label those who are in pain as causing their own problems. Irrespective of the ongoing truth about what they are going through and what is being done to them, it is not what happened to them, or the lack of justice that is the problem, it is their reaction that is causing problems. Further, these are problems they are causing themselves and others, including their own family. This assumes that if they would only move on, everything would improve. If they would be silent, everything would be better. They are expected to ignore their feelings being disregarded – for example, when Liverpool played Sheffield Wednesday at the Hillsborough ground in 1998, they arrived to find the match was sponsored by *The Sun* (Sampson, 2017).

This blame was not empowering to families who had not 'thought' themselves into the situation they found themselves in. They had been thrust into sudden grief, the kind many will thankfully never experience. They had to fight for information and navigate a legal process where their loved one, the victim, was misrepresented. For family members, the suppression of the truth and witnessing their loved one being blamed was de-humanizing and affected how they saw themselves as parents, wives and children of the victim. Further, as they looked for explanations, they blamed themselves.

Autonomy harms

Autonomy harms are those that 'result from role-deprivation and a lack of recognition or reward. Importantly, control over one's own circumstances and value [is] integral to human development or emotional wellbeing' (Canning and Tombs, 2021: 59). In this case, the families have no control over their circumstances, and yet some blamed themselves for the lack of justice.

Although difficult to comprehend when faced with families who have been through so much, it was evident that many blamed themselves in different ways. This is summed up by a mother of a victim of the Hillsborough Disaster:

> Why was I so weak? All these guilt complexes going through your head. That one time in your life when you needed to be with your son … You've brought him into the world, for Christ's sake, you needed to see him out. Why the hell wasn't I strong enough to say all this? They were powerless. (Scraton, 2016: 155)

After witnessing their loved one being blamed in the court, they felt partly responsible for the outcome, as a failure to honour their loved one. Elements of their de-humanizing treatment were viewed as within their control (Scraton and Chadwick, 2009), that they could have changed the outcome, or an element of the process, by changing their behaviour.

Honouring their loved one

Carson (1982: 296) detailed the voice of North Sea worker Richard Walker who had written in his diary on the morning of his death that he feared he would not survive. Hearing from victims, voices like Richard's, is unusual. We do not know what they experienced in the months and minutes before they were killed and they cannot defend themselves. Without the gathering of evidence and an adequate case for prosecution, those in power can control the narrative. Blaming the victim suited the needs of the company, and the costs were passed to the families of victims of safety crime, who experienced double victimization, exacerbated as they endeavoured to defend the memory of their loved one (Shover et al, 1994). For the families, their desires were not linked to recovering financial loss or protecting a corporate reputation but as the last action they could take for their dead loved one. As Angela articulated it: '[Y]ou're slapped down … you always think, this is the last thing I can do for him … [crying] sorry.' The emotions they had to deal with because of their bereavement were amplified as the memory and intentions of their loved one were attacked.

The families did not want nor expect to be in the position in which they found themselves. They expressed that their grief had been compounded by legal processes. Yvonne turned to her son, the brother of Jason, and commented, 'I have to do something here as they are just making my son a nothing.' The loved one they knew was not the person they had seen created in the court: 'That wasn't a bloke that was seen there that day, they were virtually saying he was irresponsible' (Heather). Instead of finding and revealing the truth, the court had, as Gary commented, killed his son again: 'Life will never be the same. It's an assassination of that person.' He said he wanted the court to know what was not being represented, what was stripped away: 'That was a person that had a life and has left people [who] loved him.' The long investigation and the obstruction by those with power 'due to legal privilege' exacerbated post-traumatic stress disorder and prolonged grief disorder, which the families had no control over (Matthews et al, 2019: 7).

The process had failed to hold anyone accountable – its success had come at the expense of their dead loved one as a blameworthy victim, as summed up by Carole: 'I didn't want it to seem like it was all David's fault and that was all we came away with.' David was viewed as cavalier with his life:

> [Y]ou would like them to care enough about their own life because it's caring about theirs [their children] because what's been done has hurt them, it's hurt me, it's hurt them … [I]t was like they were all trying to blame him … because no one wanted to pay out a big lump of cash, we didn't want to blame him for another reason, that's the thing [crying].

This not only sullied the truth about what happened to David but also a truth about his life:

> But it's the other side, there's nothing worse than somebody trying to say it's your fault, that's what it felt like, and it wasn't like that because you had a bloke that was really good, that worked fucking hard and if he could've done something for you, he would've done it.

Families of the victims desired a guilty verdict, as Scraton (2009) remarked, not necessarily for punishment but to publicly find out what went wrong and to put it right. Every family returned to the need for the truth, to know what happened that caused the death of their loved one and for reassurance it would not happen to another individual and another family. This was intangible because official bodies either failed to see the truth as important or deliberately complicated it for their own gain. The families found themselves fighting to maintain the innocence of their loved ones who were judged to be culpable in their absence after their death. They had to navigate the obstacles built into the criminal justice system as well as the inhumanity of the company that sought to establish their innocence by establishing the guilt of the victim.

They had to respond to bereavement and experience the lack of justice, and some took on the responsibility for themselves. As one group of families affected by safety crime summarized how they had been treated: 'Just like other victims of crime … our hearts have been torn out of our chests. The difference is we are not seen as, not acknowledged as, and not supported as the victims of crime that we are' (Families Against Corporate Killers, 2006). Families found their voices restricted and controlled and articulated that they felt disempowered when their opinions were not considered and the truth was left unexplored (Williams, 1999). In some cases, the families of victims fought back, for their own cases and for the rights of future victims.

Altering their behaviour

As in Scraton's (2009) research on Hillsborough, the quick decisions made by state agents caused the families to blame themselves for not challenging enough. Denied by officials, the families of the victims chastised themselves for trusting the authorities, considering their individual case might have ended differently had they taken more control. This added to the frustration, hopelessness and fear victims feel following traditional crimes (Spalek, 2006). Although they had little role to play in the 'theatre of law' (2009: 246), the legal proceedings were personal, as Jane puts across with the use of 'we' in the following quote: '[A]s soon as I heard his [the judge's] closing speech, I thought we'd lost it.' The reactions were one of huge disappointment and trying to come to terms with what had happened and to wonder if they could have done more.

Angela linked the lack of truth and the way she was treated by the police to her own politeness and agreeability:

> I went through a stage where I thought that if I had been different to the liaison worker, if I'd been nicer, I thought if I'd been nicer, would it have made a difference? [Crying] Sorry … I felt terrible, terrible guilt as though I hadn't done Robert any justice, but I didn't know

> what I was supposed to have done but I felt as though I should have done [something differently].

Actors in the court had little emotional connection to the victim and were less invested in how they were portrayed in the court. This was very different for the family members, who saw this as their chance to show their loved one how they felt about them:

> [Y]ou always think, this is the last thing I can do for him … [crying] sorry … It's hard to say, I think if I could go back I think I'd [have been] more, what's the word? More pushy and more aggressive, which I couldn't have done at the time, looking back you think you can do things, I think we should have. (Carole)

These effects were long lasting. The families took on an unreasonable amount of guilt as a result of the legal process they had been thrown into. The guilt and pain endured long after the formal process had ended and was apparent when I spoke to the families some three years or more after the official process. It is impossible to say whether this will dissipate or worsen in the decades that follow.

What was normal procedure to corporations and legal professionals was bewildering and confusing to the families in this research. Rights they had, for example being able to view their loved one at the morgue, were often denied, which led families to blame themselves: 'I don't know why I didn't stand there and say I need to see him properly' (Jane). Edna Murray, whose son died in the Hillsborough Disaster, had similar thoughts: 'They were behind glass. I didn't question anything that happened. Why didn't I? I didn't understand. We were not allowed to touch them' (Jones, 2017: 17). The daughter of a father who was not allowed to touch his dead son described it as something which 'broke his heart and his spirit' (Jones, 2017: 9).

Most of the family members blamed and chastised themselves for trusting official agencies, and for not doing more themselves. For example: 'I put all my faith in our justice system and that was so ignorant of me' (Yvonne), and even though many realized 'there was nothing else you could do' (Carole), the guilt that they felt in hindsight, that they ought to have realized earlier and acted differently on behalf of their loved ones, remained long after the corporations had been found innocent. This was inextricably linked to their own autonomy, despite the reality that they were not in control of the circumstances within which they found themselves.

Janet Alder was told directly that 'if I wanted to have continuing liaison with the prosecuting team then I should consider more carefully how I put my comments to them' (Alder and Glazebrook, 2024: 203). The mother of Gareth Myatt feels she has failed her son because no one has been held accountable for his death (Willow, 2014). Similarly, a daughter of a victim of the Hillsborough Disaster considered the peace of her father to be her responsibility: 'I only hope my father can rest in peace knowing that I did everything that I possibly could to be his voice and make sure his truth was heard' (Jones, 2017: 38). A mother referred to what she owed her daughters: 'Now that they have been found unlawfully killed, I owe it to my daughters to get accountability, otherwise it would have been better never to have had the unlawful killing outcome' (Jones, 2017: 87). It is hard to understand how a bereaved parent or sibling would take any responsibility for what has been done to them, but it was a common theme and resulted in the most emotional responses from family members.

Conclusion

This chapter considered the effects of the suppressed truth and the push for the victim to be invisible using a social harm framework to partly redress this under-researched invisible crime (Davies et al, 2014). Physical, emotional and psychological harms were explored, both those that led up to the death of the victims and the treatment of their families who navigated the legal process. As Chapters 2 and 3 documented, the families had to endure a protracted process which sought to silence the truth of what led up to the death of their loved ones. Their calls to change this were silenced in favour of the de-humanization and blaming of the victim. Chapter 4 demonstrated how this process created secondary victims of the families and worked to push any potential perpetrators away from punishment. After their death, families had to endure the theatre of law (Scraton, 2009), which worked to find the perpetrator innocent and their loved one blameworthy.

As 'assassinated' victims who were unwelcome in the procedure, they suffered additional and unnecessary harms. Children of the victims began experiencing the effects of grief, which the mothers had to cope with in addition to the legal process. The delays prolonged the pain of not knowing what happened to their loved one, all of which led to illness. Attending hospital appointments added to the distress and harms experienced by those already dealing with the sudden loss of a loved one. Family members' identities were affected as harms of recognition; their questions about the injustice of the process were rebuffed by those in charge, who, in turn, questioned their motives, wishing instead for their silence.

The chapter established that family members questioned their own behaviour and whether justice could have been achieved had they acted differently. Even though they had no control, many still became very upset and expressed that they should have done more. This is an autonomy harm that was the ultimate consequential harm, following being silenced, then de-humanized. By ignoring the harms of safety and state corporate crime as not within the remit of criminology, the discipline too becomes complicit in this silencing. It contributes to the belief that the state will protect future victims. For example, an article looking at the *Titanic* disaster expresses disbelief at the callousness of owners of the liner who portrayed themselves as victims, reassuring readers that '[i]f it happened today the owners would very likely have been charged with corporate manslaughter and have to pay out tens of millions of pounds in compensation' (Enoch, 2020). The notion that those who die at the hands of corporations leads to harsh punishment and resplendent compensation requires continued challenge. Several families mobilized to take up this challenge this on behalf of future victims. This, and the links to social harm and zemiology activism, will be explored in the Conclusion.

Conclusion: Alternative Social Arrangements as the Counter to Invisibility and Harm

Chapter 5 considered the harms caused to families as secondary victims when they witness the suppression of the truth and are pushed to invisibility. The de-humanizing treatment led some to blame themselves and question whether they could have done things differently to alter both their treatment and the outcome. This chapter examines the response of secondary victims when they create or join groups to support and/or alter the representation and treatment of other victims in order to 'Remember the dead and fight for the living', as encapsulated in the slogan of the campaign group Families Against Corporate Killers (FACK). The chapter will demonstrate why and how families, and those concerned, have mobilized collectively to form groups in response to the obstacles they encountered, including the suppression and de-humanization identified and explored in the previous chapters.

This chapter challenges Sutherland's reference to the white-collar victim in relation to their 'weakness' against the 'power' of the white-collar criminal (1940: 9). This positioning of the victim is in keeping with the context of criminology during Sutherland's time: concerned with the perpetrator and finding the causes of crime to enable reforms of the criminal justice system (Scraton, 1987). In the decades that followed, critical criminologists have worked with survivors and families of victims to push for change and in support of each other. In this way, they fought back. This chapter will look at the various responses of such individuals and the successes linked to groups including the Centre for Corporate Accountability (CCA), Disaster Action (DA), the Simon Jones Memorial Campaign (SJMC) and FACK. Families and survivors who are harmed may be pushed to be invisible, but they do not accept this (Copson, 2011). Groups have intervened and found solace in connecting with others to challenge the system they encountered (Pemberton, 2016). Many do, at the worst time of their lives, fight to make themselves heard, as part of grassroots organizations (Canning and Tombs, 2021).

Organized resentment and weakness of victims

Where Sutherland had struggled to maintain focus on white-collar criminals, groups started by bereaved families, with support from academics and activists, demanded the attention of the press and the government. Their testimonies 'were transformed into public issues' and were a 'spur to … political action' (Rolston, 2000: 319). A number of families of victims and survivors have been instrumental in resisting the treatment they received via the creation of campaigns in response to the Hillsborough Disaster, deaths in custody and Grenfell.

As discussed previously, it was the efforts of Jimmy Kelly's family, together with several other families whose loved ones had been killed (Blair Peach and Liddle Towers), that led to the creation of INQUEST (Ryan, 1996). With input from MP Michael Meacher, they listed the changes they wanted to be made (Ryan, 1996). INQUEST continue to carry out casework directly with those bereaved, campaign, gather knowledge that is widely used (as in this book) and work towards social justice. They continue to operate independently on the government, relying on external funding.

The month after the Hillsborough Disaster, the Hillsborough Family Support Group was founded by and for bereaved families. In 1998, members left this group to join with 'Survivors and Supporters of Justice for All' to create the 'Hillsborough Justice Campaign' (HJC) following the collapse of the Stuart-Smith Inquiry and calls for a private prosecution (Sampson, 2017). This group set up a shop across the road from Anfield and sold campaigning materials such as 'Don't Buy *The Sun*' stickers (Road, nd). In the early 1990s, Anne Williams set up 'Hope for Hillsborough (for Justice)' to raise funds and awareness and to seek justice (Cooper and Lasley, 2021: 13). This group became a part of the HJC prior to Anne's death. Those affected worked hard to keep 'alive the names and memory of those who had died' (Sampson, 2017: 181). Fundraising continued, with concerts and high-profile public figures donating money and time. Key matches were boycotted and mass protests organized including the singing of 'Justice for the 96' and holding up a mosaic that spelt 'The Truth' for six minutes at the start of an FA Cup match against Arsenal in 2006. This was in protest at Kelvin MacKenzie, who was the editor of *The Sun* when it printed a front page that wrongfully vilified survivors and victims of the Hillsborough Disaster. MacKenzie was due to appear on the BBC after he appeared at an after-dinner event in November and repeated that *The Sun* had told the truth and that he was not sorry (Sampson, 2017). Peter Hooton, a survivor of the Hillsborough Disaster, recalled that public opinion began to turn in 2011 because of 'a campaign that started with meetings in back rooms and flyers outside the ground, but now it was instant news with Twitter and Instagram' (Sampson,

2017: 286). The families have now joined together in a coalition made up of activists, leaders and people who all want justice under the umbrella of 'Hillsborough Law Now'.

Community groups had mobilized prior to the Grenfell Fire. Website and blogs already existed, including the Grenfell Action Group, which formed in 2010. Charles (2019: 175) notes that the fire happened in the midst of other grassroots campaigns, and years after the Grenfell Action Group had raised concerns about fire safety. After the fire, a number of organizations united through a 'shared pain that has "entwined lives in a substantial and sustained way"' (Charles, 2019: 177). Grenfell United was created days after the fire and works with INQUEST to fight for justice, articulating what many families in this research also felt: 'We are still fighting for change. It's a battle because we are fighting against a government, a system, institutions and corporations that do not care … Grenfell was no accident, every single death could and should have been avoided. Those responsible must be brought to justice' (Grenfell United, nd).

Similar to the existing groups in the previous section who respond to deaths at the hands of public institutions, there was a moment in time when there were many groups that mobilized around safety crimes relating to private institutions. These will be detailed in the next section.

Collective struggle and refusal

The pain the families in this research experienced was unnecessary and cruel. In order to save the company from an unlawful killing verdict or the directors from a manslaughter conviction, the family had to be forgotten. The truth they desired had to be suppressed to find the company innocent. This increased the pain they experienced as their loved one was misrepresented and blamed. The legal system they had expected to represent their interests took control further away from them (Christie, 1977; Walklate, 1989). They found little comfort in official state processes, and many left the legal system stunned. Rather than finding out their experiences were unique, some families discovered there were many other victims and families who had experienced the same or worse. Not all of the families affected by safety crime created or joined groups, but there were some in this research who met with others to work for a common cause to counter the suppression they had experienced (Williams, 1999).

Many families found that the extreme emotions they experienced because of their grief and anger were too huge to do nothing, that they were 'inescapable' and left untreated could have 'become destructive' (Eyre and Dix, 2014: 21). Bereaved families spoke to others, found solace in working collectively, and campaigned out of a need to refocus their feelings. All of the groups acted in direct response to the justice system. All felt the legal system had not delivered appropriate justice and joined with others to change the system for future victims. Had the justice system represented their interests, the movements would not have been created or would have had very different aims.

The aims of collective action

The aims of the groups were centred on changing the social, legal and political landscape to prevent other people being victims. As with support and campaign groups in general, the legal system had failed or was failing their loved one. They were under represented, which they sought to change (Goodey, 2005).

All of the groups had very similar aims. First, they saw what had happened to those killed because of safety crime as preventable and wanted the law to change so that corporations would be held accountable. The groups used their collective power to call on the criminal justice system to respond (Miers, 1985). Second, for many of the groups, this meant ensuring the current law that existed worked to its full capabilities. Third, the majority of the groups wanted to support others who were bereaved. These three aims represent what had been lacking for the bereaved families. Their success or otherwise in achieving these aims, and whether they counteracted the invisibility of safety crime, will be examined in the next section. Every group attempted to change the law, to ensure the law that existed worked and offered emotional support to the families of victims.

Challenging hegemony, changing the law

The victims of safety crime were isolated and suffered the effects very personally (Tombs and Whyte, 2015). They remained lone voices that state agencies did not pay attention to, as one mother expressed: 'He [an employee of the Crown Prosecution Service (CPS)] was just fobbing me off and we knew this' (Yvonne). This altered when families combined with others who confirmed and legitimized their struggle. With others, they found themselves in a position where they could demand more. A member of one group reflected: 'It is much easier for the Government to fob off single individuals than family groups with a clear and determined purpose' (Dix cited in Eyre and Dix, 2014).

Groups such as the CCA, DA and the SJMC were active in the period between the Corporate Manslaughter Law being proposed in the 1990s and it becoming legislation in 2007. As groups, they represented the interests of families and friends of victims and survivors, which included those created in the high-profile disasters in the 1980s and 1990s. These disasters raised public awareness and press interest, which the groups responded to and together, as part of the corporate accountability movement, called for a change in the law (Tombs and Whyte, 2003c). Though promised when Labour was in opposition, the Corporate Manslaughter and Corporate Homicide Act 2007 took 13 years to become law, which Tombs describes as a '13-year struggle' (2013: 65). During that time, government regularly consulted those who could be prosecuted by the law such as the Confederation of British Industry (Tombs, 2013: 65) The groups featured in this research existed as a counter to this, even though their views were not sought officially. In particular, the CCA followed the law closely, writing to the agencies directly, raising issues in the press and continually trying to engage the government. The CCA effectively pressurized the government through the Health and Safety Executive, highlighting the truth using statistics and the testimonies of families as well as comments ministers had previously made to attempt to hold them to account. For example, David Bergman, director of the CCA, commented in the national press: 'The government agreed four years ago to reform this archaic law' (Bergman, 2001: para 11).

When the Corporate Manslaughter Law caused conflict between groups because of the proposal to introduce immunity for crown bodies, the centre sought legal advice and stood in solidarity with other groups rather than splintering and dividing the individuals involved. Together, the groups were able to act in opposition to government and business groups that supported de-regulation. For a time, they challenged corporations and government claims of science and fact and engaged in crucial counter-hegemonic research that interest groups are rarely able to do. Their existence set an alternative to dominant narratives that attempted to undermine the existence of corporate harm (Snider, 2003a).

As part of a dominant group, corporations were able to deny facts and claim their interests were more legitimate than the claims of workers and families (Tombs, 1991). This was countered by the visibility of the corporate accountability movement, who in numbers called for change and raised awareness. The groups were 'knowledges from below … it is the reappearance of what people know at a local level, of these disqualified knowledges that [make] the critique possible' (Foucault, 2003: 7, 8). This is similar to the testimonies of the families in the interviews in this research, which 'brings into play the desubjugated knowledges' (Foucault, 2003: 11) that have been purposefully hidden or dismissed. It is rediscovering truths that have been lost, truths the victims and families of victims have had to bear. Though the state may refuse to acknowledge they exist and resist legislation, their appearance and presence countered this. As a collective, they were better able to represent the interests of the victims that continued to be created through state inaction.

'Recent social movements opposing corporate capital are important and may signify an end to quiescence' (Snider, 2003a: 64), notably in the ways their existence points to truths that are counter to what members of the public believe to be true, for example that corporations are over-regulated and frequently sued for minor mistakes. As part of a social movement, the groups could question why they were not consulted in the creation of the Corporate Manslaughter Act, drawing attention to the disparity, something that would otherwise have gone unquestioned.

The influence of campaign groups has been noted by researchers following the collapse of the Rana Plaza factory in Bangladesh in 2013 in which over 1,100 people were killed (Reinecke and Donaghey, 2015). In the aftermath, a coalition of groups was created that supported the unions. This led to an agreement between brands, unions and the campaign groups that should increase the safety of workers, which only came about because of 'the heat they feel from unions and campaigners' (Hazards, 2015: 8).

Ensuring the current law works

Groups such as FACK and DA operated to ensure the law as it existed worked as intended. By understanding and interrogating rights, they attempted to ensure that the lack of power of individuals and the lack of knowledge of state agents would not lead to further injustice. A large part of this was raising awareness of safety crime and countering the invisibility many families suffered from. To change the construction of workplace deaths as accidents, groups tried to be as visible as possible (Williams, 1999).

The most visible group was the SJMC, which made activism a central part of their campaign, scaling cranes, shutting down major roads and handing out literature to raise awareness of recent issues related to safety crime such as the dangers of working for a subcontractor. They engaged in high-visibility campaigns and were expressive at various points, for example on the victim's birthday when they forcibly shut down the agency and company who employed him. In similar ways, FACK campaigned on workplace deaths in general. They tried to reach workers by encouraging employees to join unions. As part of a group and by connecting with others, they were doing exactly the opposite of what they had been encouraged to do as individuals.

Providing emotional support

One of the biggest successes the individuals involved in the various groups had was in reducing some of the de-humanization they experienced through the criminal justice system. Families met with others who had had similar or worse experiences. Isolated as individuals, most did not know of anyone who had had similar experiences. Many families became excluded from their previous lives in numerous ways as their families and friends failed to understand what they were going through. The opportunity to create or join a group offered them a chance to create new bonds after their lives had been irrevocably changed (Williams, 1999). Together, they could influence the process in ways they had been prevented from doing so previously: 'What I have gained is a sense of satisfaction for being able to use my own tragic experience to make a difference to the lives of others' (Watkins quoted in Eyre and Dix, 2015: 116). Matthews et al (2019) found families greatly appreciated such groups because the support was coming from people who had experienced the same loss rather than the authorities or other members of their family who were also affected.

They did not need to explain to the people in the group how they felt and were not expected to have moved on. They were not judged or silenced by friends who grew uncomfortable but were able to discuss what had happened to their loved ones without shame and could share their memories without worry. The families found the way their loved one was portrayed in the court was not unique, that it was not personal to them but personal to the nature of the crime committed against them. There were others who had all experienced much the same process, which was of comfort to some members of the groups but also increased feelings of anger and hurt.

Measuring success

Success is difficult to measure. The members had given up large amounts of time, money and their own emotional well-being to be part of various groups. None wanted to belong to such groups but were compelled to become members because of their experiences. Individuals can campaign for years, attract new members and grow in influence (Best, 1999).

The opposition the groups pose lasts as long as they are active. The CCA were a force in the ten years they operated, more so as they grew in experience. They ran conferences that facilitated a wide network of people who connected and shared experiences, creating a wealth of information that was not being collected anywhere else, including the gathering of information on individuals killed at work. Connections with press, the HSE and ministers all halted once they closed, and the case workers, who had cases still open of families dealing with bereavement, gained employment at other organizations. That niche expertise could never be applied and utilized within other organizations as it had been wielded in the CCA.

The SJMC had much success in pushing forward the case of one victim, and it was because of their collective effort that the case was heard in the Crown Court. It had been taken as far as possible, and the parents of the victim recognized this when they concluded: 'It is no surprise that [the Director] James Martell waddled away; the miracle is that he was ever in the dock' (Hodge, 2002: para 18). The SJMC was unique because it was a highly active group made up of the victim's friends who were of a similar age (in their 20s and 30s) and created out of a pre-existing network that the victim had been a part of. The members were sure that the victim would have approved of their campaigning methods and would have done the same in their position. However, that level of campaigning would have been very difficult to maintain. Being a member of a highly active group takes a huge amount of emotional, physical and financial effort. For some, it delayed their grief. After the SJMC ceased to operate, one member expressed: 'Looking back, I wonder if I didn't get much chance to grieve because I kept on fighting … at points it was knackering' (Brooks, 2002: para 20).

DA started every annual meeting with two questions – 'has Disaster Action met its objectives?' and '[s]hould the organisation continue to exist or is it time to call a halt?' (Eyre and Dix, 2014: 167). Presumably, the members of DA decided in 2014 that the answer to the second question was 'no', and the publishing of *Collective Conviction* in 2014 was a significant part of their legacy. They reflect in *Collective Conviction* that only three of their funding applications were successful. As Dix stated in 2015: 'Disaster Action had accomplished all it could, especially given constraints around volunteers' time, availability of funding and the need for individuals to make changes in their lives' (Dix, 2015).

For members of such groups, this was not an issue of delaying 'closure' – families talked about how their lives would never be the same, and nothing would change that. For example, one father of a victim said: 'Even when we're enjoying ourselves … there's this guilt', to which his wife interrupted 'we don't really ever enjoy ourselves, nothing is the same' (FACK, 2010). However, being part of a group does require being around other people who are bereaved, other people who have been through a de-humanizing process and the feelings of anger that injustice evokes. For example, one father of a victim said that while he is involved in FACK, his wife has always been reluctant to share her feelings and commit time to such a group. Many, very naturally, move away after a period of time.

Those groups which had success in altering procedure could be linked to the extent they are connected to the government, as in Rock's (2002) study, where the methods of two groups were very different. One group in Rock's (2002) research encouraged the use of marches, whereas one worked with the Home Office. Clear differences could also be identified in the groups in this research. For example, DA maintained neutrality and were invited by the government to advise authorities on emergency planning response. In contrast, the campaigning nature of the SJMC was successful and raised the visibility of the case of the victim, but this also meant its members were never going to consult with or act in conjunction with the government (nor did they want to).

In different ways, both DA and the SJMC reached the government. On a singular issue, the SJMC did so very quickly – for example, on one occasion 30 members of the campaign blocked Southwark Bridge in London until the then head of the HSE agreed to speak to them. DA were 'consulted by the statutory and voluntary services on how people's practical and emotional needs can best be met in the aftermath of disaster', described by a retired assistant chief constable 'as that of "critical friend"' (Eyre and Dix, 2014: 141). While both groups had victories, neither was able to stop politicians 'brushing away' deaths like Simon's or see 'fundamental changes in the law and in business attitudes' (Eyre and Dix, 2014: 38). This was not a reflection of how hard the groups worked or what they sacrificed to support others but indicative of the political obstacles between a safety crime and justice.

In a newspaper article and their book, members of DA point to a success of the new law governing corporate manslaughter. When the Home Secretary introduced the second reading of the Corporate Manslaughter Bill in 2006, the passing of Maurice de Rohan, the chairman and one of the founders of DA, was marked (Eyre and Dix, 2014): 'The degree to which Maurice de Rohan, personally, and Disaster Action as a whole, succeeded in influencing government thinking is reflected in the remarks made by the then Home Secretary' (Eyre and Dix, 2014: 97). Unfortunately, what became the Corporate Manslaughter and Corporate Homicide Act 2007 has been described as a 'disappointment' (Gobert, 2008: 413), 'conservative in form' and, crucially, 'unlikely fundamentally to change efforts to hold corporations legally to account for workplace killing' (Almond and Colover, 2010, cited in Tombs, 2013: 65). There is evidence that 'one form of liability is being exchanged for another' (Tombs, 2013: 70) as corporations offer to plead guilty on corporate manslaughter charges if impunity is granted to individual directors (Tombs, 2013: 70).

The tenacity of the groups and their existence is a threat to social order. The extent to which they can have a voice has a positive effect on a neoliberal landscape that puts the priorities of profit and enterprise above the lives of individuals. There is no doubt that all of the organizations detailed in this research had an impact upon this landscape while they were active. The CCA is unable to challenge the HSE – it can no longer draw together key actors in the arena of health and safety or support family members in their fight for justice. Even though for ten years it answered Ann Elvin's desire for a helpline for those bereaved following a death at work, the centre also closed, as did the Relatives Support Group that she managed to create in the early 1990s. Currently, there is no number for relatives to call when they need help, and holding the HSE to account is now reliant upon the efforts of individuals working with charities and labour organizations such as the Institute of Employment Rights. Although it remains the case that '[r]egulation in the UK is under continued material and ideological attack'

(Tombs, 2013: 11), the defence mounted to halt this has diminished since this research began.

Together, the groups covered in this research were part of the corporate accountability movement from 1980 to at least 2010. This has countered invisibility and reduced some of the harm enacted by the justice system. They have not overcome the huge political obstacles which provided the impetus for their creation. However, their existence was and is crucial to stand in opposition to the dominant discourse, and the support they offered survivors (in the case of DA) and secondary victims is incredible.

An objective of zemiology is to challenge the harm caused and further social justice. 'If criminology began its life in the service of the state', zemiology is focused on 'challenging state power, and those agents and institutions which bolster and are supported by that power' (Canning and Tombs, 2021: 139). This involves activism and being 'a part of the solution rather than a part of the problem' (Canning and Tombs, 2021: 149). It is about using any position to support campaigning groups, social movements and individuals, from speaking in lecture theatres to protesting. All but one group featured in this chapter has now ceased to exist, but all have left a large footprint that should not be lost – open web pages, memoirs, DVDs, contributions to Select Committees. Action is necessary to ensure this is viewed collectively, to come together as part of a wider movement that constructs 'a new common sense' by 'highlighting the scale, consequences and origins of … social harms' (Tombs and Whyte, 2007: 13). Such groups lead the way and are at the forefront of resisting suppression and de-humanization.

Conclusion

Half of the family members went on to create or join groups to do something in the name of the loved one they had lost. The various groups that have been created by families, angry and frustrated at their own experiences, were examined. Many involved were able to remove or remedy some of the obstacles they had experienced as individual, bereaved family members. What they changed were the experiences of others going through the process – for example, reducing their feelings of isolation and guilt and helping them to resist suppression at every stage. To sum up, by working in a group, the families refused to become invisible. What they did not manage to change, despite overwhelming evidence, indicates what the state is willing to permit and whose interests matter the most. Change to address safety crime requires 'both political will and financial investment' (Berrington et al, 2003: 144), which the government shows no sign of providing. Instead, in a neoliberal market hegemony (Tombs and Whyte, 2003a), the system designed to respond to safety crime would prefer to 'sacrifice rather than realise … the principles of natural justice' (Scraton, 2009: 267). What was left – regulation – continues to fail to set the standard for justice and the fair treatment for the victims of safety crime, their families as secondary victims and in the deterrence of future safety crime victims.

Safety crime, as is the case with the presence of economic crime in crime, law and order agendas, 'requires consistent effort to keep it there' (Alvesalo and Tombs, 2002: 29). The groups examined in this research put much force and determination into doing this. They were consistent at being conspicuous, refusing to sit quietly and acquiesce to invisibility, as much as they were nudged by the official response. The groups were consistent too for the period they were active, which for all but one group has now come to an end. There is 'enormous positive potential' (Williams, 1999: 137) for the movement to continue, and the need for this has unfortunately only increased in the period since this research finished. Health and safety legislation has continued to be attacked, work has become more insecure, legal aid has been slashed and almost all of the groups featured in this research no longer exist. For the movement to continue, the families will need to work collectively with each other, finding commonalities with each other and with critical theorists who have a duty to highlight injustice and push for change, as Mathiesen observed: 'It cannot take place from the writing-desk alone' (1980: 301).

The seed for this book began with the realization that my loved ones were not as safe as I had assumed and that if they were killed at work, no one would be held responsible or punished. I had imagined there might be a reasonable explanation for what had led to the death of Sidney Rouse. If not, then it must be a major oversight that professionals would be rushing to put right. Life was not that cheap, surely? After speaking to the families in this research and listening to the testimonies of people I will never meet, I understand the truth is far more mundane. Summed up simply, the reason for the lack of justice for Sidney's death is the same reason his death occurred. The criminal justice process can never respond to it because it was designed to convict the relatively powerless. When faced with Sidney's sister, the process seeks her silence, but in the absence of that, it suppresses the truth of his death. As families are subject to a process that is demonstratively banally ineffective, they are further harmed, during the worst time of their lives. Then, as the ultimate final act, the process of invisibility leads the families to blame themselves for letting down the person they have lost. This is the cruellest of autonomy harms, making it almost impossible for families to return to their lives, not only bereaved but unable to 'flourish in ways that they choose' (Pemberton, 2016: 138).

The extent to which we can exercise choice on the corporations we encounter is limited. Irrespective of unemployment rates, we are unlikely to be privy to statistics on safety, nor seek them out when applying for jobs. Similarly, when corporations successfully bid for public contracts, as members of the public, we have no opportunity to refuse to be processed by those handed that power: we cannot ask for another corporation if we are taken into custody, residents of local authority housing cannot choose who clads their homes, and fans cannot decide who manages their entrance into a football ground. Corporations 'affect or … *infect* every part of our lives', and the costs fall on the most vulnerable (Tombs, 2015: 18, emphasis in original). As a steeplejack, Jason suspected the work he was being told to carry out was unsafe but was sent back into the chimney to his death; as residents in public housing, the occupants of Grenfell predicted the fire, and when it started, they were told to remain in their flats. Liverpool fans pleaded with the police as they went in and out of consciousness, as did Jimmy Mubenga when he appealed to the guards while he was being restrained. All of them recognized what was happening in the final moments of their lives but were denied the chance to change their fate by those with the power to help them. And after their death, the truth of what led to their death, both years and minutes before, was suppressed and their families de-humanized.

The state does a good job of discovering many crimes annually, crimes that make up a contemporary catalogue of 'monsters', including sex offenders, gang members, drug kingpins and violent-crime recidivists, whose existence forms an unending loop of renewed rationale for legislative action (Simon, 2007: 77), while other criminals, including rapists and corporate criminals, are highly unlikely to be prosecuted (Temkin and Krahé, 2008) but are free to cause more harm. Yet this has little effect on the fears of the public or the priorities of the state; indeed, it only becomes a political issue partly due to activism (Larcombe, 2011). The difference between common crimes and the crimes of the powerful is presented as such for good reason – the 'conditions are as they are', corporations demand respect from the public and do not evoke fear (Mathiesen, 1980: 86). Corporations and the state commit acts of harm, but they are not viewed as potentially criminal, even after harm has occurred.

As Box (1983) noted in *Power, Crime and Mystification*: 'There is more to crime and criminals than the state reveals. But most people cannot see it' (Box, 1983: 15). We do not see that we are three times more likely to be killed at work than murdered by another at home or on the street. Media coverage raises the fear of cyber-crime, altering our behaviour and leading to avoidance or the buying of personal surveillance devices such as the Ring doorbell (Brands and Van Doorn, 2022). Money is spent on protection we are unlikely to need, making billionaires out of those who market products that are 'tough on crime', allowing homeowners to protect 'themselves from intruders' (Kelly, 2023: 96). Wages are spent on monthly subscriptions that aim to arm people against the threat of common criminals, with little protection offered to mitigate the risk posed by powerful perpetrators who can cause greater harm.

The main way for workers to protect themselves is union membership, which is resisted by corporations, including Amazon, which bought the Ring doorbell for $1 billion. In 2025, managers at the Amazon site in Coventry held anti-union seminars and increased the number of disciplinary actions against employees following a ballot for recognition that was seen as 'clearing out what they see as troublemakers' (Hazards, 2025). Not wanting to cause trouble at work and a belief that we are overly protected at work continues to reduce union membership. Most of the families in this research did not question whether their loved one would be put in harm's way. Luke was 18 years old and relatively experienced for his age. His father, Ian, having worked with him for a year, knew Luke would be an asset to his next workplace, finding him to be 'a good little lad'. Crucially, as a young apprentice, his father knew that '[w]hatever you asked him to do, he would get on and do it. He just wanted to please.' The desire to be a good worker and being keen to please as a teenager starting out work, his father recognized he 'wouldn't have questioned … if he was told to give this manager a hand, he would have gone off and done it'. He was killed doing what was asked of him and helping his manager who assumed a position of trust and power.

Those with power and in positions of trust betray trust regularly; accordingly, we should fear that more than we do and move some focus away from common criminals. The research included in this book could have drawn on numerous deaths of individuals who have been killed by those with power who are not found in our prisons and never will be. We need to be sensitized to the ways we are victimized and the ways in which this affords benefits to those with power as an alternative to being 'seduced into seeing such processes as "disasters", "accidents", or "unavoidable incidents"' (Box, 1983: 223). The commonalities between these deaths point to a structure that causes harm, suppresses it and claims it is something else, located in the individual – whether that is the victim or their families.

Drawing parallels with feminist academics who look outside of the law to reduce the harm caused to women, a reduction of deaths caused by the powerful and the subsequent harms their families face is also not going to be found in the law (Ballinger, 2016: 130). The powerful are not considered potential perpetrators, as seen in the police leaving the scene immediately and/or the failure to collect evidence, the huge delays, the response of coroners and the inadequacy of the law even after a concerted and valiant movement for corporate accountability. It must be a one-off accident that was just unfortunate, with no apparent cause. If this receives push back, then it must be the fault of the person who died, as a blameworthy victim, and should the families argue against this, it must be because they too have a personal problem. An ideal victim (Christie, 1977) requires an ideal perpetrator, one who is not powerful but largely powerless.

If the worst happens, families 'want prosecution of culpable parties and clear actions taken to ensure others do not experience similar tragedies' (Matthews et al, 2019: 24). Yet the victims featured throughout this research had the slimmest chances of their families seeing justice. The powerful discourse that these deaths were accidental prevailed. It affected those working in the criminal justice system, from the police to the judges, who were reluctant to re-frame the potential perpetrator as criminals. For the officials, the powerful perpetrators had to be either victims of misfortune and witnesses to accidents, or invisible altogether from the act. This research argues that the judgements made or not made were not reflections of what happened that caused the death of the victims but were instead constructed that way.

Families countered this construction by joining with others as part of charities or campaigning groups. They resisted their invisibility and have created a legacy of resistance, testimonies and increased visibility, actively trying to prevent other people experiencing similar tragedies. People like Louise Adamson, who now speaks to corporations telling her brother's story: 'But we don't ever want it just to be another sad safety story. We know that it will help your organisation move mindsets, inspire action, and save lives' (Adamson, 2016).

Prior to her death, Pauline Campbell was arrested 15 times for standing in the way of vans trying to take more women into HMP Styal. Her campaigning led to the 'Corston Report'. These efforts are valiant, incredible and humbling; that in the face of such grief and de-humanization, families find strength to do what the criminal justice process failed to do. As part of the study of social harm and zemiology, academics have a duty to work with people like Louise and Pauline to collectively counter suppression and reduce the harm. Sidney Rouse's suffering was not inevitable, nor was it his fault. The circumstances that led up to his death and the official response are indicative of the society we live in and our position as citizens. We are not powerless in resisting the status quo, but in the absence of collective attrition, those with power will continue to benefit.

APPENDIX

Methodology and Research Questions

Research questions

The research questions developed from my confusion over what happened to Sidney Rouse and what failed to happen following his death: how could someone die so casually because of the action/inaction of a corporation, and why was no one held accountable to ensure it did not happen again? To explore this, the following questions were developed:

- What social, legal and political obstacles does safety crime face that prevent it from becoming defined and treated as a crime?
- How are the victims and families of victims of safety crime treated by law and key institutions of the criminal justice system including the police, inquests, the Health and Safety Executive (HSE) and the Crown Prosecution Service (CPS)?
- What effect does this have on the families of victims?
- Under what circumstances do families of victims seek to develop more general campaigns, with what aims and with what degrees of success?

Research groups

Research on secondary victims: interviews with families

Most of the families were contacted through a charity that was part of the social movement for corporate accountability. The Centre for Corporate Accountability (CCA) was a charity created by David Bergman, a journalist who had written a booklet in 1991 that detailed the death of Sidney Rouse. The full details on the CCA are covered in the Conclusion. One arm of the organization advised families on their rights and how they could ensure the HSE, the police and the CPS were fulfilling their legal duties. As part of this casework, they had access to 150 families. The centre agreed to identify a number of families whom they considered would be suitable for this research, that is, able and willing to discuss their experiences and with cases that are not ongoing. This resolved a practical issue of access but also overcame personal concerns I had about opening people up to the death of their loved one being considered a crime, which they may not have been aware of. The eleventh interview was chosen as a result of 'snowball' sampling.

Table A1.1 details families who were interviewed.

The names in the table are pseudonyms, chosen as popular names from the year they were born. They have been changed for anonymity and are used throughout the book to denote the remarks of each family.

Table A1.1

No	Pseudonyms of victim and family members	Age at death	Year of death	Job	Cause of death
1	Michael Diane and Peter (parents) Clare (sister)	20	2003	Electrical apprentice	Asphyxiation
2	David – Carole (ex-wife)	48	2003	Construction worker	Asphyxiation
3	Paul – Gary (father) and Liz (wife of father)	43	2005	Lorry driver	Heart attack following asphyxiation
4	Andrew – Heather (wife)	37	2002	Member of the public	Asphyxiation
5	Mark – Margaret (mother), Ken (husband of mother)	45	2005	Window cleaner	Fall from height
6	Robert – Angela (wife)	40	2005	Agency driver	Crushed
7	John – Sarah (wife)	53	2006	Volunteer	Asphyxiation
8	Phillip Jane and Steve (parents)	24	1998	Stevedore (unqualified)	Crushed
9	James Elizabeth (mother)	26	1989	Member of the public	Drown
10	Jason Yvonne (mother)	23	2002	Steeplejack	Explosion, fall
11	Luke Ian (father)	18	2004	Apprentice	Burns

In order to speak to victims of safety and corporate crime, Spalek (1999), Spalek and King (2007) and Matthews et al (2011) interviewed individuals, and the interviews were recorded and transcribed. These were useful and suitable models for this research, which sought to be led by the interviewees, collecting detailed rather than vast amounts of information. Hennink et al (2011) note that interviews are suitable when covering sensitive issues as they allow an examination of the context, reveal emotions and find the meanings people attach to their experiences (cited in Harding, 2013: 62). As a goal to 'see the world through someone else's eyes', face-to-face interviews were preferable over non-contact interviews, even if this poses a risk of bias and personal effects for the interviewer (Hennink et al, 2011, cited in Harding, 2013: 62). It suited my previous personal experience and occupation, which at that time involved encouraging people to be honest and open about their past painful experiences and share their anxieties about the future. In this, interviewing matched my capabilities and skills (Blaikie, 2004).

In a similar way that 'elite' interviewing is conducted with someone in a position of authority, the same could be said of the interviewees in this project (Gillham, 2000). While not in a position of authority, it became increasingly clear that the family members were capable of giving insightful answers and had a unique grasp of the subject matter beyond a recollection of events. For that reason, the interviews became less and less structured and control shifted carefully to the families, who could best convey their own perspective (Noaks and Wincup, 2004). For example, it was often the case that the interviews would begin with the prompt: 'tell me about your experience, starting with the moment the police first contacted you.' Prompts were still necessary for consistency, and to support the family members to recall where they were in terms of the narrative, but generally, the family members knew more about the topic and were able to structure their own knowledge and create the narrative (chronologically) as Spalek (2006) recommended. It was common for participants to divert on to other subjects, particularly to share memories of their loved ones, which I did not interrupt or cut short but increasingly encouraged.

Rapport and trust were developed through initial contact via the CCA, a telephone conversation and then contact in person (Leavy and Hesse-Biber, 2011). Time was given to introductions and general 'chit chat' rather than launching as quickly as possible into the interviews. As a female, then in my 20s, I tried to take a minimal role in the interview and simply listened, making as few prompts as possible rather than having a two-way conversation (Hennink et al, 2011). It was difficult not to agree or show (appropriate) exasperation at times; in a desire to be natural rather than cold and contrived, this was not purposely suppressed. Some attempt was made to connect informally with the interviewee to minimize any inequality that might have been felt (Hollway and Jefferson, 2000). It was important that the family member/s being interviewed should not have to feel their account had to be sanitized to protect me or become preoccupied with my welfare over their own. It was not easy to manage emotions when the people involved were clearly upset (Dickson-Swift et al, 2009), but it was essential to remain an attached observer. I felt strongly that the interview was the family members' experience, and little focus should be anywhere else; this research would not exist without their kindness, generosity and willingness to give up their time to recount the worst time of their life. My role during the time I shared with them was to listen as fully and actively as possible without causing unnecessary harm or centring my own needs and emotions.

The victims of safety crime in this research died between 1998 and 2007, during the time the CCA was open and prior to the adoption of the Corporate Manslaughter and Corporate Homicide Act 2007. While I did not want the sample to be purely based in my local county (in fact, none of them were), the wide geographical nature of the interviews, between Weymouth and Glasgow, complicated the practicalities of repeating many more. The interviews mainly took place in the homes of the families, around the dining room and kitchen tables. Two exceptions were interviews held in the social room of a rugby club and a workplace office. The families decided where was best for them, and I travelled for their convenience and to ensure they were as comfortable as possible. The interviews ended naturally, usually when the interviewees decided they had finished. There were many occasions when vital information was given after the interview had formally ended, that is, when the Dictaphone had been switched off. In those instances, I quickly made notes after I left the room. All of the interviews were recorded, with notes, and transcribed in full afterwards. This was a long process, as the shortest interview (with a family member) was 100 minutes and the longest was 213 minutes. The average interview length was 180 minutes.

Research on social movements: interviews, questionnaires and case studies

Methods for researching safety crime are underdeveloped worldwide, and so many of the problems connected to it remain unresolved (Tombs and Whyte, 2003b). Tombs and Whyte (2007) highlight two main difficulties researchers of safety crime have experienced, namely the lack of statistics available on the scope and nature of safety crime and the reliance upon extensive funding to collate the data. It is entirely predictable that corporations will resist research that seeks to uncover wrongdoing, complicating access (Noaks and Wincup, 2004). One way researchers have navigated such difficulties has been to study corporations through case studies of well-known, publicized safety crimes or those involving large financial loss or with many victims

(Tombs and Whyte, 2007). Punch (1996), Bittle and Snider (2006) and Tombs and Whyte (2007) utilized case studies as part of their research on corporate crime.

The second part of the data collection followed this route and utilized case studies with additional interviews and questionnaires. Four case studies were created using online resources, documents and in one case a book that two members of one support group had recently published to mark its closure. A further four individuals were interviewed for their connections to groups, one by Skype, one by phone and two through questionnaires, which they completed rather than being interviewed because of their own time constraints. Much of the additional information on the social movements came from webpages created by the groups to publicize their campaigns. During the progress of this research, the CCA closed, so it naturally came under examination. Before the centre closed, information was saved from their webpage as well as documents, such as newsletters. These were treated in the same manner as printed documents, since they contributed to both understanding of and a method of researching resistance.

Multiple sources were used to approach the case studies from a number of angles to verify the data (Yin, 2009, cited in Gray, 2014). For example, web resources were used with documents, newspaper reports and supported with the interviews of members of social movements. Information was sought under strict categories that could be replicated by another researcher.

While face-to-face interviews are preferable, four individuals were interviewed remotely due to practicalities and because they were adding to pre-existing information and filling in gaps that had been identified. Telephone interviews can be too focused on the aims and be time limited; however, the Skype interview proved more informal and an appropriate medium between face-to-face interviews and the telephone interview (Harding, 2013), which was more formal and minimized non-verbal feedback. The telephone was more suitable in cases that involved interviewing a solicitor rather than a bereaved family member.

Table A1.2 details those who were interviewed as part of the case studies.

Table A1.2

Number	Initials	Group	Interview address
12	LC	Solicitor	Telephone interview
13	DW	CCA	Skype interview
14	PD	Disaster Action	Semi-structured interview
15	BR	CCA	Semi-structured interview

Analysis

Thematic analysis was used for 'identifying, analysing, and reporting patterns within the data' (Braun and Clarke, 2006: 6). It was pre-determined that no interpretation should take place at the time of the interview to avoid inserting researcher bias into subsequent questions and to avoid a loss of focus in listening (Hollway and Jefferson, 2000). Interpretation was carried out post interview and sometimes afterwards with a view that critical social research should be reported as 'a story with a plot' (Harvey, 1990: 211). Each interview was transcribed in full to avoid any element of interpretation or the removal of the words of interviewees (Harding, 2013). It was important that nothing was missed and that the entire transcripts should stand without any initial interpretation. This meant the data could be used in a number of ways and re-read to check context, which happened many times. In my job at the time of the interviews, I was trained to highlight occasions when people showed heightened emotion, which I found myself doing during these interviews. This was useful upon reflection as it emphasized what really mattered to the interviewees, which could not be second guessed.

A number of themes were placed under the main topics after many readings of the transcriptions alongside the literature (Gillham, 2000). A theme was identified as something that was significant in the data and also related to the original questions (Braun and Clarke, 2006), although these did co-depend on each other. As themes were discovered, it was considered that any contradictions should be highlighted in the research and not determined by personal preconceptions (Harvey, 1990). The proposed themes were re-worked, or re-named to best represent the transcriptions, and attempted to link the statements made by the interviewees to relevant ideas within the existing corporate crime literature (Blaikie, 2004).

Ethics

Researching safety crime raises a number of ethical issues. These will be explored in this section using Gray's (2014) four considerations. First, harm could not be avoided – for example, care was paid, where possible, not to schedule the interviews on dates such as the anniversary of the victim's death. Case workers from the CCA spoke of families not wishing to be perceived as 'weak', so I did not approach them as such but emphasized they were to do only what they were comfortable with. Many family members had techniques for dealing with strong emotion. For example, one person intimated to her husband to explain about the formal identification process at the hospital, clearly negating a subject she found difficult. Second, the consent was open and transparent based on the presumption that individuals do not need to be shielded from the purpose of the research (Frisch and Watts, 1980; Gray,

2014). Nevertheless, consent was reiterated four times. Third, anonymity was ensured, and the recording materials were stored appropriately. It is true that some cases can be identified and that a description of events, places and people could lead to 'deductive disclosure' (Lee, 1993: 186). This requires existing knowledge of the topic as a whole, and in some cases it can be assumed that the individuals are not concerned with anonymity and would forgo theirs to reveal the identity of the corporation associated with their loved one's death. For example, there was never any self-censorship or questions asked by the family members about whether the names of the corporations would be removed. Some saw the interviews they gave as part of their opposition to the injustice they suffered, a chance to put across their point of view. However, the removal of names had already been assured in the ethics application to the university, perhaps a reflection that ethics has become more about protecting the identity of the researcher and the reputation of the university than those who are researched. It is true that it would be foolhardy and potentially litigious to include the names of the corporations involved, which would jeopardize the intentions of this research. By the nature of the research, the corporations in this research are unpunished and, therefore, *innocent*.

Other considerations were made as the interviews progressed that I had not considered during the initial design. Towards the end of the interviews, I was pregnant. In one interview, I was able to purposefully hide my pregnancy to minimize any considerations the interviewee may have had to my well-being and because I knew they had been pregnant at the time of their bereavement. Had they noticed, I would not have lied but felt it was something that did not need to be drawn attention to since I was able to conceal it. During two of the following interviews, hiding my pregnancy was impossible as I was heavily pregnant. While it was discussed by each family member in a natural manner and appeared not to affect the immediate emotions expressed, the participants may have considered I should be protected and altered their own behaviour. It is true, upon reflection, that these interviews were less 'emotional' than the others.

From my perspective, the initial interviews were followed by a feeling of 'numbness'. This could largely be negated with a period of quiet that often followed (for example, a car journey home or an overnight stay in a hotel). However, returning to the data after maternity evoked real emotion and sadness, which was difficult for anyone to understand as I was the only person at that point who had read the research. This was exacerbated when one of the people I had interviewed died prematurely. I felt great unease moving between listening to her recalling wonderfully fond memories of her loved one in one room and then immediately moving into the next room to be with my children and doing general tasks. Her insightful interview and clear anguish heightened the sense of injustice I felt that had provoked this research, mirroring the consequences of emotional work reported by researchers – 'difficulty sleeping, anxiety, gastro-intestinal upsets' (Dickson-Swift et al, 2009: 11). The subsequent personal questioning of the unpredictability and unjust nature of life contributed to anxiety, physical symptoms, visits to hospital and an endoscopy to investigate stomach pain.

The emotions I felt when I re-read the interviews added to my understanding of the events the family members had been thrown into. This does not mean I can speak for their needs or on their behalf. It does mean I am motivated to document their experiences as a testimony and a counter to commonly held assumptions about deaths at work; there is a responsibility to put these views across accurately and testify to their experiences. For some families, I was keenly aware that participating in the research was important. As the mother I mentioned in the previous paragraph expressed, 'I think part of the justice thing was also about talking to you, for me about doing what I think [he] would have thought was right' (Sarah).

Limitations and implications

Clearly, such a small sample raises significant issues of generalizability and representativeness. First, it should be emphasized that in one obvious sense, in fact, these families were not representative – they had in the first place been clients of the CCA. The selection therefore was in no way random and does not claim to be representative. They were selected by case workers at the CCA on the basis of their appreciation that they would be the least affected by a request to recount their experience. In this, these families may have been a sample who had come out of the process least victimized and most able to reflect upon it. These families had help in the form of an open and operational CCA, which they accessed. It has become very obvious that these victims had benefitted from that support. Second, as the interviews unfolded, it became clear that even across this limited set of cases, common themes emerged between the interviews, and perhaps most crucially, the stories and experiences elicited echoed the key themes referred to in the small amount of pre-existing research (Slapper, 1999; Tombs and Whyte, 2007; Matthews et al, 2011). This leads to doubt about whether what has been accessed was one set of rather anomalous experiences.

Case studies are criticized for not being useful for generalization and can take time to create using multiple sources (Gray, 2014). Situated as this research was at the end of the movement for corporate accountability, much of the sources have since been removed from open access or the books have gone out of print. They may be generalized, but they are specific to this time and highly valuable to document this particular period, which makes these case studies valuable, offering, as they do, in-depth information about a small subject matter during a specific era. Although case studies do not lend themselves to generalization, this is irrelevant for this research, which is focused upon insight and complexity (Blaikie, 2004).

In terms of omissions, as Matthews et al (2013) note, research is focused on English-speaking families and therefore produces a one-sided picture rooted in the Global North. There should be no excuses for this, particularly when it comes to migrant workers, who are more likely to be employed in insecure jobs without union representation. There are deliberate omissions relating to those who have lost a loved one and may have no idea that this would be viewed as social harm or corporate murder. These people are deliberately excluded for several ethical reasons. However, their existence as evidenced by the numbers of those killed at work is one to reflect upon and crucial for the final chapter of this book and ultimate invisibility.

References

Adamson, L. (2016) 'Michael's story: lessons from an entirely preventable death', Available from: https://thesheshow.com/michaels-story/

Addison, M. (2023) 'Framing stigma as an avoidable social harm that widens inequality', *The Sociological Review*, 71(2): 296–314.

Agozino, B. (2018) 'The withering away of the law: an indigenous perspective on the decolonisation of the criminal justice system and criminology', *Journal of Global Indigeneity*, 3(1), Available from: https://ro.uow.edu.au/jgi/vol3/iss1/2

Alder, J. and Glazebrook, D. (2024) *Defiance: Racial Injustice, Police Brutality, a Sister's Fight for the Truth*, Dialogue Books.

Aldini, N.C. (2024) 'State–corporate legal symbiosis and social harm: the case of the steel factory "Ilva" in Taranto, Italy', *Crime, Law, and Social Change*, 82(4): 893–914.

Allison, E. (2006) 'Shameful admission', *The Guardian*, 27 September, Available from: https://www.theguardian.com/society/2006/sep/27/crime.penal

Allison, E. and Grierson, J. (2016) 'Restraint injuries persist at youth jail where boy died 12 years ago', *The Guardian*, 5 May, Available from: https://www.theguardian.com/society/2016/may/05/restraint-injuries-youth-jails-rainsbrook-gareth-myatt

Almond, P. (2009a) 'The dangers of hanging baskets: regulatory myths and media representations of health and safety regulation', *Journal of Law and Society*, 36(3): 352–75.

Almond, P. (2009b) 'Understanding the seriousness of corporate crime: some lessons for the new corporate manslaughter offence', *Criminology & Criminal Justice*, 9(2): 145–64.

Almond, P. and Colover, S. (2012) 'Communication and social regulation', *British Journal of Criminology*, 52(5): 997–1016.

Alvesalo, A. (1999) 'Meeting the expectations of the local community on safety: what about white-collar crime?', paper presented at the 27th Annual Conference of the European Group for the Study of Deviance and Social Control, Palanga, Lithuania, 2–5 September.

Alvesalo, A. and Tombs, S. (2002) 'Working for criminalization of economic offending: contradictions for critical criminology', *Critical Criminology*, 11(1): 21–40.

Andreas, P. and Nadelmann, E. (2006) *Policing the Globe: Criminalization and Crime Control in International Relations*, Oxford University Press.

Ashton, J. (2012) 'John Ashton on witnessing the Hillsborough Disaster', BMJOpinion, Available from: https://blogs.bmj.com/bmj/2012/09/14/john-ashton-on-witnessing-the-hillsborough-disaster/

Atiles, J. (2024) 'Crimes of the powerful in Latin America and the Caribbean: toward a research agenda', *Sociology Compass*, 18(2): e13172, Available from: https://doi.org/10.1111/soc4.13172

Ayres, I. and Braithwaite, J. (1992) 'Partial-industry regulation: a monopsony standard for consumer protection', *California Law Review*, 80(1): 13–53.

Ballinger, A. (2003) 'Gender, power and the state: same as it ever was?', in R. Coleman, J. Sim, S. Tombs and D. Whyte (eds) *State, Power, Crime*, Sage, pp 20–35.

Ballinger, A. (2016) *Gender, Truth and State Power: Capitalising on Punishment*, Routledge.

BBC (2012) 'Ian Tomlinson pathologist Dr Freddy Patel struck off', [online], BBC News, 23 August, Available from: https://www.bbc.co.uk/news/uk-19355106

BBC (2014) 'Jimmy Mubenga death: timeline of the case and G4S guards' trial', 16 December, Available from: https://www.bbc.co.uk/news/uk-england-london-28153863

BBC (2019) 'London firefighters' guard-of-honour for Dany Cotton', 23 December, Available from: https://www.bbc.co.uk/news/uk-england-london-50892851

Becker, H.S. and Horowitz, I.L. (1972) 'Radical politics and sociological research: observations on methodology and ideology', *The American Journal of Sociology*, 78(1): 48–66.

Bergman, D. (1991) 'Deaths at work: accidents or corporate crime', Workers' Educational Association.

Bergman, D. (1993) 'Disasters: where the law fails; a new agenda for dealing with corporate violence', Herald Families Association.

Bergman, D. (1994) 'The perfect crime? How companies can get away with manslaughter in the workplace', West Midlands Health and Safety Centre.

Bergman, D. (2000) *The Case for Corporate Responsibility: Corporate Violence and the Criminal Justice System*, Disaster Action.

Bergman, D. (2001) 'Holding directors to account', [online], *The Guardian*, 4 December, Available from: http://www.theguardian.com/comment/story/0,3604,611676,00.html

Bergman, S. (2019) 'Business leaders more likely to be called Stephen than to be women', *Independent*, 22 August, Available from: https://www.independent.co.uk/life-style/ceo-women-business-sexism-ftse-100-a9073391.html

Bernat, I. and Whyte, D. (2017) 'State-corporate crime and the process of capital accumulation: mapping a global regime of permission from Galicia to Morecambe Bay', *Critical Criminology*, 25(1): 71–86.

Berrington, E., Jemphrey, A. and Scraton, P. (2003) 'Silencing the view from below: the institutional regulation of critical research', in S. Tombs and D. Whyte (eds) *Unmasking the Crimes of the Powerful: Scrutinizing States and Corporations*, Peter Lang, pp 129–45.

Best, J. (1999) *Random Violence*, University of California Press.

Bhandar, B. (2018) 'Organised state abandonment: the meaning of Grenfell', Sociological Review Blog, Available from: https://thesociologicalreview.org/collections/guest-essays/organised-state-abandonment/

Billingham, L. and Irwin-Rogers, K. (2022) *Against Youth Violence: A Social Harm Perspective* (1st edn), Bristol University Press.

Bittle, S. and Snider, L. (2006) 'From manslaughter to preventable accident: shaping corporate criminal liability', *Law and Policy*, 28(4): 470–96.

Blaikie, N. (2004) *Designing Social Research*, Polity.

Booth, R. (2024a) 'Firms criticised by Grenfell inquiry face calls to be banned from public contracts', *The Guardian*, 3 September, Available from: https://www.theguardian.com/uk-news/article/2024/sep/03/firms-criticised-grenfell-inquiry-face-calls-banned-public-contracts

Booth, R. (2024b) 'Grenfell Tower firefighters win £20m damages in out of court settlement', *The Guardian*, 1 February, Available from: https://www.theguardian.com/uk-news/2024/feb/01/grenfell-tower-firefighters-win-20m-damages-in-out-of-court-settlement

Booth, R. and Sinmaz, E. (2024) 'Police under pressure to accelerate criminal investigation into Grenfell fire', *The Guardian*, 4 September, Available from: https://www.theguardian.com/uk-news/article/2024/sep/04/police-under-pressure-to-accelerate-criminal-investigation-into-grenfell-fire

Bottoms, A. (2007) 'The relationship between theory and empirical observations in criminology', in R.D. King and E. Wincup (eds) *Doing Research on Crime and Justice*, Oxford University Press, pp 75–116.

Box, S. (1983) *Power, Crime and Mystification*, Tavistock.

Braithwaite, J (2002) 'Rewards and regulation', *Journal of Law and Society*, 29(1): 12–26.

Brands, J. and Van Doorn, J. (2022) 'The measurement, intensity and determinants of fear of cybercrime: a systematic review', *Computers in Human Behaviour*, 127: 107082, Available from: https://doi.org/10.1016/j.chb.2021.107082

Braun, V. and Clarke, V. (2006) 'Using thematic analysis in psychology', *Qualitative Research in Psychology*, 3(2): 77–101.

Brooks, L. (2002) 'Profit and loss', [online], *The Guardian*, 18 May, Available from: http://www.theguardian.com/lifeandstyle/2002/may/18/weekend.libbybrooks

Bukharin, N. (1929) *Imperialism and World Economy*, vol 2, International Publishers.

Burke, R.H. (2019) *An Introduction to Criminological Theory* (5th edn), Routledge.

Burnham, A. (2012) 'Andy Burnham: "I vowed to find out the truth about that day"', *Independent*, 16 September, Available from: https://www.independent.co.uk/news/uk/home-news/andy-burnham-i-vowed-to-find-out-the-truth-about-that-day-8142454.html

Cameron, D. (2012) Hansard, 12 September.

Canning, V. and Tombs, S. (2021) *From Social Harm to Zemiology: A Critical Introduction*, Routledge.

Carrington, K. and Hogg, R. (2013) 'Critical criminologies: an introduction', in R. Hogg and K. Carrington (eds) *Critical Criminology*, Routledge, pp 1–14.

Carson, W.G. (1974) 'Symbolic and instrumental dimensions of early factory legislation: a case study in the social origins of criminal law', in R. Hood (ed) *Crime, Criminology and Public Policy*, Heinemann, pp 107–38.

Carson, W.G. (1980) 'The other price of Britain's oil: regulating safety on offshore oil installations in the British sector of the North Sea', *Contemporary Crises*, 4: 239–66.

Carson, W.G. (1982) *The Other Price of Britain's Oil*, Martin Robertson.

Casale, S., Corfe, M. and Lewis, J. (2013) 'Report of the independent external review of the IPCC investigation into the death of Sean Rigg', Independent Police Complaints Commission.

Chakrabortty, A. (2017) 'Over 170 years after Engels, Britain is still a country that murders its poor', *The Guardian*, 3 July.

Charles, M. (2019) 'ComeUnity and community in the face of impunity', in D. Bulley, J. Edkins and N. El-Enany (eds) *After Grenfell: Violence, Resistance and Response*, Pluto Press, pp 167–92.

Chomsky, N. (2003) *For Reasons of State*, Penguin Books.

Christie, N. (1977) 'Conflicts as property', *British Journal of Criminology*, 17(1): 1–15.

Christie, N. (1986) 'The ideal victim', in E.A. Fattah (ed) *From Crime Policy to Victim Policy*, Macmillan Press, pp 17–30.

Christie, N. (2000) *Crime Control as Industry: Towards GULAGS, Western Style* (3rd edn), Routledge.

C4 News (2017) 4 November.

Clinard, M. and Yaegar, P. (1980) *Corporate Crime*, The Free Press.

Coleman, R. (2017) 'Academic egos and "self-forgetting"', [blog post], Available from: https://emotionalstates.wordpress.com/2017/10/17/academics-and-self-forgetting/

Coleman, C. and Moynihan, J. (1996) *Understanding Crime Data: Haunted by the Dark Figure*, Open University Press.

Coleman, R. and Sim, J. (2019) 'The state', in J. Muncie and E. McLaughlin (eds) *Sage Dictionary of Criminology* (4th edn), Sage, pp 518–22.

Coleman, R., Sim, J., Tombs, S. and Whyte, D. (2009) 'Introduction: State, power, crime', in R. Coleman, J. Sim, S. Tombs and D. Whyte (eds) *State, Power, Crime*, Sage Publications, pp 1–20.

Conn, D. (2010) 'Bradford remembered: the unheeded warnings that led to tragedy', *The Guardian*, 11 May, Available from: https://www.theguardian.com/football/david-conn-inside-sport-blog/2010/may/12/bradford-fire-david-conn

Conn, D. (2014) 'Hillsborough inquest: two CCTV tapes stolen from ground, court hears', *The Guardian*, 7 November, Available from: https://www.theguardian.com/uk-news/2014/nov/07/hillsborough-inquest-cctv-footage-stolen-sheffield-wednesday-electrician

Conn, D. (2019) 'Hillsborough safety officer fined £6,500 over safety breaches', *The Guardian*, 13 May.

Conn, D. (2021) 'South Yorkshire and West Midlands police agree payouts for Hillsborough "cover-up"', *The Guardian*, 4 June, Available from: https://www.theguardian.com/football/2021/jun/04/south-yorkshire-police-agree-payouts-for-hillsborough-cover-up

Conn, D. (2025) 'Hillsborough disaster: multiple police misconduct claims upheld, families told', *The Guardian*, 12 March.

Copson, L. (2011) 'Archaeologies of harm: criminology, critical criminology, zemiology', PhD thesis, University of Bristol.

Copson, L. (2018) 'Beyond "criminology vs zemiology": reconciling crime with social harm', in A. Boukli and J. Kotzé (eds) *Zemiology: Reconnecting Crime and Social Harm*, Springer, pp 33–56.

Copson, L. and Boukli, A. (2020) 'Queer utopias and queer criminology', *Criminology & Criminal Justice*, 20(5): 510–22.

Cressey, D.R. (1989) 'The poverty of theory in corporate crime research', in S. Laufer and F. Adler (eds) *Advances in Criminological Theory*, Transaction Publishers, pp 31–55.

Croall, H. (1989) 'Who is the white-collar criminal?', *British Journal of Criminology*, 29(2): 157–74.

Croall, H. (1992) *White Collar Crime: Criminal Justice and Criminology*, Open University Press.

Croall, H. (2003) '"Men's business"? Some gender questions about white collar crime', *Criminal Justice Matters*, 53(1): 26–7.

Croall, H. (2010) 'Economic crime and victimology: a critical appraisal', *International Journal of Victimology*, 8(2): 169–83.

Dannemiller, H.C. (2002) 'The parent's response to a child's murder', *OMEGA: Journal of Death and Dying*, 45(1): 1–21.

Davies, M., Croall, H. and Tryer, J. (2005) *Criminal Justice*, Longman.

Davies, P., Francis, P. and Wyatt, T. (2014) 'Taking invisible crimes and social harms seriously', in P. Davies, P. Francis and T. Wyatt (eds) *Invisible Crimes and Social Harms*, Palgrave Macmillan, pp 1–25.

Davis, H. and White, H. (2023) 'For a zemiology of politics', *Journal of White Collar and Corporate Crime*, 4(2): 88–99.

Dickson-Swift, V., James, E.L., Kippen, S. and Liamputtong, P. (2009) 'Researching sensitive topics: qualitative research as emotion work', *Qualitative Research*, 9(1): 61–79.

Disaster Action (DA) (1992) 'Disaster Action newsletter', 1 (Spring): 1.

Dix, P. (2015) 'Closing Disaster Action is a mark of our charity's success, not failure', [online], *The Guardian*, 11 December, Available from: https://www.theguardian.com/voluntary-sector-network/2015/dec/11/charity-closure-failure-hillsborough-disaster

Dorling, D. (2005) 'Prime suspect: murder in Britain', in P. Hillyard, C. Pantazis, S. Tombs, D. Gordon and D. Dorling (eds) *Criminal Obsessions: Why Harm Matters More than Crime*, vol 1, Crime and Society Foundation, pp 23–38.

Doyle, D.M. and McGrath, J. (2016) 'Attributing criminal responsibility for workplace fatalities and deaths in custody: corporate manslaughter in Britain and Ireland', in K. Fitz-Gibbon and S. Walklate (eds) *Homicide, Gender and Responsibility: An International Perspective*, Routledge, p 148.

Elkins, C. (2022) *Legacy of Violence: A History of the British Empire*, The Bodley Head.

Enoch, N. (2020) 'Bosses at Titanic's owner White Star Line portrayed themselves as the victims and expressed "heartfelt sympathy" to their chairman who controversially survived the disaster, board meeting documents reveal', *Daily Mail*, 6 November, Available from: https://www.dailymail.co.uk/news/article-8921703/Bosses-Titanics-owner-White-Star-Line-portrayed-victims.html

Eyre, A. and Dix, P. (2014) *Collective Conviction*, Liverpool University Press.

FACK (nd) Michael Adamson '*about us*', https://www.hazardscampaign.org.uk/fack/about/michaeladamson.pdf

Families Against Corporate Killers (FACK) (2006) 'FACK briefing paper for committee stage of the Corporate Manslaughter and Corporate Homicide Bill', 18 December.

Families Against Corporate Killers (FACK) (2010) *The Human Face of Workplace Killing*, [DVD], Bite Size Movies.

Fire Protection Association (2025) 'Possible debarring of Grenfell-linked companies paused', Fire Protection News, 17 July, Available from: https://www.thefpa.co.uk/news/possible-debarring-of-grenfell-linked-companies-paused-

Foot, P. (2012) *The Vote: How It Was Won and How It Was Undermined*, Bookmarks.

Forster, K. (2017) 'Grenfell Tower's fireproof cladding was "downgraded to save £293,000" show leaked documents', *The Independent*, 30 June.

Foucault, M. (2003) 'Society must be defended', in M. Bertani, A. Fontana, F. Ewald and A. Fontana (eds) *Lectures at the College de France*, Penguin, pp 1–22.

Fraser, N. (2000) 'Rethinking recognition', *New Left Review*, 3: 107.

Freedom of Information Request (2024) 'Prosecutions relating to manslaughter', Crown Prosecution Service, 18 June, Available from: https://www.cps.gov.uk/foi/2024/prosecutions-relating-corporate-manslaughter

Friedrichs, D.O. (2017) 'Edwin H. Sutherland: an improbable criminological key thinker: for critical criminologists and for mainstream criminologists', *Critical Criminology*, 25(1): 55–69.

Frisch, M. and Watts, D.L. (1980) 'Oral history and the presentation of class consciousness: the New York Times versus the Buffalo unemployed', *International Journal of Oral History*, 1: 88–110.

Garland, D. (1985) *Punishment and Welfare: A History of Penal Strategies*, Gower.

Garland, D. (1992) 'Criminological knowledge and its relation to power: Foucault's genealogy and criminology today', *British Journal of Criminology*, 32(4): 403–22.

Garland, D. (1997) '"Governmentality" and the problem of crime: Foucault, criminology, sociology', *Theoretical Criminology*, 1(2): 173–214.

Garside, R. (2013) 'Addressing social harm: better regulation versus social transformation' [Abordar el daño social: ¿mejor regulación o transformación social?], *Crítica penal y poder*, 5: 247–65.

Gayle, D. (2017) 'Man who died after police restraint was "gentle giant", court told', *The Guardian*, 7 February, Available from: https://www.theguardian.com/uk-news/2017/feb/07/man-died-olaseni-lewis-police-restraint-gentle-giant

Gaylord, M.S. and Galliher, J.F. (2020) *The Criminology of Edwin Sutherland*, Routledge.

Geis, G. (2016) 'The roots and variant definitions of the concept of "white-collar crime"', in S. van Slyke, M.L. Benson and F.T. Cullen (eds) *The Oxford Handbook of White-Collar Crime*, Oxford University Press, pp 25–38.

Geis, G. and Goff, C. (1983) 'Introduction', in E.H. Sutherland, *White Collar Crime: The Uncut Version*, Yale University Press, pp 1–11.

Gillham, B. (2000) *Case Study Research Methods*, Continuum.

Gilmore, R.W. (2007) *Golden Gulag: Prisons, Surplus, Crisis, and Opposition in Globalizing California*, University of California Press.

Giroux, H.A. (2005) 'The terror of neoliberalism: rethinking the significance of cultural politics', *College Literature*, 32(1): 1.

Gobert, J. (2008) 'The Corporate Manslaughter and Corporate Homicide Act 2007: thirteen years in the making but was it worth the wait?', *The Modern Law Review*, 71(3): 413–33.

Gobert, J. and Punch, M. (2003) *Rethinking Corporate Crime*, Butterworths.

Goodey, J. (2005) *Victims and Victimology*, Longman.

Gottfredson, M. and Hirschi, T. (1990) *A General Theory of Crime*, Stanford University Press.

Gouldner, A. (1973) *For Sociology: Renewal and Critique in Sociology Today*, Allen Lane.

Gray, D.E. (2014) *Doing Research in the Real World*, Sage.

Grenfell United (nd) 'About us', Available from: https://grenfellunited.org.uk/about-us

Guerry, A.-M. (1829) 'Mémoire sur les variations métérologiques comparées aux phénomènes physiologiques', *Annales d'hygiène publique et de médecine légal*, 1: 228.

Gunningham, N. and Johnstone, R. (1999) *Regulating Workplace Safety: System and Sanctions*, Oxford University Press.

Gusfield, J.R. (1967) 'Moral passage: the symbolic process in public designations of deviance', *Social Problems*, 15(2): 175–88.

Gusfield, J.R. (1970) 'Moral passage: the symbolic process in public designations of deviance', in C.A. Bersani (ed) *Crime and Delinquency: A Reader*, Macmillan.

Hancock, M. (2014) 'Our drive to cut red tape is working – both at home and in Europe', [online], *Telegraph*, 23 July, Available from: http://www.telegraph.co.uk/news/worldnews/europe/10986255/Our-drive-to-cut-red-tape-is-working-both-at-home-and-in-Europe.html

Hansard (2007) 'Gareth Myatt', 12 July, Available from: https://hansard.parliament.uk/commons/2007-07-12/debates/07071265000004/GarethMyatt

Harding, J. (2013) *Qualitative Data Analysis*, Sage.

Harding, S. (1991) *Whose Science? Whose Knowledge?: Thinking from Women's Lives*, Cornell University Press.

Hardwick, N. (2006) 'Report dated 27th February 2006, of the review into events leading up to and following the death of Christopher Adler on 1st April 1989', Stationary Office, Available from: https://assets.publishing.service.gov.uk/media/5a7c1c72ed915d1c30daaa18/0971_i.pdf.

Harvey, D. (2007) *A Brief History of Neoliberalism* (1st edn), Oxford University Press.

Harvey, L. (1990) *Critical Social Research*, Unwin Hyman.

Hattenstone, S. (2006) 'A death foretold', *The Guardian*, 1 April, Available from: https://www.theguardian.com/uk/2006/apr/01/ukcrime.prisonsandprobation1

Hazards (2015) 'He wanted to learn a trade; he ended up dead at 16, special online report', *Hazards Magazine*, September, Available from: http://www.hazards.org/deadlybusiness/cameronminshull.htm

Hazards (2025) 'Amazon union members targeted after a failed recognition vote in the face of unionbusting', *Hazards Magazine*, Available from: https://www.hazards.org/organise/outoftheshadows.htm

Hennink, M.M., Bailey, A. and Hutter, I. (2011) *Qualitative Research Methods*, Sage.

Hillyard, P. (2003) 'The "exceptional" state', in R. Coleman, J. Sim, S. Tombs and D. Whyte (eds) *State, Power, Crime*, Sage, pp 5–22.

Hillyard, P. and Tombs, S. (2005) 'Beyond criminology?', in P. Hillyard, C. Pantazis, S. Tombs, S. Pemberton, D. Gordon and D. Dorling (eds) *Criminal Obsessions: Why Harm Matters More than Crime* (no 1), Crime and Society.

Hillyard, P., Sim, J., Tombs, S. and Whyte, D. (2004) 'Leaving a "stain upon the silence": contemporary criminology and the politics of dissent', *The British Journal of Criminology*, 44(3): 369–90.

Hirschi, T. and Gottfredson, M. (1987) 'Causes of white-collar crime', *Criminology*, 25: 949–74.

Hodder, A., Williams, M., Kelly, J. and McCarthy, N. (2017) 'Does strike action stimulate trade union membership growth?', *British Journal of Industrial Relations*, 55(1): 165–86.

Hodge, N. (2002) 'British government accedes to demands for a new corporate killing offence', [online], 25 February, Available from: https://www.wsws.org/en/articles/2002/02/man-f25.html

Hollway, W. and Jefferson, T. (2000) *Doing Qualitative Research Differently*, Sage.

Iain Tomlinson Family Campaign (nd) 'Ian Tomlinson family campaign', Available from: http://www.iantomlinsonfamilycampaign.org.uk

Independent Police Complaints Commission (IPCC) (2006) 'Review into the events leading up to and following the death of Christopher Alder; vol I', 27 March, Available from: https://www.gov.uk/government/publications/review-into-the-events-leading-up-to-and-following-the-death-of-christopher-alder-vol-i

Institution of Occupational Safety and Health (2022) 'Robens report: 50 years on', Available from: https://www.ioshmagazine.com/2022/04/26/robens-report-50-years

INQUEST (2000) 'Jury concludes unlawful killing in death of Christopher Alder', Available from: https://www.inquest.org.uk/christopher-alder-inquest-concludes

INQUEST (2004) 'Death in police custody report on the death of Christopher Alder', INQUEST, Available from: http://inquest.gn.apc.org/pdf/Christopher%20Alder%20briefing.pdf

INQUEST (2007) 'INQUEST's submission to the Ministry of Justice & Department for Children, Schools and Families on the "Review of Restraint"', INQUEST, Available from: https://inquest.eu.rit.org.uk/Handlers/Download.ashx?IDMF=2971b3a6-8dab-4e6b-bcbe-9bbedfb14a95

INQUEST (2007) 'Gareth Myatt inquest verdict', INQUEST, Available from: https://www.yumpu.com/en/document/read/25016385/gareth-myatt-inquest-verdict

INQUEST (2007) 'Gareth Myatt inquest verdict: failings of the Youth Justice Board cause death of a child', Available from: https://www.inquest.org.uk/gareth-myatt-close

INQUEST (2018) 'Humberside police misconduct hearing finds that surveillance of Janet Alder was unlawful but concludes with "no case to answer" for officers involved', Available from: https://www.inquest.org.uk/alder-surveillance-conclusion

INQUEST (2023) 'Sean Rigg: police watchdog issue unprecedented apology to family, 15 years on from Brixton custody death', Available from: https://www.inquest.org.uk/sean-rigg-iopc-apology

Israel, S. (2011) 'PC Harwood: "Ian Tomlinson posed no threat to anyone"', Channel 4, 5 April, Available from: https://www.channel4.com/news/tomlinson-inquest-pc-harwood-gives-second-day-of-evidence

James, P., Tombs, S. and Whyte, D. (2012) 'An independent review of British health and safety regulation? From common sense to non-sense', *Policy Studies*, 34(1): 36–52.

Janes, L. (2018) 'The isolation of children in prison', *Prison Service Journal*, 236: 43.

Johnes, M. (2004) ' "Heads in the sand": football, politics and crowd disasters in twentieth-century Britain', *Soccer & Society*, 5(2): 134–51.

Jones, J. (2017) ' "The patronising disposition of unaccountable power": a report to ensure the pain and suffering of the Hillsborough families is not repeated', Her Majesty's Stationery Office.

Justice for Seni (2016) 'Father accuses authorities of delaying inquest into son Olaseni Lewis's police restraint death at Bethlem Royal Hospital in Beckenham', April, Available from: https://www.justiceforseni.com/2016/04/

Kelly, K.A. (2023) 'The Ring video doorbell and the entry of Amazon into the smart home: implications for consumer-initiated surveillance', *Journal of Consumer Policy*, 46(1): 95–104.

Kramer, R.C. (1985) 'Defining the concept of crime: a humanistic perspective', *Journal Sociology and Social Welfare*, 12: 469–87.

Kramer, R., Michalowski, R. and Kauzlarich, D. (2002) 'The origins and development of the concept and theory of state-corporate crime', *Crime and Delinquency*, 48(2): 263–82.

Kristensen, P., Weisæth, L. and Heir, T. (2012) 'Bereavement and mental health after sudden and violent losses: a review', *Psychiatry*, 75(1): 76–97.

Larcombe, W. (2011) 'Falling rape conviction rates: (some) feminist aims and measures for rape law', *Feminist Legal Studies*, 19(1): 27–45.

Lasslett, K. (2010) 'Crime or social harm? A dialectical perspective', *Crime, Law, Society and Change*, 54(1): 1–19.

Leavy, P.H.N.S. and Hesse-Biber, S.N. (2011) *The Practice of Qualitative Research*, Sage.

Lee, R. (1993) *Doing Research on Sensitive Topics*, Sage.

Lees, S. (1996) *Carnal Knowledge: Rape on Trial*, Penguin Books.

Levi, M. and Pithouse, A. (1992) 'The victims of fraud', in D. Downes (ed) *Unravelling Criminal Justice: Eleven British Studies*, Macmillan Press, pp 229–46.

Lewis, P. (2009a) 'Ian Tomlinson's family accuse police of cover-up over his death', *The Guardian*, 6 August, Available from: https://www.theguardian.com/uk/2009/aug/06/ian-tomlinson-family-accuse-police-of-cover-up

Lewis, P. (2009b) 'Police floated imposter theory over Ian Tomlinson's death at G20 protests', *The Guardian*, 30 June, Available from: https://www.theguardian.com/uk/2009/jun/30/ian-tomlinson-inquiry-g20-protests

Lewis, P. (2010) 'Ian Tomlinson: a story of justice denied', *The Guardian*, 22 July, Available from: https://www.theguardian.com/uk/2010/jul/22/ian-tomlinson-story-justice-denied

Lowkey (2018) Personal Interview with hip-hop artist and Non-Executive Director at Kids on the Green, 14 September.

MacLeod, G. (2018) 'The Grenfell Tower atrocity: exposing urban worlds of inequality, injustice, and an impaired democracy', *City*, 22(4): 460–89.

Mason, W. (2020) '"No one learned": interpreting a drugs crackdown operation and its consequences through the "lens" of social harm', *British Journal of Criminology*, 60(2): 382–402.

Mathiesen, T. (1980) *Law, Society and Political Action: Towards a Strategy under Late Capitalism*, Academic Press.

Matthews, L.R., Quinlan, M., Rawlings-Way, O. and Bohle, P. (2011) 'The adequacy of institutional responses to death at work: experiences of surviving families', *International Journal of Disability Management*, 60(1): 37–48.

Matthews, L.R., Bohle, P., Quinlan, M. and Rawlings-Way, O. (2012) 'Traumatic death at work: consequences for surviving families', *Work, Health and Families*, 42(4): 647–66.

Matthews, L.R., Quinlan, M.G. and Bohle, P. (2019) 'Posttraumatic stress disorder, depression, and prolonged grief disorder in families bereaved by a traumatic workplace death: the need for satisfactory information and support', *Frontiers in Psychiatry*, 10, Available from: https://doi.org/10.3389/fpsyt.2019.00609

Mawby, R. and Walklate, S. (1994) *Critical Criminology*, Sage.

Mazower, M. (2008) *Hitler's Empire: How the Nazis Ruled Europe*, Penguin Books.

McCullagh, C. (2016) 'White collar and corporate crime in and after the crisis', in D. Healy, C. Hamilton, Y. Daly and M. Butler (eds) *The Routledge Handbook of Irish Criminology*, Routledge, pp 89–105.

Melossi, D. (2008) *Controlling Crime, Controlling Society: Thinking about Crime in Europe and America*, Polity.

The Mesothelioma Center (2017) 'Mesothelioma latency period', Available from: https://www.asbestos.com/mesothelioma/latency-period/

Michael, J. and Adler, M.J. (1933) *Crime, Law and Social Science*, Brace.

Michalowski, R.J. (1985) *Order, Law, and Crime: An Introduction to Criminology*, Random House.

Michalowski, R.J. and Kramer, R.C. (1987) 'The space between the laws: the problem of corporate crime in a transnational context', *Social Problems*, 34: 34–53.

Miers, D. (1985) 'Compensation and support for victims of crime', *The British Journal of Criminology*, 25(4): 383–9.

Monaghan, K. (2015) 'Report by the Assistant Deputy Coroner Karon Monaghan QC under the Coroner's Rules 1984, Rule 43: Inquest into the Death of Jimmy Kelenda Mubenga', 31 July.

Moore-Bick, M., Nethercot, D. and Mothersole, J. (2019) 'Grenfell Tower Inquiry', House of Commons.

Moore-Bick, M., Nethercot, D. and Mothersole, J. (2024) 'Grenfell Tower Inquiry', House of Commons.

Muncie, J. (1999) 'Institutionalised intolerance: youth justice and the 1988 Crime and Disorder Act', *Critical Social Policy*, 19(2): 147–75.

Noaks, L. and Wincup, E. (2004) *Criminological Research: Understanding Qualitative Methods*, Sage.

Pantazis, C. (2008) 'The problem with criminalisation', *Criminal Justice Matters*, 74(1): 10-12.

Pantazis, C. and Pemberton, S. (2009) 'Nation states and the production of social harm: resisting the hegemony of "TINA"', in R. Coleman, J. Sim, S. Tombs and D. Whyte (eds) *State, Crime, Power*, Sage, pp 214–33.

Parker, H. (2020) 'Grieving family of Stoke-on-Trent man: our Adrian died in police custody after telling officers "I can't breathe"', *Stoke Sentinel*, 23 June, Available from: https://www.stokesentinel.co.uk/news/stoke-on-trent-news/grieving-family-stoke-trent-man-4253491

Parliament (2010) 'The death of Ian Tomlinson: decision on prosecution', UK Parliament, Available from: https://data.parliament.uk/DepositedPapers/Files/DEP2010-1570/DEP2010-1570.pdf

Parsons, S. (2018) 'The Corporate Manslaughter and Corporate Homicide Act 2007 ten years on: fit for purpose?', *The Journal of Criminal Law*, 82(4): 305–10.

Pearce, A. (2008) *Playing it Safe: The Crazy World of Britain's Health and Safety Regulations*, Friday Books.

Pearce, F. (1976) *Crimes of the Powerful*, Pluto Press.

Pearce, F. (1990) '"Responsible corporations" and regulatory agencies', *The Political Quarterly*, 61(4): 415–30.

Pearce, F. (2003) 'Foreword: Holy wars and spiritual revitalization', in S. Tombs and D. Whyte (eds) *Unmasking the Crimes of the Powerful: Scrutinizing States and Corporations*, Peter Lang, pp ix–xv.

Pearce, F. and Tombs, S. (1989) 'Bhopal: Union Carbide and the hubris of the capitalist technocracy', *Social Justice*, 16(2): 116–45.

Pearce, F. and Tombs, S. (1993) 'US capital versus the Third World Union Carbide and Bhopal', in F. Pearce and M. Woodiwiss (eds) *Global Crime Connections*, Macmillan Press, pp 187–211.

Pearce, F. and Tombs, S. (1997) 'Hazards, law and class: contextualizing the regulation of corporate crime', *Social & Legal Studies*, 6(1): 79–107.

Pearce, F. and Tombs, S. (1998) *Toxic Capitalism: Corporate Crime and the Chemical Industry*, Ashgate.

Pearce, F. and Tombs, S. (2012) *Bhopal: Flowers at the Altar of Profit and Power*, CrimeTalk Books (e-book).

Peck, J. (2010) 'Zombie neoliberalism and the ambidextrous state', *Theoretical Criminology*, 14(1): 104–10.

Pemberton, S. (2007) 'Social harm future(s): exploring the potential of the social harm approach', *Crime, Law and Social Change*, 48(1–2): 27–41.

Pemberton, S. (2008a) 'Where next? The future of the social harm perspective', in P. Hillyard, C. Pantazis, S. Tombs, S. Pemberton, D. Gordon and D. Dorling (eds) *Criminal Obsessions: Why Harm Matters More than Crime* (no 1), Crime and Society Foundation, pp 70–90.

Pemberton, S. (2008b) 'Demystifying deaths in police custody: challenging state talk', *Social and Legal Studies*, 17(2).

Pemberton, S.A. (2016) *Harmful Societies: Understanding Social Harm*. Policy Press.

Prasad, R. (2023) 'I can't breathe: race, death and British policing', INQUEST, Available from: https://www.inquest.org.uk/i-cant-breathe-race-death-british-policing

Presser, L. and Sandberg, S. (2019) 'Narrative criminology as critical criminology', *Critical Criminology*, 27(1): 131–43.

Punch, M. (1996) *Dirty Business: Explaining Corporate Misconduct*, Sage.

Punch, M. (2009) 'Why corporations kill – and get away with it: the failure of law to cope with crime in organizations', in A. Nollkaemper and H. van der Wilt (eds) *System Criminality in International Law*, Cambridge University Press, pp 42–69.

Quetelet, A. (1984) 'On moral statistics and the principles which should form the basis of it', *Deviance and Society*, 8(1): 13–41.

Raymen, T. (2022) *The Enigma of Social Harm: The Problem of Liberalism*, Routledge.

Reiman, J. (1998) *The Rich Get Richer and the Poor Get Prison*, Allyn and Bacon.

Reinecke, J. and Donaghey, J. (2015) 'After Rana Plaza: building coalitional power for labour rights between unions and (consumption-based) social movement organisations', *Organization*, 22(5): 720–40.

Riding, J. (2024) 'Police investigating Grenfell fire say trials will not begin until at least mid-2027', Inside Housing, Available from: https://www.insidehousing.co.uk/news/police-investigating-grenfell-fire-say-trials-will-not-begin-until-at-least-mid-2027-86599

Rigg, D. (2019) 'Time to take a stand? The law on all-seated stadiums in England and Wales and the case for change', *The International Sports Law Journal*, 18(3–4): 210–18.

Road, A. (nd) *The Hillsborough Groups*, https://www.anfieldroad.com/lfc-info/the-hillsborough-groups/

Rock, P. (1998) *After Homicide: Practical and Political Responses to Bereavement*, Clarendon Press.

Rock, P. (2002) 'On becoming a victim', in C. Hoyle and R. Wilson (eds) *New Visions of Crime Victims*, Hart Publishing, pp 1–23.

Rolston, B. (2000) *Unfinished Business: State Killings and the Quest for Truth*, Beyond the Pale Publications.

Roper, V. (2018) 'The Corporate Manslaughter and Corporate Homicide Act 2007: a 10-year review', *The Journal of Criminal Law*, 82(1): 48–75.

Ruggiero, V. (2015) *Power and Crime*, Routledge.

Ryan, M. (1996) *Lobbying from Below*, Routledge.

Sabbagh, D. (2018) 'MPs pass mental health restraint bill after filibuster fears', *The Guardian*, 6 July, Available from: https://www.theguardian.com/law/2018/jul/06/olaseni-lewis-mother-urges-mps-to-pass-filibustered-mental-health-bill

Sampson, K. (2017) *Hillsborough Voices: The Real Story Told by the People Themselves*, Ebury Press.

Sanders, A. and Young, R. (2000) *Criminal Justice*, Butterworths.

Scraton, P. (1987) *Law, Order and the Authoritarian State: Readings in Critical Criminology*, Open University Press.

Scraton, P. (1999) 'Policing with contempt: the degrading of truth and denial of justice in the aftermath of the Hillsborough Disaster', *Journal of Law and Society*, 26(3): 273–97.
Scraton, P. (2002) 'Lost lives, hidden voices: "truth" and controversial deaths', *Race & Class*, 44(1): 107–18.
Scraton, P. (2004) 'Death on the terraces: the contexts and injustices of the 1989 Hillsborough Disaster', *Soccer & Society*, 5(2): 183–200.
Scraton, P. (2009) *Hillsborough: The Truth*, Mainstream.
Scraton, P. (2013) 'The legacy of Hillsborough: liberating truth, challenging power', *Race & Class*, 55(2): 1–27.
Scraton, P. (2019) 'Boris Johnson: Liverpool, lies and bigotry', Institute of Race Relations, Available from: https://irr.org.uk/article/boris-johnson-liverpool-lies-and-bigotry/
Scraton, P. and Chadwick, K. (1987) *In the Arms of the Law: Coroners' Inquests and Deaths in Custody*, Pluto.
Scraton, P. and Chadwick, K. (2009) *The Theoretical and Political Priorities of Critical Criminology*, Willan.
Sellin, T. and Wolfgang, M.E. (1964) *The Measurement of Delinquency*, Wiley.
Shapiro, S.P. (1983) 'The new moral entrepreneurs: corporate crime crusaders', *Contemporary Sociology*, 12: 304–7.
Shapiro, S.P. (1990) 'Collaring the crime, not the criminal: reconsidering the concept of white-collar crime', *Sociological Review*, 55(3): 346–65.
Shears, D. (2018) 'Rich pickings?', *Hazards Magazine*, 143, Available from: https://www.hazards.org/insecure/richpickings.htm
Shover, N., Litton Fox, G. and Mills, M. (1994) 'Long-term consequences of victimization by white collar crime', *Justice Quarterly*, 11(1): 75–98.
Sim, J. (2010) 'Thinking about state violence: Joe Sim explores how idealised constructions of the normal and the pathological legitimate state violence', *Criminal Justice Matters*, 82(1): 6–7.
Sim, J. (2023) 'Punishment in "this hard land": conceptualising the prison in power, crime and mystification', in D.G. Scott and J. Sim (eds) Demy*stifying Power, Crime and Social Harm: Critical Criminological Perspectives*, Palgrave Macmillan, pp 507–30.
Sim, J., Scraton, P. and Gordon, P. (1987) 'Introduction: Crime, the state, and critical analysis', in P. Scraton (ed) *Law, Order, and the Authoritarian State*, Open University Press, pp 1–70.
Simon, J. (2007) *Governing through Crime: How the War on Crime Transformed American Democracy and Created a Culture of Fear*, Oxford University Press.
Sinmaz, E. and Booth, R. (2024) 'Grenfell survivors and bereaved demand justice as report published', *The Guardian*, 4 September, Available from: https://www.theguardian.com/uk-news/article/2024/sep/04/survivors-and-bereaved-respond-to-long-awaited-grenfell-inquiry-report

Slapper, G. (1993) 'Corporate manslaughter: an examination of the determinants of prosecutorial policy', *Social and Legal Studies*, 2(4): 423–43.

Slapper, G. (1999) *Blood in the Bank*, Ashgate.

Slapper, G. and Tombs, S. (1999) *Corporate Crime*, Longman.

Smart, C. (1990) 'Feminist approaches to criminology or postmodern woman meets atavistic man', in L. Gelsthorpe and A. Morris (eds) *Feminist Perspectives in Criminology*, Open University Press, pp 70–84.

Smart, C. (1995) *Law, Crime and Sexuality: Essays in Feminism*, Sage.

Smith, L. (2007) 'Nobody can hurt him now', *The Guardian*, 4 July, Available from: https://www.theguardian.com/society/2007/jul/04/youthjustice.prisons

Snell, K. and Tombs, S. (2011) '"How do you get your voice heard when no-one will let you?" Victimization at work', *Criminology & Criminal Justice*, 11(3): 207–23.

Snider, L. (2003a) 'Researching corporate crime', in S. Tombs and D. Whyte (eds) *Unmasking the Crimes of the Powerful: Scrutinizing States and Corporations*, Peter Lang, pp 49–69.

Snider, L. (2003b) 'Constituting the punishable woman: atavistic man incarcerates postmodern woman', *British Journal of Criminology*, 43(2): 354–78.

Spalek, B. (1999) 'Exploring the impact of financial crime: a study looking into the effects of the Maxwell scandal upon the Maxwell pensioners', *International Review of Victimology*, 6(3): 213–30.

Spalek, B. (2006) *Crime Victims: Theory, Policy and Practice*, Macmillan.

Spalek, B. and King, S. (2007) 'Farepak victims speak out: an exploration of the harms caused by the collapse of Farepak', *Criminal Justice Matters*, 71(1): 8–10.

Soliman, F. (2021) 'States of exception, human rights, and social harm: towards a border zemiology', *Theoretical Criminology*, 25(2): 228–48.

Solnit, R. (2004) *Hope in the Dark: The Untold History of People Power*, Canongate.

Stec, A.A., Dickens, K., Barnes, J.L.J. and Bedford, C. (2019) 'Environmental contamination following the Grenfell Tower Fire', *Chemosphere*, 226: 576–86.

Sutherland, E.H. (1939) 'Crime and the man', *Journal of Criminal Law and Criminology*, 29(6) (March–April): 911–14.

Sutherland, E.H. (1940) 'White-collar criminality', *American Sociological Review*, 5(1): 1–12.

Sutherland, E.H. (1941) 'Crime and business', *The Annals of the American Academy of Political and Social Science*, 217(1): 112–18.

Sutherland, E.H. (1945) 'Is "white-collar crime" crime?', *American Sociological Review*, 10: 132–9.

Sutherland, E. (1983) *White Collar Crime*, Holt, Reinhart and Winston.

Symonds, T. (2022) 'Grenfell: why are families still waiting for justice?', BBC News, 14 June, Available from: https://www.bbc.co.uk/news/uk-61724373

Tappan, P. (1947) 'Who is criminal?', *American Sociological Review*, 12(1): 96–102.

Tappan, P. (1977) 'Who is criminal?', in G. Geis and R.F. Meier (eds) *White Collar Crime: Offenses in Business, Politics, and the Professions*, The Free Press, pp 272–81.

Tauri, J.M. (2018) 'The master's tools will never dismantle the master's house: an indigenous critique of criminology', *Journal of Global Indigeneity*, 3(1), Available from: https://www.journalofglobalindigeneity.com/article/33223-the-master-s-tools-will-never-dismantle-the-master-s-house-an-indigenous-critique-of-criminology

Temkin, J. and Krahé, B. (2008) *Sexual Assault and the Justice Gap: A Question of Attitude*, vol 5, Bloomsbury Publishing.

Temkin, J., Gray, J.M. and Barrett, J. (2016) 'Different functions of rape myth use in court: findings from a trial observation study', *Feminist Criminology*, 13(2): 205–26.

Thompson, J. (2009) 'Asda delivers storming full-year sales but profits slip', *Independent*, 8 November, Available from: https://www.independent.co.uk/news/business/news/asda-delivers-storming-fullyear-sales-but-profits-slip-1817208.html

Todd, S. (2015) *The People: The Rise and Fall of the Working Class*, John Murray.

Tombs, S. (1991) 'Injury and ill-health in the chemical industry: de-centring the accident-prone victim', *Industrial Crisis Quarterly*, 5: 59–75.

Tombs, S. (1999) 'Health and safety crimes: (in)visibility and the problems of knowing', in P. Davies, P. Francis and V. Jupp (eds) *Invisible Crimes: Their Victims and Their Regulation*, Macmillan, pp 77–104.

Tombs, S. (2005) 'Workplace harm and the illusions of law', in D. Dorling, D. Gordon, P. Hillyard, C. Pantazis, S. Pemberton and S. Tombs (eds) *Criminal Obsessions*, Crime and Society Foundation, pp 39–59.

Tombs, S. (2013) 'Still killing with impunity: corporate criminal law reform in the UK', *Policy and Practice in Health and Safety*, 11(2): 63–80.

Tombs, S. (2015) 'Crisis, what crisis? Regulation and the academic orthodoxy', *The Howard Journal of Crime and Justice,* 54(1): 57–72.

Tombs, S. (2017) *Social Protection after the Crisis: Regulation without Enforcement*, Policy Press.

Tombs, S. (2018) 'The UK's corporate killing law: un/fit for purpose?', *Criminology & Criminal Justice*, 18(4): 488–507.

Tombs, S. (2018) 'For pragmatism and politics: crime, social harm and zemiology', in A. Boukli and J. Kotzé (eds) *Zemiology: Reconnecting Crime and Social Harm*, Springer, pp 11–31.

Tombs, S. (2019) 'The poor get prison … Grenfell as a site of crime?', Available from: https://ccseljmu.wordpress.com/2019/12/06/the-poor-get-prison-grenfell-as-a-site-of-crime/

Tombs, S. (2020) 'Home as a site of state-corporate violence: Grenfell Tower, aetiologies and aftermaths', *Howard Journal of Crime and Justice*, 59(2): 120–42.

Tombs, S. and Whyte, D. (2002) 'Unmasking crimes of the powerful', *Critical Criminology*, 11(3): 217–36.

Tombs, S. and Whyte, D. (2003a) 'Scrutinizing the powerful: crime, contemporary political economy, and critical social research', in S. Tombs and D. Whyte (eds) *Unmasking the Crimes of the Powerful: Scrutinizing States and Corporations*, Peter Lang, pp 3–49.

Tombs, S. and Whyte, D. (2003b) 'Researching the crimes of the powerful: establishing some rules of engagement', in S. Tombs and D. Whyte (eds) *Unmasking the Crimes of the Powerful: Scrutinizing States and Corporations*, Peter Lang, pp 261–73.

Tombs, S. and Whyte, D. (2003c) 'Two steps forward, one step back: towards accountability for workplace deaths?', *Policy and Practice in Health and Safety*, 1(1): 9–30.

Tombs, S. and Whyte, D. (2007) *Safety Crimes*, Willan Publishing.

Tombs, S. and Whyte, D. (2010) 'A deadly consensus: worker safety and regulatory degradation under New Labour', *British Journal of Criminology*, 50(1): 46–65.

Tombs, S. and Whyte, D. (2015) *The Corporate Criminal: Why Corporations Must Be Abolished*, Routledge.

Tran, M. and Pulham, S. (1999) '26 dead in west London train crash', [online], *The Guardian*, 5 October, Available from: https://www.theguardian.com/uk/1999/oct/05/ladbrokegrove.transport

Travers, R. (2023) 'Inquest touching the death of Aisha Cleary', UK Parliament, HM Coroners Office, Available from: https://www.surreycc.gov.uk/__data/assets/pdf_file/0003/346557/A-Cleary-Findings-and-Conclusion-28-July-2023.pdf

Tucker, P. (2017) 'The Grenfell Tower Fire was the end result of a disdainful housing policy', *The Guardian*, 20 June, Available from: https://www.theguardian.com/commentisfree/2017/jun/20/grenfell-fire-housing-policy-social-housing-tenants

UK Parliament (2012) 'Report of the Hillsborough Independent Panel', Available from: https://www.gov.uk/government/publications/the-report-of-the-hillsborough-independent-panel

Walker, P. (2012) 'Ian Tomlinson seemed deliberately obstructive, police officer tells court', *The Guardian*, 2 July, Available from: https://www.theguardian.com/uk/2012/jul/02/ian-tomlinson-police-officer-court

Walker, P. (2013) 'Lakanal House tower block fire: deaths "could have been prevented"', [online], *The Guardian*, 28 March, Available from: https://www.theguardian.com/uk/2013/mar/28/lakanal-house-fire-deaths-prevented#:~:text=Those%20who%20died%20could%20all,escape%20routes%20along%20communal%20balconies

Walklate, S. (1989) *Victimology: The Victim and the Criminal Justice Process*, Unwin Hyman.

Walklate, S. (2007) 'Researching victims', in R.D. King and E. Wincup (eds) *Doing Research on Crime and Justice*, Oxford University Press, pp 25–42.

Webber, F. (2014) 'Justice blindfolded? The case of Jimmy Mubenga', 16 December, Available from: https://irr.org.uk/article/justice-blindfolded-the-case-of-jimmy-mubenga/

Wells, C. (1995) *Negotiating Tragedy: Law and Disasters*, Sweet Maxwell.

Wells, C. (2001) *Corporations and Criminal Responsibility*, Oxford University Press.

Wells, C. (2009) 'Bribery: corporate liability under the Draft Bill 2009', *Criminal Law Review*, 7: 479–87.

Whyte, D. (2007) 'Victims of corporate crime', in S. Walklate (ed) *Handbook of Victims and Victimology*, Willan Publishing, p 446.

Whyte, D. (2015) *How Corrupt Is Britain?*, Pluto Press.

Williams, B. (1999) *Working with Victims of Crime: Policies, Politics and Practice*, Athenaeum Press.

Willow, C. (2014) 'Gareth Myatt died 10 years ago, but prison restraint on children continues', *The Guardian*, 19 April, Available from: https://www.theguardian.com/commentisfree/2014/apr/19/gareth-myatt-died-prison-restraint-children-rainsbrook

Wolmar, C. (2001) *Broken Rails*, Arum Press.

Wright, E. (2023) 'Decolonizing zemiology: outlining and remedying the blindness to (post)colonialism within the study of social harm', *Critical Criminology*, 31: 127–44.

Wright, G. and Hill, J. (2004) 'Victims, crime and criminal justice', in J. Muncie and D. Wilson (eds) *Student Handbook of Criminal Justice and Criminology*, Cavendish Publishing, pp 105–22.

Yar, M. (2012) 'Recognition as the grounds of a general theory of crime as social harm?', in S. O'Neill and N.H. Smith (eds) *Recognition Theory as Social Research: Investigating the Dynamics of Social Conflict*, Palgrave, pp 109–26.

Yin, R.K. (2009) *Case Study Research* (3rd edn), Sage.

Index